Giuseppe Riva, Brenda K. Wiederhold, Pietro Cipresso (Eds.)

The Psychology of Social Networking

Identity and Relationships in Online Communities

Giuseppe Riva, Brenda K. Wiederhold,
Pietro Cipresso (Eds.)

The Psychology of Social Networking:

Identity and Relationships in Online Communities

Managing Editor: Aneta Przepiórka

Language Editor: Matthew Coleshill

DE GRUYTER
OPEN

ISBN: 978-3-11-047384-1
e-ISBN: 978-3-11-047385-8

Published by De Gruyter Open Ltd, Warsaw/Berlin
Part of Walter de Gruyter GmbH, Berlin/Boston
The book is published with open access at www.degruyter.com.

Library of Congress Cataloging-in-Publication Data
A CIP catalog record for this book has been applied for at the Library of Congress.

Managing Editor: Aneta Przepiórka
Language Editor: Matthew Coleshill

www.degruyteropen.com

Cover illustration: iStock/ Daniel Rodr ├iguez Quintana

Contents

List of contributing authors

Giuseppe Riva, Ph.D.
IRCCS Istituto Auxologico Italiano and Catholic University of Milan
giuseppe.riva@unicatt.it

Brenda K. Wiederhold, Ph.D., MBA, BCB, BCN
CEO, Interactive Media Institute, a 501c3 non-profit
President, Virtual Reality Medical Center
b@imi-europe.eu

Pietro Cipresso, Ph.D.
IRCCS Istituto Auxologico Italiano
p.cipresso@auxologico.it

Nicholas David Bowman, Ph.D.
West Virginia University
Nicholas.Bowman@mail.wvu.edu

Jaime Banks, Ph.D.
West Virginia University
jabanks@mail.wvu.edu

Edward Paul Downs, Ph.D.
University of Minnesota-Duluth
epdowns@d.umn.edu

Sean Young, PhD
Executive Director of the University of California Institute for Prediction Technology (UCIPT) and the UCLA Center for Digital Behavior (CDB), as well as Assistant Professor of Family Medicine, UCLA.
youngsean@ucla.edu

Jamie Guillory, PhD
Center for Health Policy Science & Tobacco Research
RTI International
jamieguillory@gmail.com

Jeffrey T. Hancock, PhD
Department of Communication
Stanford University
jeffreyhancock@gmail.com

Jesse Fox, Ph.D.
The Ohio State University
fox.775@osu.edu

Elizabeth Sillence, Ph.D.
Department of Psychology, Faculty of Health and Life Sciences, Northumbria University
elizabeth.sillence@northumbria.ac.uk

Hui-Tzu Grace Chou, Ph.D.
Utah Valley University
chougr@uvu.edu

Ron Hammond, Ph.D.
Utah Valley University
ronh@uvu.edu

Ryan C. Martin, Ph.D.
University of Wisconsin-Green Bay
martinr@uwgb.edu

Lauren E. Vieaux
University of Wisconsin-Green Bay

Megan Moreno, MD, MSEd, MPH
University of Washington and Seattle Children's Research Institute
mamoreno@uw.edu

Natalie Goniu, BSN
University of Wisconsin Madison
goniu@wisc.edu

Peter Moreno, MS, JD
University of Washington
psmoreno@uw.edu

Doug Diekema, MD, MPH
University of Washington and Seattle Children's Research Institute
Doug.diekema@seattlechildrens.org

Shengli Deng, Ph.D.
School of Information Management, Wuhan University
victorydc@sina.com

Noella Edelmann, BA(Hons), MSc, MAS
Centre for E-Governance, Danube University Krems
noella.edelmann@donau-uni.ac.at

Ma. Regina M. Hechanova, Ph.D.
Ateneo de Manila University
rhechanova@ateneo.edu

Antover P. Tuliao, M.A.
University of Nebraska - Lincoln
antover.tuliao@gmail.com

Arsenio S. Alianan, Ph.D.
Ateneo de Manila University
aalianan@ateneo.edu

Lota A. Teh, Ph.D.
Ateneo de Manila University
lateh@ateneo.edu

Jen-Wei Chang, Ph.D.
Department of Electrical Engineering, Graduate Institute of Communication Engineering, National Taiwan University
jenweichang@ntu.edu.tw

Chun-Chia Lee, Ph.D.
Department of Information Management, Fooyin University
ft031@fy.edu.tw

Silvia Casale,
Department of Health Sciences, Psychology and Psychiatry Unit, University of Florence, Italy
silvia.casale@unifi.it

Caterina Primi,
Department of NEUROFARBA, Section of Psychology, University of Florence, Italy
primi@unifi.it

Giulia Fioravanti,
Department of Health Sciences, Psychology and Psychiatry Unit, University of Florence, Italy
giulia.fioravanti@unifi.it

Selim Gunuc, Ph.D.
Computer Education and Instructional Technology Department
Educational Faculty
Yuzuncu Yil University
selimgunuc@hotmail.com

Ozge Karakus, Ph.D.
Computer Education and Instructional Technology Department
Educational Faculty
Eskisehir Osmangazi Univeristy
ozgeekarakus@gmail.com

Hatice Ferhan Odabasi, Ph.D.
Computer Education and Instructional Technology Department
Educational Faculty
Anadolu University
fodabasi@anadolu.edu.tr

Mike Yao, Ph.D.
City University of Hong Kong
mike.yao@cityu.edu.hk

Olatz Lopez-Fernandez, Ph.D.
University of Barcelona
olatzlopez@ub.edu

José A. Carmona-Torres, Ph.D.
University of Almería (Spain)
jacarmona@ual.es

Adolfo J. Cangas, Ph.D.
University of Almería (Spain)
ajcangas@ual.es

Roberto Zárate, Ph.D.
University of California at Los Angeles (UCLA) (USA)
rzarate@ucla.edu

Ari Ucar
University of California at Los Angeles (UCLA) (USA)
ariaucar2692@gmail.com

Alvaro I. Langer, Ph.D
RedGesam Clinical Center and Pontifical Catholic University of Chile
alvaro.langer@gmail.com

Meagan Ramsey, Ph.D.
University of Utah
meagan.ramsey@psych.utah.edu

Ann M. Oberhauser, Ph.D.
Iowa State University
annober@iastate.edu

D'Arcy J. Reynolds Jr.
University of Southern Indiana
dreynolds1@usi.edu

Gregor Petrič, Ph.D.
Faculty of Social Sciences, University of Ljubljana
gregor.petric@fdv.uni-lj.si

Amy L. Gentzler, Ph.D.
West Virginia University
amy.gentzler@mail.wvu.edu

Lise Haddouk, Lecturer in Psychology,
Rouen University
lise.haddouk@gmail.com

Christa Nieuwboer, Ph.D.
Fontys University of Applied Sciences
c.nieuwboer@fontys.nl

Ruben Fukkink, Ph.D.
University of Amsterdam
r.fukkink@uva.nl

Danilo Garcia, Ph.D. Assistant Professor
Blekinge Centre of Competence, Blekinge County Council, Karlskrona, Sweden
Department of Psychology, University of Gothenburg, Gothenburg, Sweden
Department of Psychology, Lund University, Lund, Sweden
Network for Empowerment and Well-Being, Sweden
Anthropedia Foundation, Washington, Missouri, USA
Institute of Neuroscience and Physiology, Centre for Ethics, Law and Mental Health (CELAM), University of Gothenburg, Gothenburg, Sweden
danilo.garcia@icloud.com

Oscar N. E. Kjell, M. Sc.
Department of Psychology, Lund University, Lund, Sweden
Network for Empowerment and Well-Being, Sweden
oscar.kjell@psy.lu.se

Sverker Sikström, Ph. D. Professor
Department of Psychology, Lund University, Lund, Sweden
Network for Empowerment and Well-Being, Sweden
sverker.sikstrom@psy.lu.se

Lina Gega, PhD
Northumbria University at Newcastle
lina.gega@northumbria.ac.uk

David Fowler, DClinPsych
University of Sussex
D.Fowler@sussex.ac.uk

Richard White, Ph.D.
University of Exeter, UK
rw440@exeter.ac.uk

Andrew O'Neill, BSc(Hons)
University of South Africa
andrew.uk.oneill@gmail.com

Leanne M. Casey, PhD.
Griffith University and Menzies Health Institute - Queensland
l.casey@griffith.edu.au

Bonnie A.Clough, BPsySc (Hons.)
Institute for Resilient Regions, University of Southern Queensland BPsySc (Hons.)
Bonnie.Clough@usq.edu.au

Nicole Muscanell, Ph.D.
Pennsylvania State university, York
nlm19@psu.edu

Rosanna Guadagno, Ph.D
University of Texas, Dallas
Rosanna.Guadagno@utdallas.edu

Giuseppe Riva, Brenda K. Wiederhold, Pietro Cipresso

Introduction

The proposal of this book in the scientific panorama was to produce an edited collection of original chapters to provide a core and supplementary text with a number of well-recognized co-authors. There was a need for such a book as currently no all-encompassing compilation of diverse online behaviors from a social media perspective exists. Therefore, this collection makes a unique contribution to the rapidly growing area of cyberpsychology and has the additional advantage of being written in a sufficiently accessible way to appeal to cross-over disciplines, Internet service businesses ,and lay individuals alike who are interested in understanding the effects (positive and negative) of social media on individual, interpersonal, and societal behavior. Despite the continued rise of interest in the area of cyberpsychology, there is currently a dearth of reference works that can be recommended for the rapidly increasing number of core and modular courses being offered at both the undergraduate and postgraduate levels. Even fewer books have the range of expertise offered by the contributing authors in this collection, who come from diverse backgrounds to provide a good cross-over reference for other disciplines to which psychological theory and research is essential to understanding human behavior from a wide and varied approach. In order to achieve this, a number of the chapters contributed by experts from areas such as technology and the social sciences.

The opening paper by C.C. Nieuwboer and R.G. Fukkink discusses current variety of online services for parents, distinguishing between peer support and professional support. They focus on the design characteristics of these web-based resources and explain two major trends that give direction to future research and development.

Next, Regina M. Hechanova et al. in their paper "Online Counselling for Migrant Workers: Challenges and Opportunities" summarize research on online counseling, particularly for Filipino migrant workers. They present opportunities and challenges encountered by both counselees and counselors in online counseling and discuss the prospects for technology-mediated interventions in addressing the psychosocial needs of migrant workers.

After that there is a paper "Using Facebook: Good for Friendship But Not So Good for Intimate Relationships" by Ron Hammond and Hui-Tzu Grace Chou that examines the impact of using Facebook on the satisfaction with and quality of intimate relationships. Their study indicated that using Facebook is negatively related to the satisfaction with, and quality of, intimate relationships.

Later, a paper entitled "Communicatively integrated model of online community: A conceptual framework and empirical validation on a case of a health-related online community" by Gregor Petrič provides an alternative perspective on one of the key questions in online community research—How is online community possible? The hypotheses are tested on a sample of users from the biggest online health community in Slovenia. The authors conclude that a sense of virtual community is strongly associated with the quality of communication within that community.

Researchers Jamie Guillory and Jeffrey T. Hancock in their paper titled “Effects of Network Connections on Deception and Halo Effects in Linkedin” used two experiments to explore the pervasive influence that social relationships have on how we construct our self-presentations and how others form perceptions of our self-presentations on social networking websites.

After that there is a paper by Jesse Fox “The Dark Side of Social Networking Sites in Romantic Relationships” that evaluates the potential harmful effects of social networking sites. The author concludes that social networking sites can be a source of stress and relational turbulence for romantic partners from the early stages of dating to the post-breakup phase.

Next, researchers Leanne M. Casey and Bonnie A. Clough in their paper “Making and Keeping the Connection: Improving Consumer Attitudes and Engagement in E-Mental Health Interventions” discuss consumer attitudes toward e-mental health services, as well as the efficacy and use of strategies to improve attitudes and enhance engagement with such online services. Researchers assert that despite a lack of awareness about e-mental health services, individuals are receptive to gaining more information about these treatment options. Further, the effectiveness of e-mental health therapies depends on client engagement with these services.

After that there is a paper by Lise Haddouk entitled “Intersubjectivity in Video Interview”, which discusses how videoconferencing enables the introduction of an important element from the point of view of “sensoriality”: the body image, which engages the subjects’ interaction in a different way than in a written or verbal exchange. She concludes that the “virtual” doesn’t oppose the real, but that they similarly enable the emergence of the mental reality, and can also reach the same level of the symbolic as it is understood in psychoanalysis.

Next, Megan A. Moreno et al. present their paper “Institutional Review Board and Regulatory Considerations for Social Media Research”. They present a review of common risks inherent in social media research and consider how researchers can consider these risks when writing research protocols. Finally, it summarizes that social media websites are immensely popular and present new opportunities for research as well as new challenges for Institutional Review Boards.

After that Megan A. Moreno et al. describes “Media Theories and the Facebook Influence Model”, which illustrates key constructs that contribute to influence, incorporating perspectives of older adolescent Facebook users. She asserts that Facebook provides a novel lens for understanding behavioral influence in the context of existing behavioral theory.

Later, in “Social Networking and Romantic Relationships: A Review of Jealousy and Related Emotions” Nicole L. Muscanell and Rosanna E. Guadagno focus on contemporary research examining the use of SNSs and the resulting impact on jealousy and related emotions in the context of romantic relationships. Specifically, they review the way couples utilize their social media profiles, individual differences, such as gender differences in the experience of jealousy, and the role of social media on actual relationship outcomes. Finally, the paper summarizes that there is a combination of factors that may influence whether individuals are likely to experience SNS-related jealousy or related emotions.

Noella Edelmann follows with a paper titled "What is Lurking? A Literature Review of Research on Lurking" which provides an understanding of the phenomenon of online lurking by defining lurking and showing that lurkers are both active and valuable online participants. The paper emphasizes that the understanding of lurkers, their activities and value in the online environment is important when studying online environments, particularly in terms of the interpretation of online research and results.

Later, a paper by Sean D. Young and Alexander H. Jordan titled "Can Social Media Photos Influence College Students' Sexual Health Behaviors?" presents the potential for such investigations to shed light on the social psychological complexity of online social networks and pave the way for interventions that improve student health behaviors and wellbeing. They provide evidence that Facebook – in particular viewing peer photos – may influence college students' perceptions of sexual health behavior norms among their peers, which may in turn influence students' own sexual health behaviors.

Selim Gunuc et al. then examine "Social Networks as a Communication Tool from Children's Perspective: A Twitter Experience" focusing on the effects of social networks on the lifestyles and behaviors of people both psychologically and socially by linking theory and practice. Researchers assert that Twitter is a promising tool in educational contexts. They also discuss what major arrangements are needed in educational contexts in order to benefit from everything that Twitter has to offer.

Shengli Deng in her paper "The Influence of Extraversion on Individuals' SNS Use" presents a model to elucidate how extraversion, an important dimension of personality, affects the perceptions of Internet users and their continuance intention. She asserts that a significant relationship between extraversion and critical mass indicates that extraverts are more likely to be accompanied by similar SNS users.

Finally, Riva et al. conclude the collection by highlighting the complex nature of social media in defining what a social network is. In particular, Riva and colleagues try to understand the complexity arising by parsing technology and identity, and the relationship in-between. Social networks are different from previous media in terms of two opportunities. The first is the ability to visibly use social networks. The second is the possibility to decide how to present oneself to the people who make up the network (impression management).

Danilo Garcia, Oscar N. E. Kjell, Sverker Sikström

1 A Collective Picture of What Makes People Happy: Words Representing Social Relationships, not Money, are Recurrent with the Word 'Happiness' in Online Newspapers

Abstract: The Internet allows people to freely navigate through news and use that information to reinforce or support their own beliefs in, for example, different social networks. In this chapter we suggest that the representation of current predominant views in the news can be seen as collective expressions within a society. Seeing that the notion of what makes individuals happy has been of increasing interest in recent decades, we analyze the word happiness in online news. We first present research on the co-occurrence of the word happiness with other words in online newspapers. Among other findings, words representing people (e.g., "mom", "grandmother", "you"/"me", "us"/"them") often appear with the word happiness. Words like "iPhone", "millions" and "Google" on the other hand, almost never appear with the word happiness. Secondly, using words with predefined sets of psycholinguistic characteristics (i.e., word-norms measuring social relationships, money, and material things) we further examine differences between sets of articles including the word happiness and a random set of articles not including this word. The results revealed that the "happy" dataset was significantly related to social relationships word-norm, while the "neutral" dataset was related to the money word-norm. However, the "happy" dataset was also related to the material things word-norm. In sum, there is a relatively coherent understanding among members of a society concerning what makes us happy: relationships, not money; meanwhile there is a more complex relationship when it comes to material things. The semantic method used here, which is particularly suitable for analyzing large amounts of data, seems to be able to quantify collective ideas in online news that might be expressed through different social networks.

1.1 Introduction

The Internet allows people to freely navigate through online news and use that information to reinforce or support their own beliefs (Tewksbury & Althaus, 2000; Althaus & Tewksbury, 2002). Along this thinking, we have earlier suggested (Garcia & Sikström, 2013a) that current and predominant views in a society tend to perpetuate themselves through, besides inter- and intrapersonal conversations, narratives in newspapers, popular songs and books, movies, and television, and in recent decades, even in blogs and other online media (see Landauer, 2008). This representation can be seen as the vox populi (or the voice of the people) in a certain culture; a notion that becomes part of that culture's knowledge about the world (Giles, 2003). From a statistical point of view, because we share experiences with many others, there should be relatively good agreement among members of a society concerning different topics (Landauer, 2008). The semantic knowledge of specific topics and abstract ideas become the current and predominant views of society's collective picture of specific topics, recursively feeding on itself (Landauer, 2008). See Figure 1.1.

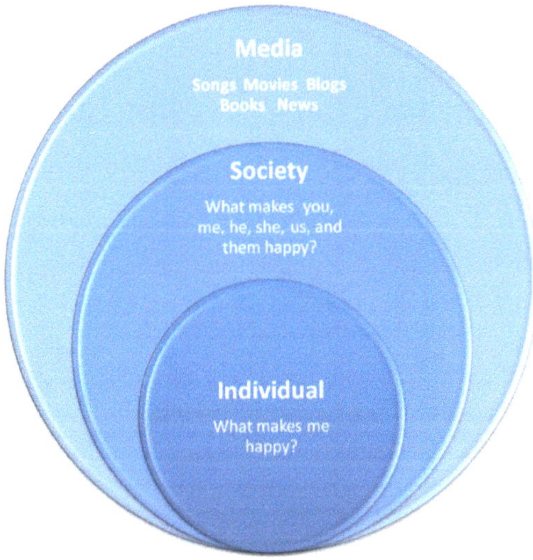

Figure 1.1. The individual's and society's ideas about happiness expressed in the media, which generates a collective theory of happiness; in turn, feeding the original ideas found at the individual and society levels

In the first part of this chapter we present how we tested our suggestions by analyzing the co-occurrence of the word happiness (lycka in Swedish) with other words in Swedish online newspapers (Garcia & Sikström, 2013a). The notion of happiness has for decades been of scientific and also of popular interest, and thus a natural choice for our study. Specifically, we hypothesized that by investigating the frequency or infrequency of the word happiness in relation to other words in the same language, we would be able to quantify a collective picture of "what makes people happy". This picture might be a belief or notion shared by the many and the one, but not necessary accurate in what really makes people happy (see for example Gilbert, 2007, who suggests that humans are actually inaccurate at imagining how happy we will be in the future or if we get things which we assume will make us happy). Although measurement of people's subjective experience of happiness using self-report is a cumulated or a collective result based on a large number of individuals (Gilbert,

2007), it is different from our proposed quantification of a collective theory of "what makes us happy". This is analogous to the difference between commuting to work by public transport and driving your own car, in which the former is a collective type of transport available for everyone. In other words, this representation of "what makes us happy" is collective in nature because it is a picture communicated by relatively few individuals to the masses. In the second part of this chapter we expand our earlier research by using words with predefined sets of psycholinguistic characteristics (i.e., word-norms) to further examine differences between sets of articles including the word happiness ("happy" dataset) and a random set ("neutral" dataset) of articles not including this word.

1.2 The Co-Occurrence of the Word Happiness With Other Words in Online Newspapers

In our original article (Garcia & Sikström, 2013), news articles were collected from the fifty largest daily newspapers in Sweden published online during 2010. These online newspapers are in most cases also published in printed format, making them representative of public media in Sweden. We randomly selected 3,000 of these articles that included the Swedish word "lycka" for the "happy" dataset, and 3,000 articles that did not include this word for the "neutral" dataset.

The data were analyzed with words as the basic unit of analysis. In total there were 1,065,429 words in the "happy" dataset, 493,927 words in the "neutral" dataset, and 93,093 unique words in both datasets. A frequency vector was generated consisting of the number of occurrences of each unique word in the "happy" dataset, and a similar vector was generated for the "neutral" dataset. For each unique word, a 2-by-2 chi-square test was conducted, consisting of four frequencies: the frequencies of the word in the two datasets and the number of remaining words in the two datasets. The resulting p-values were corrected for multiple comparisons using the Bonferroni method (i.e., multiplying each p-value by N). Words that were significant (at the 0.05 level) were selected for further analyses. The resulting significant words were divided into different word classes. Due to the large number of significant words, we find it appropriate to only present the p-value, whilst omitting other data that are typically presented in chi-square analysis, such as the chi-square value and the number of occurrences in each cell. In Table 1, the words are ordered by increasing p-values, where these Bonferroni corrected p-values were in the range $0.00001 < p < 0.05$. The total number of words, in all chi-square tests, is the sum of the words in both datasets. In Table 1, we present the results for pronouns, proper names, and nouns.

Table 1.1. Words discriminating between articles including or not including the word happiness (Printed with permission from D. Garcia and S. Sikström)

Word classes	"Happy" dataset Articles including the word happiness	"Neutral" dataset Articles NOT including the word happiness
Proper nouns	Victoria Tommy Daniel Anna Werner Samuelsson MFF Westling Salem Alfsson Jari VM Rydström Runo Thoralf Fakir Mats Kay v75 Kojer Swärd Linda Jim Tidholm Lagerbäck Svante Jonsson Johan Nigeria Iphoto Drogba Petri Eva Smith Zlatan Falkehed United Stellan Alice Taylor Kalmar Patrik Falk Bergendahl Degerfors Argentina Gustavsson Eric Franzen Hammarby Astrid Kuba Modo	Google Windows IT ipad iphone Microsoft Apple EU HP IDG Office Mac Microsofts Intel Sony Asus IBM Googles Facebook Strömsund Nokia Apples HTC Oracle Samsung IDC SAP Yahoo TT Eskilstuna Dell Linux Toshiba Mcafee Teliasonera Carnegie +143 more words.
Pronouns	Jag (I) du (you) min (my) mig (me) ni (you) dig (you) det (it) din (yours) hon (she) mitt (mine) mina (mine) han (he) man (one) henne (her) er (you) honom (him) varandra (each other) ditt (yours) dina (yours) hans (his) hennes (hers) oss (us) dem (them) vem (who) vi (we) dom (them)	–
Nouns	livet (life) människor (people) fråga (question) kram (hug) kärlek (love) pappa (dad) kronprinsessan (the Crown Princess) hjärtans (heart's) mormor (grandma') mamma (mom) hälsningar (greetings) dag (day) monarkin (the monarchy) deklarationen (the income-tax return) hälsning (greeting) kungen (the king) kramar (hugs) glädje (joy) fotboll (football) stadion (stadium) jobbannons (job ad) bröllopet (the wedding) brudparet (the wedding couple) dotter (daugther) hjärta (heart) lyckan (the happiness) coach (coach) familj (family) tränare (trainer) deklaration (income-tax return) chatten (the chat) träningen (the workout) spelarna (players) sambo (living-together) spelare (player) moderator (moderator) muslimer (muslims) piller (pills) prins (prince) son (son) låten (the song) bröllop (wedding) mat (food) familjen (the family) känslor (feelings) barn (children) svar (answer) vänner (friends) talet (the speech) puss (kiss) drömmar (dreams) frågor (questions) mobbning (bullying) guld (gold) artist (artist) webbplats (website) lillen (the kid) avdraget (the deduction) tjej (girl) kärleken (the love) scenen (the stage) karriär (carreer) längtan (the longing) mens (menstruation) lag (team) dröm (dream) landslaget (the national team) make (husband) scen (scene) uppskov (deferral).	procent (percent) kronor (crowns) miljoner (millions) polisen (the police) kvartalet (the quarter) miljarder (billions) företaget (the company) användare (user) vd (CEO) dollar (dollar) företag (company) usb (usb) datorer (computers) företagets (the company's) kunder (customers) data (data) marknaden(the market) funktioner (features/functions) kommunen (municipality) bolaget (the company) skärm (screen) tum (inch) app (app) leverantörer (suppliers) gigabyte (gigabytes) branden (the fire) servrar (servers) leverantören (the supplier) mkr (million of crowns) system (system) tillverkare (manufacturer) januari (January) affärer (business) bolaget (the company) +373 more words.

Note. The words are divided into the word classes proper nouns, pronouns, and nouns (other word classes are removed). The words are ordered by increasing p-values in the range $0.000001 < p < 0.05$ and only the approximately 40 most significant words are included. All words are significant following corrections for multiple comparisons (Bonferroni). English translation of pronouns and nouns in parentheses

Proper names associated with the "happy" dataset were almost exclusively names of people, where the Swedish Crown Princess' name "Victoria" was the most discriminative word followed by proper names associated with sports, especially soccer, for example, Zlatan, Lagerbäck (the former coach of Sweden's national soccer team), Drogba, Argentina, and Nigeria. Proper names discriminative for the "neutral" dataset were almost exclusively company names, where the most significant companies were in the IT field. Although these results were obviously inflated by the overrepresentation of the Swedish royal wedding and the FIFA World Cup in the media during 2010, the results with regard to relationships are in accordance with current findings suggesting that happy individuals always report strong positive social relationships (Diener & Seligman, 2002, 2004). Moreover, research on widows (Lucas, Clark, Georgellis & Diener, 2003) and divorced people (Clark, Diener, Georgellis & Lucas, 2008) has shown great declines in happiness precisely before and after the loss of a significant other. Also in line with this, the results regarding pronouns show that almost all pronouns discriminated between the datasets, and all of the significant pronouns were associated with the "happy" dataset (e.g., I, you, mine, me, yours, and she) and the results regarding nouns associated with the "happy" dataset were largely semantically related to love or people (e.g., people, hug, love, dad, grandmother, mom). In contrast, the "neutral" dataset was associated with nouns representing money or companies (e.g., crowns, millions, billions).

These results lead us to suggest that a collective theory of "what makes us happy" reflects research based on self-reports showing that people who put more value in love and relationships rather than money are happy (Diener & Biswas-Diener, 2002). On a larger level, research has only found small correlations between income and happiness within nations—the correlations are larger in poor nations, and the risk of unhappiness is much higher for people living in poverty. Moreover, economic growth in most economically developed societies has been accompanied by only small increases in happiness levels (Diener & Seligman, 2002). In other words, as long as basic needs are met, money or material things do not seem to increase happiness levels. Accordingly, our results do not mean that money and material things make us unhappy, rather that specific words representing money and material things are not associated with happiness in the media.

Our study was an addition to recent research on happiness using large datasets of texts (e.g., Dodds & Danforth, 2010; Dodds, Harris, Kloumann, Bliss & Danforth, 2011; Garcia & Sikström, 2013ab; 2014; Schwartz, Eichstaedt, Kern, Dziurzynski, Ramones et al., 2013) and also complemented self-reporting techniques by offering an approach to the investigation on how "what makes us happy" is presented through the mass media to large segments of a society at the same time. Earlier theories of individual unconsciousness and consciousness have suggested that humans possess a collective level of awareness or knowledge. Carl Jung (1968), for example, proposed a collective unconscious consisting of memories accumulated throughout human history. These memories are represented in archetypes that are expressed in the symbols, myths, and beliefs found in many cultures, such as the image of a god, an evil force, the hero, the good mother, and the quest for self-unity and wholeness. Similarly, the French sociologist Émile Durkheim (1965) coined the term collective consciousness, which refers to the shared beliefs and moral attitudes that serve as a unifying force within a society. Determining whether this representation of happiness in our study is implicit (as Jung's theorized collective unconscious) or explicit is beyond the scope of our current research. Nevertheless, although at a collective level people probably understand the influence of close and warm relationships on their own happiness, they might not be consciously aware that such relationships are necessary for happiness (Lyubomirsky, 2007). After all, the importance of social relationships to a happy life is indeed epitomized in a simplified and larger-than-life manner in the standard ending of many fairy tales: "...and they lived happily ever after". Likewise, most people seem to understand that money can't buy happiness.....or love, as in the in the famous Beatles song "Can't buy me love". Moreover, we have suggested that the representation of a collective picture of "what makes us happy" in the media seems to be a notion that does not fit with theories of happiness focusing on individual differences (e.g., the theory of "Virtues in Action" by Peterson & Seligman, 2004) or for determining whether focusing on intentional activities is related to a happy life (e.g., Diener & Oishi, 2005).

In sum, our findings seem to mirror a collective theory of "what makes us happy" or an agreement among members of a community about what makes people happy: relationships, not money or material things. This picture is presented to all members of the society through newspapers and other media, making it collective in nature. Because this information is accessible through the Internet, it might be used by readers to reinforce or support their own beliefs and express those beliefs when social networking. In the next part of this chapter, we present new analyses of the same dataset using quantitative semantics and words with predefined sets of psycholinguistic characteristics (i.e., word-norms) measuring social relationships, money, and material things. We use this approach to further investigate if a collective picture of "what make us happy" suggests that social relationships, rather than money are of more importance in enabling happiness.

1.3 Measuring Happiness' Relationship to Social Relationships, Money, And Material Things: The Word-Norm Approach

The method we employed to quantitatively re-analyse the news texts and word-norms is called Latent Semantic Analysis (LSA; Landauer & Dumais, 1997). This method involves applying an algorithm to create semantic representations of the various semantic based contents. In short, the LSA-algorithm assumes that words that occur close to each other in text can be used as a source of information; which is used to create multi-dimensional semantic representations. That is, the context that words occur in normally consists of a meaning that more often than not corresponds to the meaning of the word (Landauer & Dumais, 1997; Landauer, 2008; Landauer, McNamara, Dennis & Kintsch, 2008). As a result, the content can be represented as a vector in a multi-dimensional semantic space. In turn, the semantic representations of single words can be used to summarize larger text by adding the representations, and normalizing the length of the vectors to one. The similarity between semantic representations can be measured by the cosines of the angle between the vectors, which is mathematically equivalent to multiplying each dimension with each other and adding the resulting products. This similarity measure can then be used in standard statistical procedures such as correlations, regressions, t-tests, analysis of variance, etc (for studies applying regression analysis using semantic representations see: Karlsson, Sikström & Willander, 2013; Garcia & Sikström, 2013ab, 2014; Gustafsson, Sikström & Lindholm, in press; Rosenberg, Sikström & Garcia, 2013; Roll, Mårtensson, Sikström, Apt, Arnling-Bååth & Horne, 2011). Semantic representations for the text content under investigation, which here includes the word contexts from the articles as well as the word-norms, were carried out using Semantic Excel, which is a web-based software developed by the last author of this chapter (S. Sikström). This software is specifically developed to create and analyse semantic representations and can be found at: www.semanticexcel.com.

The use of word-norms to analyze the previously used news dataset allowed us to emulate the interaction between readers and the text in the online newspapers. Participants, seen as readers of news, were asked to generate words they associated to hypothesis-relevant key words: "social relationships" (the Swedish word: sociala relationer); "money" (the Swedish word: pengar); and "material things" (the Swedish word: "materiella ting"). These word-norms enabled us to examine which of the happiness or random-word contexts they related the most to. Thus we could hypothesize that the social relationships word-norm will relate more to the happiness contexts than to the random-word contexts — the opposite pattern will occur for the money and material things word-norms.

1.3.1 Methods

1.3.1.1 Participants and procedure

We recruited participants using the social network Facebook. The sample consisted of 10 females and 5 males. The age ranged from 22 to 64 years with a mean age of 34 (sd = ±12.7) years. Participants had a wide range of employment or study interest: 8 participants reported to study (2 philosophy, 2 law, 1 psychology, 1 ethnology, 1 graphic design, and 1 did not give an answer), 6 being employed (2 teacher, 1 PhD student, 1 economist, 1 carpenter and 1 dentist) and 1 being retired (from being a teacher). In the beginning of the study participants were informed about their right to withdraw at any time and that there responses will be kept confidential, after which they were asked to consent to the study. They were subsequently asked to spend approximately two to three minutes generating words that they associated with the key words that they were provided; these were introduced in random order between participants. The survey took approximately five minutes; at the end of the survey participants were thanked and debriefed.

1.3.1.2 Creating Semantic Representations

To create high quality semantic representations one typically needs a larger dataset than what is usually collected in experimental studies. Therefore we first created a word space using a very large text corpus; and then use this as a foundation for the analyses of the experimental data. The word space that comes with the semantic excel software was used (www.semanticexcel.com). This space was created using a Google N-gram database for Swedish text, which is based on 1 Terabyte of text data (see the Google N-gram project: http://ngrams.googlelabs.com). From this database, a co-occurrence matrix was made comprised of 5-grams contexts; the rows consisted of the 120000 most common words and the columns of the 10000 most common words in the N-gram database. We did not use a stemming algorithm, mainly because word stems contain additional information that might be lost during stemming, and also because the large size of the Google N-gram database makes the space large enough to provide sufficient data on words with unusual stems. Each cell in the co-occurrence matrix represented the frequency of the 4 context words in the N-gram on the columns relative to one target word on the rows. Finally, the cells where normalized by calculating the logarithm plus one.

Singular value decomposition was applied to compress the information of the matrix whilst preserving as much information as possible. This final matrix is called the semantic representation of each word. A synonym test was used to establish the best solution of dimensions; the highest score (and hence the optimal number of dimensions) was found at 256 dimensions. Accordingly, the current analysis yielded a semantic quantification that represents the most frequent words used in the Swedish N-gram database, where each word is best described with a high dimensional vector normalized to the length of one.

1.3.1.3 Creating Semantic Scales: The word-norms

The number of words associated with social relationships was 171, including words such as 'friend', 'support', 'enemies', and 'activities'. Money included 203 words, such as, 'wealth', 'power', 'society', and 'possibilities'. Material things consisted of 156 words, such as, 'joy', 'jealousy', 'craving', and 'abundance'. Words generated by more than one participant (for example 'friendship', 'value'; 'consumption') were kept in for the analyses, so that duplicated words were weighted heavier than non-duplicated words. Words that were misspelt but where the meaning was clearly understandable were corrected prior the analyses; 1 'word' within the material things dataset was unrecognizable and thus removed. The final three lists of words were separately summarized by aggregating their associated semantic representation, and then normalized to the length of one. This procedure created three word-norms related to social relations, money, and material things.

1.3.1.4 Applying the semantic scales on articles including/not including the word Happiness

Two sets were created. Articles including the word happiness (i.e., "lycka" in Swedish) and articles not including this word. This dataset included 1867 random documents and 4185 happiness documents. The words in each article were summarized by aggregating their associated semantic representation, and then normalized to the length of one. This procedure created a semantic representation for each article. We then measured the semantic similarity between the semantic representation of the articles, with the semantic representations related to social relations, money, and material things. The semantic similarity was measured by the cosines of the angel between the two associated semantic representations (i.e., vectors), which can be mathematically calculated as the dot product (Landauer, McNamara, Dennis & Kintsch, 2008). We call the resulting values the semantic scale or word-norms of social relations, money, and material things respectively. These scales were calculated for each article.

1.3.2 Results

Social relationships. The analysis examining the one-tailed hypothesis that the value on the social relationship semantic scale is higher for happiness contexts (mean = 0.301; sd = 0.0443) compared to random contexts (mean = 0.228; sd = 0.052), revealed a significant difference as measured by a t-test in the hypothesized direction ($p < .0001$; $t = 56.233$).

Money. The analysis examining the one-tailed hypothesis stating that the money-norm will be more related with the random (mean = 0.251; sd = 0.048), as compared with the happiness (mean = 0.249; sd = 0.0401) word contexts were also significant ($p = .032$; $t = 1.859$) and therefore accepted.

Material things. In direct contrast to the one-tailed hypothesis, the analysis revealed that material things were in fact significantly more related to happiness (mean = 0.256; sd = 0.039749) rather than the random (mean = 0.218; sd = 0.034) word contexts. Hence the hypothesis was rejected ($p < .0001$; $t = -36.4455$).

1.3.3 Discussion

Overall the results supported the hypothesis in that happiness contexts, as compared with random-words contexts, relate more to the concept of social relationships and less with the concept of money. However, the results from the material things word-norm was, in contrast to the hypothesis, related to happiness, as compared with random words contexts; leading to some interesting enquiries. This result, for example, might reflect that substantial parts of public domains embrace and uphold a consumer society and that this 'way of life' is depicted as a happy life. It might also illustrate that the relationship between happiness and money versus material things appear to be rather intricate and complex.

A visual inspection of the words included in the material thing word-norm appears to indicate that it might capture, at least, two rather separate aspects. In our original article (Garcia & Sikström, 2013a) we labelled material things those words representing advanced technologies (e.g., iPad, computer) and company names (e.g. Windows, Sony and even 'company'). This is in accordance with some of the words in the material things word-norm presented here (e.g., computers, buy, fashion, commercial, cars, boats, diamonds, etc); which clearly overlap with the money word-norm. Noticeable, the material things word-norm also included positive emotion words (e.g. joy, satisfying, fun, and wonderful); whilst also taping into what perhaps could be categorized as a wider sense of basic needs for life and perhaps even happiness (e.g., life, need, choice availability, house, the home, identity, and fellowship). The results appear to tap into what Aristotle (trans. 2009) exclaimed: "The life of money-making is one undertaken under compulsion, and wealth is evidently not the good we are seeking; for it is merely useful and for the sake of something else" (p.7). Perhaps the material things word-norm taps in to this 'something else'; such as basic needs for a healthy and long-lasting happy life. In other words, it is what you do with the money that influences your level of well-being and happiness; such as spending it on safety and leisure time with important others; rather than consuming goods that lead to an ever ending increase in wants and desires (e.g., Easterlin, 1974; Lyubomirsky, 2007).

1.4 Limitations, Strenghts, And Suggestions For Future Studies

It might be worth highlighting the consideration of using comparison contexts. That is, it might be useful to select more than the current random-word contexts employed in this study. For example, as we here examined happiness in the context of datasets including this specific emotion and compared with unspecific random-words datasets, it could be argued that our findings to some degree reflect emotions in general rather than happiness specifically. That is, emotions are inherently ascribed to humans as a characteristic and are not applied to material things or for example companies, as these do not experience emotions. Although it should be noted that countries such as

Argentina, Nigeria, and Kuba were associated with the happiness contexts. However, future research could create several comparison contexts; for example, including random contexts constrained to emotion-contexts that include various emotion words or alternatively compare specific emotions such as happiness and unhappiness-contexts. This would further bring nuances and details of the nature to any concept under investigation. However, it is worth pointing out that the word-norm analysis actually showed that, although emotions are not ascribed to immaterial things, the material things word-norm was actually related to happiness context but not related to the random words contexts.

Similarly it is important to remember that overall happiness contexts are more related to social relationships than random words; however, certain kinds of social relationships are probably harmful and decrease happiness (e.g., see how depressive symptoms spread person-to-person through social networks, Rosenquist, Fowler & Christakis, 2011). Hence as a follow up, future research should examine word-norms that are more detailed, such as 'supportive social relationships' versus 'destructive social relationships' in, for example, happiness versus unhappiness contexts.

Furthermore, our new results also illustrate the strengths of using LSA in conjunction with our previous method investigating the frequency of words (Garcia & Sikström, 2013a). This approach is suitable in highlighting the Text-Norm specific interaction. That is, it can emulate the interplay between the one who made the text in the first place and how different groups of readers (e.g., students, laymen, or experts) might interpret it differently. It is important to point out that the collective picture of "what makes us happy" as represented in the online news (i.e., that relationships not money makes us happy) from our original study, is not necessarily what people actually use when networking. The results using the word-norms actually suggest that people might express happiness on the Internet by associating happiness to plain material things (e.g., computers, buy, fashion, cars, boats, diamonds, etc), positive emotion words (e.g. joy, satisfying, fun, and wonderful), identity and basic needs (e.g., life, need, choice availability, house, the home, identity, and fellowship).

1.5 Concluding Remarks

With regard to a collective picture of "what makes us happy", there is a relatively coherent understanding among members of a society concerning what makes us happy: relationship, not money. Nevertheless, there is a more complex relationship when it comes to material things. From a methodological perspective, the different approaches used here seem to be able to quantify collective ideas in online news, blogs, and other type of Internet medium. These methods can be suggested to study how people express themselves through different social networks. Using word-norms can be a straightforward and sound way to complement keywords interpretations. Mainly because the research then becomes more distanced from the interpretation processes, whilst at the same time it can reflect different interactions, such as between different texts (e.g., news articles, blogs, and twitter) and various readers (laypersons, students, or difference experts). Indeed, we believe it might be worth pointing out that this norm-based approach has the potential to constitute a sound complement in examining and interpreting keywords that are different between word texts, in particularly for analysis of large datasets.

> "I cannot think it unlikely that there is such a total book
> on some shelf in the universe. I pray to the unknown gods
> that some man--even a single man, tens of centuries ago--
> has perused and read this book. If the honor and wisdom
> and joy of such a reading are not to be my own,
> then let them be for others. Let heaven exist,
> though my own place may be in hell.
> Let me be tortured and battered and annihilated,
> but let there be one instant, one creature,
> wherein thy enormous Library may find its justification."
>
> In "The Library of Babel" by Jorge Luis Borges.

Acknowledgements: The development of this Chapter was funded by a grant from The Swedish Research Council (Dnr. 2015-01229).

References

Althaus, S. L., & Tewksbury, D. (2002). Agenda setting and the "new" news: Patterns of issue importance among readers of the paper and online versions of the New York Times. Communication Research, 29, 180-107.

Aristotle. (2009) The Nicomachean Ethics. (Ross, D, Trans.). Oxford Univesity Press.

Clark, A., Diener, E., Georgellis, Y., & Lucas, R. E. (2008). Lags and leads in life satisfaction. A test of the baseline hypothesis. Economic Journal, 118, F222-F443.

Diener, E., & Biswas-Diener, R. (2002). Will money increase subjective well-being? A literature review and guide to needed research. Social Indicators Research, 57, 119-169.

Diener, E., & Biswas-Diener, R. (2008) Happiness – Unlocking the mysteries of psychological wealth. Oxford: Blackwell Publishing.

Diener, E., & Oishi, S. (2005). The nonobvious social psychology of happiness. Psychology Inquiry, 16, 162-167.

Diener, E., & Seligman, M. E. P. (2002). Very happy people. Psychological Science, 13, 80-83.

Diener, E., & Seligman, M. E. P. (2004). Beyond Money. Toward and economy of well-being. Psychological Science in the Public Interest, 5, 1-32.

Dodds, P. S., & Danforth, C. M. (2010). Measuring the happiness of large-scale written expression: Songs, blogs, and presidents. Journal of Happiness Studies, 11, 441-456.

Dodds, P. S., Harris, K. D., Kloumann, I. M., Bliss, C. A., & Danforth, C. M. (2011). Temporal Patterns of Happiness and Information in a Global Social Network: Hedonometrics and Twitter. PLoS ONE, 6: e26752. doi:10.1371/journal.pone.0026752.

Durkheim, E. (1965) The elementary forms of religious life (J. W. Swain, Trans.). New York: Free Press. (Original work published 1915).
Eastelin R.A. (1974) Does economic growth improve the human lot? Some empirical evidence. Nations and households in economic growth, 89-125.
Garcia, D., & Sikström, S. (2013a). A Collective Theory of Happiness: Words Related to the Word Happiness in Swedish Online Newspapers. Cyberpsychology, Behavior, and Social Networking, 16, 469–472. DOI: 10.1089/cyber.2012.0535.
Garcia, D., & Sikström, S. (2013b). Quantifying the Semantic Representations in Adolescents' Memories of Positive and Negative Life Events. Journal of Happiness Studies, 14, 1309–1323. DOI: 10.1007/s10902-012-9385-8.
Garcia, D., & Sikström, S. (2014). The Dark Side of Facebook – Dark Triad of Personality Predicts Semantic Representation of Status Updates. Personality and Individual Differences, 67, 92–94 DOI: 10.1016/j.paid.2013.10.001.
Gilbert, D. (2007) Stumbling on happiness. London: Harpercollins Publishers.
Giles, D. (2003) Media Psychology. Hillsdale, NJ: Lawrence Erlbaum.
Jung, C. (1968) Archetypes of the collective unconscious. In: C, Jung, Collected Works of C. G. Jung, Vol. 9, Part 1 (2nd ed.). Princeton University Press.
Landauer, T. K. (2008). LSA as a theory of meaning. In T. K. Landauer, D. S. McNamara, S. Dennis, and W. Kintsch. (Eds.) Handbook of Latent Semantic Analysis. Mahwah: Lawrence Erlbaum Associates.
Landauer, T. K., & Dumais, S. (1997). A solution to Plato's problem: The latent semantic analysis theory of acquisition, induction, and representation of knowledge. Psychological Review, 104, 211–240.
Landauer, T. K., McNamara, D. S., Dennis, S., & Kintsch, W. (2008). Handbook of latent semantic analysis. Mahwah: Lawrence Erlbaum Associates.
Lucas, R. E., Clark, A. E., Georgellis, Y., & Diener, E. (2003). Re-examining adaptation and the setpoint model of happiness: Reactions to changes in marital status. Journal of Personality and Social Psychology, 84, 527-539.
Lyubomirsky, S. (2007) The How of Happiness. A Scientific approach to getting the life you want. New York: Penguin Press.
Peterson, C., & Seligman, M. E. P. (2004) Character strengths and virtues: A handbook and classification. Oxford: Oxford University Press.
Rosenquist, J.N., Fowler, J.H., & Christakis, N.A. (2011) Social network determinants of depression. Molecular Psychiatry, 16, 273–281.
Schwartz, H. A., Eichstaedt, J. C., Kern, M. L., Dziurzynski, L., Ramones, S. M., et al. (2013). Personality, Gender, and Age in the Language of Social Media: The Open- Vocabulary Approach. PLoS ONE 8(9): e73791. doi:10.1371/journal.pone.0073791.
Tewksbury, D., Althaus, S. L. (2000) Differences in knowledge acquisition among readers of the paper and online versions of a national newspaper. Journalism & Mass Communication Quarterly, 77, 457-79.

D'Arcy J. Reynolds, Jr., William B. Stiles, Terry Hanley

2 The Online Calming Effect: Does the Internet Provide a More Comfortable Modality for Conducting Psychotherapy?

Abstract: This chapter proposes the hypothesis that online therapeutic work may be relatively less arousing than face-to-face work. It focuses on a study in which the impact of exchanges of online therapy text exchanges were compared to previously published results in face-to-face therapy using both aggregate benchmarking and mixed effects modeling. Therapists (N = 30) and clients (N = 30) engaged in online therapy were recruited from private practitioner sites, e-clinics, online counseling centers, and mental health related discussion boards. In a naturalistic design, they each visited an online site weekly and completed the Session Evaluation Questionnaire, a standard impact measure, for at least six weeks. Results indicated that the impact of text therapy was similar to or even more positive than that of face-to-face therapy. Of particular interest, online participants gave much lower SEQ Arousal ratings compared to their face-to-face counterparts, consistent with previous results. We call our hypothesis the online calming effect. This study's small size and naturalistic design impose limitations on its sensitivity and generalizability, but its suggestion of an online calming effect is intriguing.

This research was supported by grant 05.1207 from the Ohio Department of Mental Health. We thank Chelsi Day, Elizabeth Lawton, Erin Hoffman, Beth Linkhart, Carlyn Porter, and Emily Verkamp for data collection; Britt Carr and Christian Ratterman for help with the website conceptualization, implementation, and testing; John Bailer and Michael Hughes for statistical consultation; and Art Cooksey, Jason Zack, and John Grohol for recruitment assistance.

Disclosure Statement: All authors assert that no competing financial interests exist.

Correspondence and requests for reprints concerning this article should be addressed to D'Arcy J. Reynolds, Jr., Department of Psychology, University of Southern Indiana, Evansville, IN, 47712, 812-461-5242 (voice), 812-465-7152 (fax), dreynolds1@usi.edu (e-mail).

With the advent of the Internet, online practitioners have used successively more sophisticated computer-mediated tools to provide psychotherapy. Currently, the most common modality for Internet psychotherapy is asynchronous text-based email, although synchronous text-based chat services are becoming more popular (Finn & Barak, 2010; the International Society for Mental Health Online, 2011). Typically such services vary in cost, with asynchronous therapy conducted through email ranging from $25 to $125 per email exchange and text chat or webcams costing $1.75 to $4.99 per minute (Grohol, 2011). Despite technological advances increasing the availability of modalities such as videoconferencing, these services are often viewed as costly and thus less attractive (e.g., Barak & Grohol, 2011; Heinlen, Welfel, Richmond, & Rak, 2003).

Studies examining the characteristics of online therapists have found that online therapists are predominantly middle-aged, highly educated, competent, North American, cognitive-behavioral, and experienced (Chester & Glass, 2006). Furthermore, they have commonly developed online therapeutic skills through informal means such as textbooks, rather than formal training, and they are satisfied with their practice and believed it to be effective (Finn & Barak, 2010). Where the characteristics of online clients have been explored, clients have been predominately female (Chester & Glass; DuBois, 2004). They commonly thought that online counseling would be free of charge (DuBois) and sought short-term therapy mostly for 'relationship issues,' 'family issues,' 'mood disorders,' and 'anxiety' (Chester & Glass).

Some of the challenges of the online environment for therapy include the missing non-verbal communication, the increased opportunity for miscommunication, the time delay present when using e-mail, the computer skill deficiency of either the counselor or client, the inability to intervene when there is a crisis, the cultural clashes that may occur, the question of identity (are they really who they say they are?), and the vulnerability of sending sensitive material over the internet (Rochlen, Zack & Speyer, 2004). However, the distinctive opportunities of providing therapy in an online environment include that it is convenient and increases access for clients, the client may feel safer and thus disinhibited by the online environment, e-mail provides a meditative 'zone of reflection', writing is therapeutic, individuals report feeling close to others they meet online (this has been described by Lombard & Ditton [1997] as 'Telepresence'), and it provides immediate access to internet-based resources (Rochlen et al.).

Studies examining the effectiveness of online therapy consistently demonstrate strong support for such practice (Barak & Grohol, 2011). A meta-analysis of the outcomes of 92 internet delivered therapy studies found such work to have a medium effect size (0.53) which is enduring in nature (Barak, Hen, Boniel-Nissim, & Shapira, 2008). Additionally, this study found no significant differences between therapy delivered face-to-face and a web-based therapeutic intervention. Such compelling findings appear to have countered many of the early critical reports that questioned the therapeutic effectiveness or even the appropriateness of using e-mail as a therapeutic endeavor (e.g., Maheu & Gordon, 2000).

Online therapy is arguably less stimulus rich than conventional face-to-face therapy (i.e., it lacks the nonverbal cues), but it need not lead to a lesser quality of interaction (Grohol, 1999). Anecdotal reports have suggested that clients and therapists perceive text therapy as similar to traditional therapy. For example, Fenichel and his colleagues (2002) remarked on the "similarity between a text-based transcript and a comparable office session," noting "the expressiveness and depth of the text-based communication" (¶ 26). A systematic review of empirical investigations indicated that online therapy seems to be at least equivalent to face-to-face therapy in terms of therapeutic alliance and that there is a relation between the therapeutic alliance and online therapy outcome (Sucala et al., 2012). Thus, there is a need to examine differences in processes between online therapy and face-to-face therapy (Mallen, Vogel, Rochlen, & Day, 2005).

This chapter focuses on a hypothesis involving session impact. Session impact encompasses participants' evaluations of their session and participants' post-session affective state (Stiles et al., 1994). It may be distinguished from in-session behaviors (e.g., the therapists' verbal interventions) and from long-term outcome (cf. Rosen & Proctor, 1981). Measures of session impact offer an immediate index of the interpersonal climate, sense of progress, affect following therapeutic encounters, and consumer satisfaction.

Our hypothesis suggests that online therapeutic work may be relatively less arousing than face-to-face work. We call this the online calming effect, manifested as lower post-session arousal among online therapy participants. We suggest that clients tend to experience the online environment as more comfortable and less threatening than the face-to-face milieu (Cohen & Kerr, 1998; Littell, Milliken, Stroup, & Wolfinger, 1996). Preliminary analyses were consistent with these expectations (Reynolds, Stiles, & Grohol, 2006). Our study extended previous descriptive investigations, which have used cross-sectional designs (Cook & Doyle, 2002; Leibert, Archer, Munson, & York, 2006; Preschl, Maercker, & Wagner, 2011), by examining online processes longitudinally.

Psychotherapy centrally involves building a relationship, and doing therapy online by text is in some ways analogous to cultivating relationships in social networking. The online calming effect may be considered as an analogue of the social safety of interacting online in social networking. On the other hand, therapy and social relationships also have different norms that determine the commonly discussed content. Online therapy is private and intimate, and it provides clients with permission to unburden themselves, so the content is typically troubled. In contrast, social networking often involves large, public, and impersonal networks and tends to constrain members to positive self-presentations to secure desired social rewards; this tends to yield mainly untroubled content (Day, 2013; Forest &Wood, 2012).

Arousal represents a major dimension of mood states across a wide range of situations (Russell, 1978, 1979). In a practical sense, everything is arousing or calming to some degree. Although the arousing impact of face-to-face psychotherapy sessions has not yet been widely investigated, arousal is likely important in something as emotionally potent as confronting troubled content in face-to-face therapy. For example, it might be connected with tendencies to put therapeutic learnings into practice or to act upon personal changes in the short term (Stiles et al., 1994). A relatively calming influence of the online environment has been suggested by participants' ratings in two studies of online psychotherapy.

In the first study, Cohen and Kerr (1998) measured participants' anxiety before and after a single meeting of traditional face-to-face psychotherapy and synchronous text-based computer-mediated psychotherapy (chat therapy). Clients scored higher on post-session arousal after face-to-face sessions than after online sessions, but showed no differences on other impact scales. Conceivably, the exposure to the online environment during their therapy sessions may have accounted for clients decreased arousal ratings.

A second study further suggested the online calming effect by directly examining online psychotherapy. Using a naturalistic design, Reynolds, Stiles, Bailer, and Hughes (2013) investigated 30 therapists and 30 clients who each visited an online site weekly and reported on at least 6 weeks of either e-mail or text chat therapeutic exchanges. Both preliminary analyses based on a partial sample (Reynolds et al., 2006), and analysis of the full sample (Reynolds et al., 2013) found modestly and substantially lower arousal ratings of online therapists and clients (respectively) relative to their face-to-face counterparts. The remainder of this chapter focuses on this second study.

2.1 How the Study Was Conducted

2.1.1 Participants

Participants were 30 therapists and 30 clients engaged in online therapy. Therapists each saw either 1 to 2 clients (mode = 1 client) for a total of 394 therapist-rated weeks of exchanges. Clients (N = 30) contributed a total of 475 client-rated weeks of exchanges. A subset of participants included both members of the therapeutic dyad: 10 online therapists and 13 clients; the other 20 therapists and 17 clients participated alone.

All therapists were English speaking and used e-mail (n = 17 therapists), text chat (n = 10 therapists), or both (n = 3 therapists) to communicate with their clients. They were licensed to practice in the United States (n = 20 therapists), completed post-secondary education, female (70%), Caucasian (90%), 28 to 62 years (Mdn = 48), married/partnered (67%), and used a Cognitive/Behavioral (33%) or Eclectic/Integrative (27%) theoretical orientation.

The 30 clients were 19 to 55 (Mdn = 43) years old with 83% female, 73% Caucasian, 40% married/partnered or 30% divorced/separated, 97% completed high school, and depression (12 clients) was the most common self-reported presenting problem.

2.1.2 Measurement of Session Impact

Session impact was measured using the Session Evaluation Questionnaire (SEQ, Form 5; Stiles, Gordon, & Lani, 2002). The SEQ consists of 21 seven point bipolar adjective items. The stem "The therapeutic exchanges this week were:" precede the first 11 session evaluation items which include five depth subscale items, five smoothness subscale items, and one global evaluation item. The stem "Based on the therapeutic exchanges this week, I feel:" precedes the second 10 post-session mood items which include five positivity subscale items and five arousal subscale items. The arousal subscale included the items moving-still, excited-calm, fast-slow, energetic-peaceful, and aroused-quiet.

2.1.3 Procedure

Participants were recruited online from private practitioner sites, e-clinics, online counseling centers, and mental health-related discussion boards. Interested therapists had the option to invite current clients to take part. However, either the therapists or the clients could participate alone. Many of the therapists chose to report on their therapeutic interactions without approaching their clients about their potential participation.

On their initial visit to the study's online site, participants completed a consent form and then the demographic forms. They could then choose to enter their weekly data immediately or logout to complete their ratings later. At the status screen, therapists could request an e-mail invitation to register be sent to their clients.

A weekly e-mail with an embedded link to the log-in screen was sent to all participants who had yet to complete the forms for the previous week. When they logged in, participants were presented with links for the prior 2 weeks. For a completed week, participants entered either the number of weekly text-chat exchanges or the number of e-mails that they sent and received and completed the SEQ, along with other measures not considered in this chapter.

2.1.4 Data Analysis Strategy

To assess the similarity of online process with face-to-face process, we compared the distributions of online therapy scale scores with distributions of face-to-face therapy values obtained in previously published studies. This comparison represents an aggregate benchmarking strategy used previously in psychotherapy outcome studies (Barkham et al, 2001; Sperry, Brill, Howard, & Grissom, 1996). At its simplest, benchmarking refers to "the establishment of reference points that can be used to interpret data" being mindful of comparing similar sets of information (Sperry et al., p. 143).

In addition to benchmarking, we employed linear mixed modeling analytic techniques (Littell et al., 1996) to estimate client-therapist text exchange trajectories. The use of a mixed effects modeling strategy has the advantages of accommodating the correlation of multiple measurements, estimating population relationship and participant-specific trajectories, and describing psychotherapy as a linear trend (Crits-Christoph et al., 1998). Separate analyses were performed on therapists' ratings and clients' ratings for each of the four impact subscales.

We estimated two parameters for the therapists' and clients' raw weekly ratings. The initial score (the SEQ subscale scores estimated for the participant reported start date of their online exchanges) and the slope (the estimated mean change in SEQ subscale scores per day) were averaged across therapists and then clients (i.e., one average for therapists and another average for clients). The estimated initial score and slope for the average client and average therapist provided the basis for the population-level effects.

2.2 Results

2.2.1 Session Impact Averages, Variability, and Reliability

2.2.1.1 Index means and standard deviations

The means of all subscales were above the midpoint (midpoint was 4.0 for all SEQ indexes; Tab.2.1). Standard deviations of the therapists clustered around 1.0 with clients' standard deviations slightly higher.

2.2.1.2 Internal consistency of the subscales

The alpha coefficients showed that the 5 item SEQ indexes were in the .80s and .90s, except that arousal was .45 for therapists and .46 for clients (Tab.2.1).

2.2.2 Comparing Online Session Impact Averages with Face-to-Face Averages

Online therapist SEQ scores were greater than those of face-to-face therapists, with the notable exception of arousal scores. Similarly, online clients' SEQ scores were comparable to or greater than those of their face-to-face counterparts (Tab.2.1).

2.2.3 Participant Form Completion Latency

Whereas participants in the face-to-face studies always completed the paper-and-pencil forms immediately after their sessions (e.g., Stiles & Snow, 1984, p. 6), participants in the current study completed their online forms from immediately to two weeks after their given week of online exchanges. However, comparisons between forms completed early (within two days following their exchanges) and late (more than two days following their exchanges) provided no evidence that the participants' delay led to systematically higher or lower scores on the SEQ.

Table 2.1. Therapists' and Clients' Means, Standard Deviations, Internal Consistency Reliabilities (Coefficient Alpha), and Previous Studies' Range of Means and Standard Deviations for Session Evaluation Questionnaire (SEQ) Indexes

					Means of previous studies[a]		Standard deviations of previous studies[a]	
Index	**No. items**	**Alpha**	*M*	*SD*	*Median*	*Range*	*Median*	*Range*
Therapist								
SEQ								
Depth	5	0.88	5.31	0.96	4.80	4.25 – 5.10	1.01	0.41 – 1.08
Smoothness	5	0.92	5.09	1.36	4.20	3.86 – 4.52	1.03	0.56 – 1.20
Positivity	5	0.85	5.49	1.03	4.59	4.38 – 5.16	0.93	0.49 – 1.01
Arousal	5	0.45	4.05	0.75	4.43	4.18 – 4.58	0.96	0.80 – 1.05
Client								
SEQ								
Depth	5	0.94	5.51	1.54	5.20	4.65 – 5.85	0.85	0.58 – 1.29
Smoothness	5	0.92	4.83	1.69	4.35	4.13 – 5.28	1.30	0.76 – 1.47
Positivity	5	0.92	5.03	1.72	4.62	4.38 – 4.88	0.86	0.70 – 1.44
Arousal	5	0.46	4.20	0.96	4.22	4.12 – 4.40	0.92	0.64 – 1.28

Note. N = 394 weeks of exchanges for therapists and N = 475 weeks of exchanges for clients. Indexes were calculated as the mean of therapists' and clients' ratings on constituent items. SEQ items could range from 1 to 7. Alpha = internal consistency measured by coefficient alpha.
[a]The means are from prior studies employing the SEQ (Cummings, Slemon, & Hallberg, 1993; Dill-Standiford, Stiles, & Rorer, 1988; Kivlighan, Angelone, & Swafford, 1991; Nocita & Stiles, 1986; Reynolds et al., 1996; Stiles et al., 1994; Stiles, Shapiro, & Firth-Cozens, 1988; Stiles and Snow, 1984; Tryon, 1990).

2.2.4 Population-level Participants' Initial Scores and Slopes

Using the obtained scores and the reported session dates, we estimated an initial score for each participant on each scale at their reported treatment start date. These initial scores for therapist and client ratings on session impact subscales averaged near but mostly above the midpoint of each subscale. As a clear exception, therapists' estimated population-level arousal initial scores were low and clients' estimated population-level arousal initial scores were especially low (i.e., 4.30 and 3.92 respectively) given that therapists and clients session evaluation subscales' estimated intercepts were generally between 4.0 and 5.5. Average therapists' and clients' slope or rates of change per day ranged from -0.0002 to 0.0010 units of session impact per day with none significantly increasing or decreasing. Specifically, therapists' population-level arousal slopes were negative, indicating that their arousal tended to decrease across sessions.

2.3 Discussion

Online clients and therapists rated their session impacts as equally or more deep, smooth, and positive than therapists and clients in studies of face-to-face therapy (Tab.2.1). We hasten to acknowledge that these comparisons were not based on random assignment, and there were many potentially confounding differences.

The proposed online calming effect, manifested in the modestly and substantially lower arousal ratings of online therapists and clients (respectively) relative to their face-to-face counterparts, was potentially observed. Given the very low reliability of the arousal findings, readers are asked to consider the online calming effect as speculative. Nevertheless, the suggestion for such an online calming effect included the following observations. First, therapists' arousal responses were numerically lower and clients' arousal responses were in the lower range of previously published face-to-face study means (Tab.2.1). Second, therapists' estimated population-level arousal initial scores were low, clients' estimated population-level arousal initial scores were especially low. Third, therapists' population-level arousal slopes were negative, indicating that their arousal tended to decrease across sessions. With these findings in mind, we consider several possible explanations consistent with the emerging empirical literature.

2.3.1 The Online Calming Effect Hypothesis

The online calming effect proposes that therapists and clients experience the online environment as more comfortable and less threatening than the face-to-face milieu. Cohen and Kerr's (1998) online clients rated their mood "right now" as less aroused than their face-to-face clients. Likewise, in this chapter's featured study (reported by Reynolds et al., 2013), online therapists and clients who were exposed to the online environment during their therapeutic exchanges, reported modestly (therapists) or substantially (clients) lower arousal ratings than clients in benchmark studies of face-to-face therapy.

Anecdotally, some of our clients anonymously stated that they were able to tolerate online therapy better than face-to-face therapy consistent with the interpretation that clients' experience a calming influence of the online environment.

Clinically, if the our proposed hypothesis is supported by further research, it may suggest a basis for triage. Therapists might take advantage of the proposed online calming effect by addressing client problems that are relatively accessible with lower emotional arousal by adding online therapy into their repertoire of services (Carryer & Greenberg, 2010). The online calming effect may be accentuated for more experienced therapists given that they may employ more effective or time-tested techniques to remain emotionally grounded and centered during their sessions which attenuate their internal arousal (Hersoug et al., 2001). If online therapy is experienced as more comfortable, it may offer a less threatening alternative to face-to-face psychotherapy, especially for those new to online therapy who wrestle with anxiety disorders like social anxiety disorder (Suler, 2010).

This speculation dovetails with the social networking literature whereby people have evidenced a preference for online social interaction based on the belief that they are safer, more efficacious, more confident, and more comfortable in computer-mediated communication than face-to-face interactions (Caplan, 2003). People with this preference for online social interaction often have psychosocial difficulties (such as social anxiety, shyness, and reduced self-esteem) and are drawn to interpersonal aspects of the Internet (Caplan & High, 2010).

An alternative explanation of online participants' lower Aarousal ratings is the longer delay in reporting (Reynolds & Stiles, 2007). Most of the previous face-to-face participants completed the SEQ immediately after their sessions (e.g., Stiles & Snow, 1984, p. 6 and Cummings et al., 1993, p. 159) whereas most of our online participants did so later. In principle, the activating influence of online participants' therapeutic encounter could have decreased with the greater time from their online exchanges so that their scores underestimated their actual post-session degree of arousal. However, comparisons between forms completed early and late provided no evidence that reporting delay affected arousal levels (see Reynolds et al., 2013).

2.3.2 Limitations and Practice Implications

The proposed online calming effect hypothesis is very tentative, given the limited number of participants, their narrow demographics, the limited number of therapist orientations represented, the restricted presenting problem range of the clients, and the relatively low reliability of the crucial arousal index. Also, we cannot rule out possible self-selection biases because our participants volunteered to take part in this study and because clients self-selected to enter online rather than face-to-face therapy. Further, our lack of a randomized comparison group admits the possibility that other phenomenon (such as poor stimulus quality resulting from lack of nonverbal cues) rather than the online calming effect may be responsible for the lower arousal ratings we observed in online therapy. Finally, we note that some authors have suggested that arousal may be important to the therapeutic change process (Greenberg & Safran,

1989; Mahoney, 1991; Robins & Hayes, 1993), opening the possibility that an online calming effect might not necessarily be desirable for effective therapy.

On the other hand, our results offer qualified encouragement for future therapists and clients who are considering using online therapy. Finding that impacts of online therapy are at least as positive as those of face-to-face therapy support the argument that online text exchanges can be a legitimate manner of conducting psychotherapy.

References

References marked with an asterisk indicate studies included in the comparison analysis.

Barak, A., & Grohol, J. M. (2011). Current and future trends in Internet-supported mental health interventions. Journal of Technology in Human Services, 29, 155-196.

Barak, A., Hen, L., Boniel-Nissim, M., & Shapira, N. (2008). A comprehensive review and a meta-analysis of the effectiveness of internet-based psychotherapeutic interventions. Journal of Technology in Human Services, 26, 109-160.

Barkham, M., Margison, F., Leach, C., Lucock, M., Mellor-Clark, J., Evans, C., ... McGrath, G. (2001). Service profiling and outcomes benchmarking using the CORE-OM: Toward practice-based evidence in the psychological therapies. Journal of Consulting and Clinical Psychology, 69(2), 184-196.

Caplan, S. E. (2003). Preference for online social interaction: A theory of problematic Internet use and psychosocial well-being. Communication Research, 30, 625–648.

Caplan, S. E., & High, A. (2010). Online social interaction, psychosocial well-being, and problematic internet use. In K. Young & C. Nabuco de Abrue (Eds.), Internet addiction: A handbook for evaluation and treatment (pp. 35–53). Hoboken, NJ: John Wiley & Sons Inc.

Carryer, J. R., & Greenberg, L. S. (2010). Optimal levels of emotional arousal in experiential therapy of depression. Journal of Consulting and Clinical Psychology, 78(2), 190–199.

Chester, A., & Glass, C. A. (2006). Online counseling: A descriptive analysis of therapy services. British Journal of Guidance & Counselling, 34(2), 145-160.

Cohen, G. E., & Kerr, B. A. (1998). Computer-mediated counseling: An empirical study of a new mental health treatment. Computers in human services, 15, 13-26.

Cook, J. E., & Doyle, C. (2002). Working alliance in online therapy as compared to face-to-face therapy: Preliminary Results. CyberPsychology & Behavior, 5, 95-105.

Crits-Christoph, P., Siqueland, L., Chittams, J., Barber, J. P., Beck, A. T., Frank, A., ... Woody, G. (1998). Training in cognitive, supportive-expressive, and drug counseling therapies for cocaine dependence. Journal of Consulting and Clinical Psychology, 66(3), 484-492.

*Cummings, A. L., Slemon, A. G., & Hallberg, E. T. (1993). Session evaluation and recall of important events as a function of counselor experience. Journal of Counseling Psychology, 40(2), 156-165.

Day, S. (2013). Self-disclosure on Facebook: How much do we really reveal? Journal of Applied Computing and Information Technology, 17(1).

*Dill-Standiford, T. J., Stiles, W. B., & Rorer, L. G. (1988). Counselor-client agreement on session impact. Journal of Counseling Psychology, 35(1), 47-55.

DuBois, D. (2004). Clinical and demographic features of the online counselling client population. Counselling and Psychotherapy Research, 4(1), 18-22.

Fenichel, M., Suler, J., Barak, A., Zelvin, E., Jones, G., Munro, K., ... Walker-Schmucker, W. (2002). Myths and Realities of Online Clinical Work. CyberPsychology & Behavior, 5(5), 481-497.

Finn, J., & Barak, A. (2010). A descriptive study of e-counsellor attitudes, ethics, and practice. Counselling and Psychotherapy Research, 10, 268–277.

Forest, A. L., & Wood, J. V. (2012). When social networking is not working: Individuals with low self-esteem recognize but do not reap the benefits of self-disclosure on Facebook. Psychological Science, 23(3), 295–302.

Greenberg, L. S., & Safran, J. D. (1989). Emotion in psychotherapy. American Psychologist, 44(1), 19-29.

Grohol, J. M. (1999). Too much time online: Internet addiction or healthy social interactions? CyberPsychology & Behavior, 2, 395-401.

Grohol, J. M. (2011). Best practices in e-therapy: Typical costs and pricing for online therapy. Retrieved from http://psychcentral.com/etherapy/costs-of-etherapy.htm

Heinlen, K. T., Welfel, E. R., Richmond, E. N., & Rak, C. F. (2003). The scope of webcounseling: A survey of services and compliance with NBCC standards for the ethical practice of webcounseling. Journal of Counseling and Development, 18, 62-70.

International Society for Mental Health Online. (2011). Membership survey. Retrieved from https://www.surveymonkey.com/sr.aspx?sm=LSxnP3JXsNljwFO0kHFXjGOglk3uN5jmwT2_2fQqryiDU_3d

*Kivlighan, D. M., Jr., Angelone, E. O., & Swafford, K. G. (1991). Live supervision in individual psychotherapy: Effects of therapist's intention use and client's evaluation of session effect and working alliance. Professional Psychology: Research and Practice, 22(6), 489-495.

Lombard, M., & Ditton, T. (1997). At the heart of it all: The concept of presence. Journal of Computer Mediated Communication, 3(2). doi:10.1111/j.1083-6101.1997.tb00072.x

Leibert, T., Archer, J., Jr., Munson, J., & York, G. (2006). An exploratory study of client perceptions of Internet counseling and the therapeutic alliance. Journal of Mental Health Counseling, 28, 69-83.

Littell, R. C., Milliken, G. A., Stroup, W. W., & Wolfinger, R. D. (1996). SAS system for mixed models. Cary, NC: SAS Institute.

Maheu, M. M., & Gordon, B. L. (2000). Counseling and therapy on the Internet. Professional Psychology: Research and Practice, 31, 484-489.

Mahoney, M. J. (1991). Human change processes: The scientific foundations of psychotherapy. New York, NY: Basic Books.

Mallen, M. J., Vogel, D. L., Rochlen, A. B., & Day, S. X. (2005). Online counseling: Reviewing the literature from a counseling psychology framework. The Counseling Psychologist, 33, 819-871.

*Nocita, A., & Stiles, W. B. (1986). Client introversion and counseling session impact. Journal of Counseling Psychology, 33(3), 235-241.

Preschl, B., Maercker, A., & Wagner, B. (2011). The working alliance in a randomized controlled trial comparing online with face-to-face cognitive-behavioral therapy for depression. BMC Psychiatry, 11(189). doi: 10.1186/1471-244X-11-189

Reynolds, D. J., Jr., & Stiles, W. B. (2007). Online data collection for psychotherapy process research. CyberPsychology & Behavior, 10, 92-99.

Reynolds, D. J., Jr., Stiles, W. B., Bailer, A. J., & Hughes, M. R. (2013). Impact of exchanges and client–therapist alliance in online-text psychotherapy. Cyberpsychology, Behavior, and Social Networking, 16(5), 370-377.

Reynolds, D. J., Jr., Stiles, W. B., & Grohol, J. M. (2006). An investigation of session impact and alliance in internet based psychotherapy: Preliminary results. Counselling and Psychotherapy Research, 6, 164-168.

*Reynolds, S., Stiles, W. B., Barkham, M., Shapiro, D. A., Hardy, G. E., & Rees, A. (1996). Acceleration of changes in session impact during contrasting time-limited psychotherapies. Journal of Consulting and Clinical Psychology, 64(3), 577-586.

Robins, C. J., & Hayes, A. M. (1993). An appraisal of cognitive therapy. Journal of Consulting and Clinical Psychology, 61(2), 205-214.

Rochlen, A., Zack, J. & Speyer, C. (2004). Online therapy: Review of relevant definitions, debates, and current empirical support. Journal of Clinical Psychology, 60(3), 269–283.

Rosen, A., & Proctor, E. K. (1981). Distinctions between treatment outcomes and their implications for treatment evaluation. Journal of Consulting and Clinical Psychology, 49, 418-425.

Russell, J. A. (1978). Evidence of convergent validity on the dimensions of affect. Journal of Personality and Social Psychology, 36(10), 1152-1168.

Russell, J. A. (1979). Affective space is bipolar. Journal of Personality and Social Psychology, 37(3), 345-356.

Sperry, L., Brill, P. L., Howard, K. I., & Grissom, G. R. (1996). Treatment outcomes in psychotherapy and psychiatric interventions. New York, NY: Brunner/Mazel.

Stiles, W. B., Gordon, L. E., & Lani, J. A. (2002). Session evaluation and the session evaluation questionnaire. In G. S. Tryon (Ed.), Counseling based on process research: Applying what we know (p. 325-343). Boston, MA: Allyn and Bacon.

*Stiles, W. B., Reynolds, S., Hardy, G. E., Rees, A., Barkham, M., & Shapiro, D. A. (1994). Evaluation and description of psychotherapy sessions by clients using the session evaluation questionnaire and the session impacts scale. Journal of Counseling Psychology, 41, 175-185.

*Stiles, W. B., Shapiro, D. A., & Firth-Cozens, J. A. (1988). Do sessions of different treatments have different impacts? Journal of Counseling Psychology, 35(4), 391-396.

*Stiles, W. B., & Snow, J. S. (1984). Counseling session impact as viewed by novice counselors and their clients. Journal of Counseling Psychology, 31, 3-12.

Sucala, M., Schnur, J. B., Constantino, M. J., Miller, S. J., Brackman, E. H., & Montgomery, G. H. (2012). The therapeutic relationship in e-therapy for mental health: A systematic review. Journal of Medical Internet Research, 14(4):e110.

Suler J. (2010). The psychology of text relationships. In R. Kraus, G. Stricker, & C. Speyer (Eds.), Online counseling: A handbook for mental health professionals (p. 22-53). San Diego, CA: Elsevier.

*Tryon, G. S. (1990). Session depth and smoothness in relation to the concept of engagement in counseling. Journal of Counseling Psychology, 37(3), 248-253.

Hui-Tzu Grace Chou, Ron Hammond

3 Feeling Anxious without It: Characteristics of People Prone to Facebook Addiction

Abstract: Previous research has found that Facebook can provide its users with a place for self-presentation and increase their perceived social support, self-esteem, and subjective well-being. It is argued in this research that the margin of gratification Facebook brings to its users is lower for those who are higher in subjective well-being or self-esteem and higher for those feeling lonely, shy, or concerned with others' perceptions of them. Therefore, those with low subjective well-being or low self-esteem, and those feeling lonely, shy, or concerned about how others perceive them, are hypothesized to feel more anxious than their counterparts if they cannot use Facebook for three days. Using a probability sample, undergraduate students at a state university in Utah were solicited to take an online survey in April and May 2012. The findings supported all of the hypotheses. The results indicated that those with high subjective well-being or high self-esteem are less likely to have the problem of Facebook addiction, while those people feeling lonely, shy, or concerned with others' perceptions of them are more likely to have this problem.

3.1 Introduction and Literature Review

Previous research has indicated that Facebook brings some benefits to its users, such as strengthening perceived social and emotional support (Ellison, Steinfield, & Lampe, 2007; Manago, Taylor, & Greenfield, 2012), boosting self-esteem (Gonzales & Hancock, 2011; Valkenburg, Peter, Schouten, 2006), and enhancing subjective well-being (Kim & Lee, 2011). In addition, Facebook provides a place for self-presentation (Nadkarni & Hofmann, 2012) and entertainment (Special, Li-Barber, 2012). Because of the benefits Facebook provides to its users, some people gradually become addicted to it. For example, on June 19, 2014, when Facebook was down for a brief period of time, many people around the world experienced some anxiety. The purpose of this research is to identify the people who are prone to Facebook addiction; specifically, this study identifies the characteristics of individuals who would feel anxious if they could not use Facebook for three days.

One reason why some people get addicted to Facebook is because of the rewards they receive when using it. As mentioned above, Facebook can increase individuals' happiness or subjective well-being (Kim & Lee, 2011). Individuals who already have a high level of subjective well-being, however, may experience less reward from Facebook than their counterparts of low subjective well-being. Put differently, the margin of gratification Facebook contributes to the former is lower than that to the latter. Therefore, happy people are less likely to feel anxious if they cannot use Facebook.

In the same way, if Facebook is used to boost self-esteem, those with low self-esteem might find using Facebook more rewarding than those with high self-esteem, since Facebook brings a larger margin of gratification to the former. As previous research has found, those low in self-esteem spend a greater amount of time on Facebook (Kalpidou, Costin, & Morris 2011; Mehdizadeh, 2010), have a higher frequency of logins or updates on their Facebook page (Mehdizadeh, 2010), accumulate a larger number of Facebook friends (Lee, et al. 2012), and include more strangers on their Facebook page than those with high self-esteem (Acar, 2008). Therefore, they are more likely to feel anxious if their access to Facebook is denied. Based on this argument, the first two hypotheses were formulated:

> Hypothesis 1. Those who are happy are less likely to feel anxious if they cannot use Facebook for three days.
> Hypothesis 2. Those who have high self-esteem are less likely to feel anxious if they cannot use Facebook for three days.

Another benefit Facebook brings to its users is perceived social and emotional support (Ellison, Steinfield, & Lampe, 2007; Manago, Taylor, & Greenfield, 2012). Following the logic of margin of gratification, those who feel lonely or shy might find Facebook more attractive. Previous research has found that those who feel lonely are more likely to use Facebook (Ryan & Xenos, 2011), and they also have more Facebook friends than their counterparts (Skues, Williams, & Wise); shy people spend more time on Facebook (Orr, et al., 2009) and express more favorable attitudes toward Facebook (Orr, et al., 2009). Therefore, when Facebook access becomes unavailable, lonely or shy people are more likely to feel anxious than their counterparts. Based on the arguments above, the following two hypotheses were formulated:

> Hypothesis 3. Those who feel lonely are more likely to feel anxious if they cannot use Facebook for three days.
> Hypothesis 4. Those who are shy are more likely to feel anxious if they cannot use Facebook for three days.

Facebook provides a place for self-presentation (Nadkarni & Hofmann, 2012). Previous research has identified various strategies that internet users employ to present themselves in a favorable way, such as presenting an ideal self (Ellison, Heino, & Gibbs, 2006), managing the styles of their languages (Adkins & Brashers, 1995; Ellison, Heino, & Gibbs, 2006; Lea & Spears, 1992; Walther, 2007), carefully selecting pictures (Ellison, Heino, & Gibbs, 2006), highlighting positive attributes (Ellison, Heino, & Gibbs, 2006), showing connections with certain people or symbols

(Dominick, 1999; Schau & Gilly, 1999; Walther, et al., 2008), or having deeper self-disclosures (Tidwell & Walther, 2002). For those who are concerned about others' perceptions of them (high self-monitors), Facebook serves as a platform where they can present a desirable image as well as a channel through which they can receive others' approval. A relevant study found that those with a need to feel popular disclose more information on Facebook (Christofides, Muise, & Desmarais, 2012). Therefore, if they cannot use Facebook, they will lose one platform of self-presentation and one channel of social approval, which might make them anxious. Based on the argument above, the following hypothesis was formulated:

> Hypothesis 5. Those who are concerned about how others perceive them are more likely to feel anxious if they cannot use Facebook for three days.

Previous research has found that the use of Facebook is related to certain demographic variables. For example, women have more Facebook friends than men (Acar, 2008), spend more time on Facebook than men (Acar, 2008), and are more likely than men to report losing sleep because of Facebook (Thompson & Lougheed, 2012), and feel addicted to Facebook (Thompson & Lougheed, 2012). Adolescents spend more time on Facebook than adults (Christofides, Muise, & Desmarais, 2012), and they also disclose more information on Facebook than adults (Christofides, Muise, & Desmarais, 2012). Therefore, gender and age, as well as marital status, were included in this research, and the frequency distribution of these demographic variables was mentioned previously in this chapter.

3.2 Method

3.2.1 Participants

An online questionnaire was sent to undergraduate students at a state university in Utah through the university's Institutional Research Department in April and May 2012. A probability sample of 8,000 students enrolled in Fall 2011 was chosen for this research; 1,059 of them responded to the survey, and 830 completed all of the questions asked in the survey. Among these participants, 44% were men, and 84.3% were White. The mean age was 27.71. About 10% of the respondents were single with a steady dating partner, and 31% were married at the time of the survey. The demographic information is presented in the Appendix.

3.2.2 Measures

The dependent variable, Facebook addiction, was measured by this statement, "I would feel very anxious if I could not use Facebook for 3 days." Strongly disagree was coded as 1; disagree was coded as 2; Don't know was coded as 3; Agree was coded as 4; and Strongly Agree was coded as 5. The independent variables were all measured by a 5-point Likert scale. Respondents were asked to rate their level of agreement with some statements, and 1 indicated strongly disagree; 2 indicated disagree; 3 indicated don't know or no opinion; 4 indicated agree; and 5 indicated strongly agree. Happiness or subjective well-being was measured by the statement, "I am a very happy person" (mean = 4.15; standard deviation = .79); self-esteem was measured by the statement, "I believe I can succeed in everything I do" (mean = 4.00; standard deviation = .89); self-monitor was measured by the statement, "I am very concerned about how others perceive me" (mean = 2.9; standard deviation = 1.18); loneliness was measured by the statement, "I feel very lonely" (mean = 2.29, standard deviation = 1.16); and shyness was measured by the statement, "I am very shy" (mean = 2.48; standard deviation = 1.20).

3.3 Results

Among the 830 respondents who answered all of the questions, the majority of them indicated that they strongly disagree (56.6%) or disagree (29%), while 61 (or 7.3%) indicated that they agree, and 9 (or 1.1%) indicated that they strongly agree with the statement, "I feel very anxious if I could not use Facebook for 3 days." In other words, 70 (or 8.4%) of the respondents appear to have had the problem of Facebook addiction; that is, they would feel very anxious if they could not use Facebook for 3 days.

The bivariate correlation coefficients are presented in Table 1. As predicted in hypotheses 1 and 2, happy people ($r = -.11$; $p < .01$) and those with higher self-esteem ($r = -.14$; $p < .001$) were less likely to feel anxious if they could not use Facebook for 3 days. Also, as predicted in hypotheses 3, 4, and 5, those feeling lonely ($r = .21$; $p < .001$), shy ($r = .11$; $p < .01$), or concerned about how others perceive them ($r = .23$; $p < .001$) were more addicted to Facebook. In addition, married, male, and older people were less likely to have the problem of Facebook addiction. A cross-tab analysis between gender and Facebook addiction revealed that women were twice as likely as men to experience Facebook addiction: About 11.3% of female participants and 4.6% of male participants would feel very anxious if they could not use Facebook for 3 days ($t = 3.70$, $p < .001$).

Table 3.1. Bi-variate correlation coefficient matrix

Variables	1.	2.	3.	4.	5.	6.	7.	8.	9.	10.
1. Feeling anxious without using Facebook	1.00									
2. Subjective well-being	-.11**	1.00								
3. Self-esteem	-.14***	.43***	1.00							
4. Loneliness	.21***	-.42***	-.28***	1.00						
5. Shyness	.11**	-.35***	-.23***	.46***	1.00					
6. Self-monitor	.23***	-.15***	-.12***	.41***	.26***	1.00				
7. Dating	.05	-.05	-.07*	-.01	.02	.05	1.00			
8. Married	-.07*	.10**	.09*	-.28***	-.14***	-.10**	-.23***	1.00		
9. Gender (male)	-.14***	-.04	.06	-.05	-.02	-.11**	-.05	.03	1.00	
10. Age	-.10**	-.04	-.00	-.07*	-.08*	-.10**	-.15***	.32***	.03	1.00

* p<0.05; ** p<0.01; *** p<0.001

Since Facebook addiction was related to gender, age, and marital status, and was also related to some independent variables, these demographic variables were controlled in the multiple regression analysis. The results of the multiple regression analysis are presented in Table 2. After controlling for the demographic variables, the association between Facebook addiction and these independent variables remained significant. As predicted in hypotheses 1 and 2, those with higher subjective well-being ($\beta = -.11$; $p < .01$) or higher self-esteem ($\beta = -.13$; $p < .001$) were less likely to feel anxious if they could not use Facebook for 3 days. In addition, those feeling lonely ($\beta = .21$; $p < .001$), shy ($\beta = .10$; $p < .05$), or concerned about how others perceived them ($\beta=.21$; $p<.001$) were more likely to have the problem of Facebook addiction, as expected in hypotheses 3, 4, and 5. Men were less likely than women, and older people were less likely than younger people to be addicted to Facebook.

Table 3.2. Multiple Regression Analysis of Facebook Addiction on Selected Independent Variables (Standardized Coefficients)

Independent variables					
Subjective well-being	-.11**				
Self-esteem		-.13***			
Loneliness			.21***		
Shyness				.10*	
Self-monitor					.21***
Dating	.02	.02	.04	.02	.02
Married	-.03	-.04	.02	-.04	-.03
Gender (male)	-.13***	-.11**	-.11**	-.12**	-.10**
Age	-.09*	-.08*	-.07	-.07	-.06
F-value	5.84***	6.45***	9.70***	5.45***	10.91***
R^2	.04	.04	.06	.04	.07
N	717	714	710	707	710

* p<0.05; ** p<0.01; *** p<0.001

3.4 Discussion and Conclusions

As previous research has found, Facebook can provide its users a place for self-presentation and increase their perceived social support, self-esteem, and subjective well-being. Based on previous research, in this study it was anticipated that the margin of gratification Facebook brings to its users would be low for those who were high in subjective well-being or self-esteem, and high for those feeling lonely, shy, or concerned about others' perceptions of them. The findings of this study supported these hypotheses. That is, people with high subjective well-being or high self-esteem were less likely to feel anxious if they could not use Facebook for three days, and people feeling lonely, shy, or concerned about how others perceived them were prone to Facebook addiction. In addition, women and younger people were more likely than men and older people to feel anxious if they could not use Facebook for three days, indicating that Facebook brought a higher margin of gratification to them than to their counterparts.

The results of this research imply that Facebook outage might serve as an assessment for individuals' psychological states. Compared with their counterparts, those who feel anxious without access to Facebook are less happy, have lower self-esteem, tend to feel lonely or shy, and have concern about how others perceive them.

While using Facebook might satisfy their needs, they can also think about alternative activities that enrich their lives, as well as find out some causes of their psychological traits that are associated with Facebook addition. Either way, when Facebook is down, some alternatives rise up.

The current research has two major limitations. First, this research used a single question for each of the dependent and independent variables. Although this research did shed some light on the possible connections between personalities and Facebook addiction, future research could advance this study by using an established measurement of Facebook addiction, as well as some personality characteristics, such as happiness, self-esteem, loneliness, shyness, and self-monitoring. Second, although this research used a probability sample, recruiting undergraduate students taking classes from various academic disciplines, the participants' homogeneity limits the generalization of the results. Therefore, future research should examine people of different age groups and ethnic backgrounds, and people living outside Utah, to see whether similar patterns appear. These two major limitations open up opportunities for future research.

References

Acar, A. (2008). Antecedents and consequences of online social networking behavior: The case of Facebook. Journal of Website Promotion, 3, 62-83.

Adkins, M., & Brashers, D. (1995). The power of language in computer-mediated groups. Management Communication Quarterly, 8, 289-322.

Christofides E, Muise A, & Desmarais S. (2012). Hey mom, what's on your Facebook? Comparing Facebook disclosure and privacy in adolescents and adults. Social Psychological and Personality Science, 3, 48-54.

Dominick, J. (1999). Who do you think you are? Personal home pages and self-presentation on the world wide web. Journalism & Mass Communication Quarterly, 76, 646-658.

Ellison, N., Heino, R., & Gibbs ,J. (2006). Managing impressions online: Self-presentation processes in the online dating environment. Journal of Computer-Mediated Communication, 11, http://jcmc.indiana.edu/vol11/issue2/ellison.html (accessed March 1, 2011).

Ellison, N.B., Steinfield, C., & Lampe C. (2007). The benefits of Facebook "Friends:" Social capital and college students' use of online social network sites. Journal of Computer-Mediated Communication, 12, 1143-1168.

Gonzales, A.L., Hancock, J.T. (2011). Mirror, mirror on my Facebook wall: Effects of exposure to Facebook on self-esteem. CyberPsychology, Behavior, and Social Networking, 14, 79-83.

Kalpidou, M., Costin, D., & Morris, J. (2011). The relationship between Facebook and the well-being of undergraduate college students. CyberPsychology, Behavior, and Social Networking, 14, 183-189.

Kim, J., & Lee, J.E.R. (2011). The Facebook paths to happiness: Effects of the number of Facebook friends and self-presentation on subjective well-being. CyberPsychology, Behavior, and Social Networking, 14, 359-364.

Lea, M., & Spears, R. (1992). Paralanguage and social perception in computer-mediated communication. Journal of Organizational Computing, 2, 321-341.

Lee, J.E.R., Moor, D.C., Park, E.A., et al. (2012). Who wants to be "friend-rich"? Social compensatory friending on Facebook and the moderating role of public self-consciousness. Computers in Human Behavior, 28, 1036-1043.

Manago, A.M., Taylor, T., & Greenfield, P.M. (2012). Me and My 400 Friends: The anatomy of college students' Facebook networks, their communication patterns, and well-being. Development Psychology, 48, 369-380.

Mehdizadeh, S. (2010). Self-presentation 2.0: Narcissism and self-esteem on Facebook. CyberPsychology, Behavior, and Social Networking, 13, 357-364.

Nadkarni, A., & Hofmann, S. (2012). Why do people use Facebook. Personality and Individual Differences, 52, 243-249.

Orr, E., Sisic, M., Ross, C., et al. (2009). The influence of shyness on the use of Facebook in an undergraduate sample. CyberPsychology & Behavior, 12, 337-339.

Ryan, T., & Xenos, S. (2011). Who uses Facebook? An investigation into the relationship between the Big Five, shyness, narcissism, loneliness, and Facebook usage. Computers in Human Behavior, 27, 1658-1664.

Schau, H.J., & Gilly, M.C. (2003). We are what we post? Self-presentation in personal web space. Journal of Consumer Research, 30, 385-404.

Skues, J., Williams, B., & Wise, L. (2012). The effects of personality traits, self-esteem, loneliness, and narcissism on Facebook use among university students. Computers in Human Behavior, 28, 2414-2419.

Special, W., & Li-Barber, K.T. (2012). Self-disclosure and student satisfaction with Facebook. Computers in Human Behavior, 28, 624-630.

Thompson, S., & Lougheed, E. (2012). Frazzled by Facebook? An exploratory study of gender differences in social network communication among undergraduate men and women. College Student Journal, 46, 88-98.

Tidwell, L.C., & Walther, J.B. (2002). Computer-mediated communication effects on disclosure, impressions, and interpersonal evaluations: Getting to know one another a bit at a time. Human Communication Research, 28, 317-348.

Valkenburg, P.M., Peter, J., & Schouten, A.P. (2006). Friend networking sites and their relationship to adolescents' well-being and social self-esteem. CyberPsychology & Behavior, 9, 484-590.

Walther, J.B. (2007). Selective self-presentation in computer-mediated communication: Hyperpersonal dimensions of technology, language, and cognition. Computers in Human Behavior, 23, 2538-57.

Walther, J.B., Van Der Heide, B., Kim, S., Westerman, D., & Tong, S.T. (2008). The role of friends' appearance and behavior: Are we known by the company we keep? Human Communication Research, 3, 28-49.

Appendix:
Operationalization of Variables, Mean, and Standard Deviation

Variables	Survey items and coding	Min.	Max.	Mean	St.d.
1. Facebook addiction	Please rate your level of agreement with this statement, "I feel very anxious if I could not use Facebook for 3 days." 1. Strongly disagree; 2. Disagree; 3. Don't know. 4. Agree; 5. Strongly agree.	1	5	1.67	.95
2. Subjective well-being	Please rate your level of agreement with this statement, "I am a very happy person." 1. Strongly disagree; 2. Disagree; 3. Don't know. 4. Agree; 5. Strongly agree.	1	5	4.15	.79
3. Self-esteem	Please rate your level of agreement with this statement, "I believe I can succeed in everything I do." 1. Strongly disagree; 2. Disagree; 3. Don't know. 4. Agree; 5. Strongly agree.	1	5	4.00	.89
4. Loneliness	Please rate your level of agreement with this statement, "I feel lonely" 1. Strongly disagree; 2. Disagree; 3. Don't know. 4. Agree; 5. Strongly agree.	1	5	2.29	1.16
5. Shyness	Please rate your level of agreement with this statement, "I am very shy." 1. Strongly disagree; 2. Disagree; 3. Don't know. 4. Agree; 5. Strongly agree.	1	5	2.48	1.20
6. Self-monitor	Please rate your level of agreement with this statement, "I am very concerned about how others perceive me." 1. Strongly disagree; 2. Disagree; 3. Don't know. 4. Agree; 5. Strongly agree.	1	5	2.90	1.18
7. Dating	What is your current marital status: single with a steady dating partner was coded as 1; others were coded as 0.	0	1	.10	.30
8. Married	What is your current marital status: married was coded as 1; others were coded as 0.	0	1	.31	.46
9. Gender (male)	What is your gender? 1. Male; 0. Female	0	1	.44	.50
10. Age	What is your age?	18	73	27.71	9.14

Jen-Wei Chang, Chun-Chia Lee

4 What Determinants Matter When Users Engage in Particular Collaborative Storytelling Websites? Exploring Attractive Gamification Features and Design Guidelines

Abstract: Gamification refers to the incorporation of game mechanics into non-game settings, which aims to increase user's engagement with the product or service and facilitate certain behaviors. Gamification receives considerable attention for various social networking services and product design. Specifically, gamification is considered as the predictor of the user's engagement with collaborative storytelling websites. Although previous studies have mentioned a broad range of factors that may influence gamification, they neither depicted the actual design features nor relative attractiveness among them. In line with this, the present aims to identify attractive gamification features for collaborative storytelling websites. We first constructed a hierarchical system structure of gamification design for collaborative storytelling websites and conducted a focus group interview with eighteen frequent users to identify 35 gamification features. Following this, the relative attractiveness of these gamification features was determined by administrating an online survey to 6333 collaborative storytelling websites users. The results indicated that the top 10 most attractive gamification features could account for more than 50% of attractiveness among these 35 gamification features. The feature of unpredictable time pressure is important to website users, yet was not revealed in previous studies. Based on these findings a number of design guidelines were created for gamification in collaborative storytelling websites.

4.1 Introduction

As a text based social networking service, a collaborative storytelling website allows users, without limitations of time and place, to collaborate on shared stories.[1-3] At present popular collaborative storytelling websites such as Protagonize.com, Storybird.com, and Flickspin.com always attract myriads of users to discuss and collaborate on stories online. In collaborative storytelling websites, users can not only work together in teams to create collaborative stories but also feed off of each other's ideas, devising more creative stories together. Importantly, collaborative storytelling websites have educational potential by providing story materials and support to help users develop interpersonal and story-related skills through organizing, communicating, evaluating, and transforming life experience into words.[2] Moreover, collaborative storytelling websites provide connection with other social networking services such as instant messengers, Facebook, and Twitter, which not only amplify its social influence between users, but facilitate more user to user interactions and negotiations.[4] Thus, collaborative storytelling websites have received considerable attention from both educators and internet researchers.

Some studies have considered gamification design as one critical factor that contributes to the success of collaborative storytelling websites because of its fun and interactivity.[5, 6] The definition of gamification refers to the incorporation of game mechanics into non-game settings, which aims to increase user's engagement with the product or service and facilitate certain behaviors.[7] Recently, gamification is widely used for increasing user's interaction and engagement in a variety of domains such as business and marketing, [8] health and wellness,[9] education and training,[7]corporate and vocational training,[10] as well as public policy and the government.[10] So far collaborative storytelling websites effectively attract and maintain users via various gamification designs, such as leaderboards and badges.[7] Moreover, the gamification features attract uses by providing fun and flow experience as users create and collaborate on stories together, which result in more daily users and higher average time spent on sites.[5] Gamification essentially functions as entertainment which makes collaborative storytelling website users enjoy actively participating and engaging with others. Consequently, gamification plays a critical role in the survival of collaborative storytelling sites.

Prior studies have been conducted to identify the influences of gamification. Many studies have examined the role of achievement aspects (such as goal setting and status) in facilitating gamification design through increasing user's self-efficacy and recognition.[5, 9-11] Some scholars have argued that the gamification design relies heavily on the support of interpersonal relationship aspects.[12-16] Furthermore, other studies have examined how role-playing aspects foster user's engagement with products or services through increasing self-identity and fun. [17-19] While aforementioned studies have mentioned a broad range of factors that may influence gamification, these studies depicted neither the actual design features (design guidelines) nor relative attractiveness of them. Identifying the attractive design features for gamification could establish significant milestones in how to make attractive collaborative storytelling websites.

This study aims to identify gamification features for collaborative storytelling websites. Following this, the relative attractiveness of these gamification features will be examined. Doing so would help website developers focus on those aspects with the greatest weight and identify the best design strategy for improving websites' attractiveness through gamification.

4.2 Systematic framework of gamification design

In this study, we first attempted to construct a hierarchical model to represent the systematic structure of gamification design. After reviewing gamification factors from relevant literatures, we then conducted a discussion with four website designers on these factors and corresponding design mechanics for collaborative storytelling websites. Therefore, through this process, some factors may be excluded because they are lacking corresponding design mechanics for collaborative storytelling websites. All gamification factors discussed in this study can be divided into three main components: achievement, interpersonal relationship, and role-playing. Achievement means users are motivated by a need to achieve goals or accomplish something through difficult tasks and repeated efforts, including such design factors as rewards, goal setting, reputation, and status.[5, 9-11] Interpersonal relationship refers to the process that facilitates the formation of social networks that connects users with whom the user interacts, including instruction, competition, and altruism.[12-16] Role-playing refers user sees the world based on the viewpoint of their role, including such design factors as group identification, self-expression, and time pressure.[17-19] The role and user are not only closely interconnected with each other but also allow users to accomplish their goals at the personal and social levels. Various sets of gamification features associated with each design factor in the second level are linked to the third level. The hierarchical framework of gamification design in this study is shown in Figure 4.1.

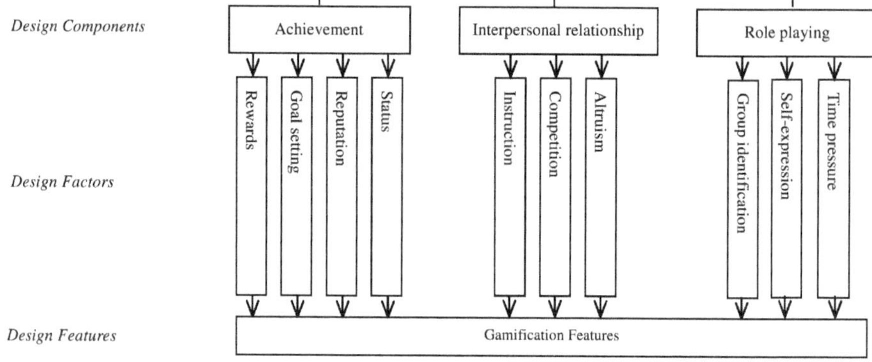

Figure 4.1 Hierarchical system structure of gamification of collaborative story telling websites

4.2.1 Achievement

Rewards. Rewards refer to the gamification factors that satisfies users shared need and motivates them to implement certain behaviors. [10, 17] For example, users are motivated to create more stories with others in order to receive more and more rewards from websites. At present, gamification design mechanics of rewards includes tangible reward (i.e. points or virtual currency) and intangible rewards (praise or recognition from others) that users can see and use to benefit themselves.[10] The rewards mechanism operates in terms of earning points or the equivalent (like frequent-flyer miles) and effectively forms a reward-behavior cycle.[19] That is, the more time a user invests in the expected behaviors, the more rewards they will receive from websites.

Goal setting. Goal setting is related to the most motivating goals that are just out of comfortable reach.[20] Users always conduct certain behaviors toward a specified goal because the fun and interest of goal seeking is often the primary reward itself.[21] In the context of collaborative storytelling websites, user's goals may comprise personal level goals (i.e. individual achievement and learning) or group level goals (i.e. group achievement and belonging). So far the gamification design mechanics of goal setting mainly operates in two ways, explicit signs (i.e. trophies and badges) and progress towards goals (i.e. progress bars or percentage).[10]

Reputation. Reputation refers to the system that facilitates user's behaviors based on the estimation of recognition held by other users.[21-23] The idea of a reputation has been widely adopted by online shopping websites, such as eBay and Amazon.com, to increase the reliability of systems, reduce risks between users, and help users decide whether to interact with other users based on the experiences of third-party users. In the setting of collaborative storytelling websites, reputation can be seen as an effective tool for determining the trustworthiness of users or the reliability of story. For the moment gamification design mechanics of reputation include special titles or highlighted personal profiles within the community.[7]

Status. As users join a social group, status refers to the user's need for recognition, fame, prestige, attention, and other user's respect.[10, 21] Status serves as user's desire to be recognized and foster users to achieve goals enthusiastically. For collaborative storytelling websites, the status also represents user's contribution on creating stories and participating in websites' activities. A quantified approach is often used for representing design mechanics about user's status, such as experience points and level-up.[10]

4.2.2 Interpersonal relationship

Instruction. As new users (also called newbies) enter into a system, some instructions are required to teach them the social norms.[21, 24] Instruction not only functions as the social shaping of user activities but also assists users in mastering the whole system in an efficient way. In the context of collaborative storytelling websites,instruction helps users to learn communication and teamwork skills as they collaborate with others. "Nonce helper" and billboard is usually used for representing the gamification mechanics of instruction in collaborative storytelling websites.[3]

Competition. Competition refers to the user's desire to compete with others, including reaching high scores in order to defeat others, with the winning user receiving a prize or benefit.[10, 11]Thus, users enjoy the striving for the advantages of winning and will go on competing with others. The gamification design mechanics of competition is leaderboards, which lists winners among all competitors.[10]

Altruism. Altruism is user's desire to bridge and maintain relationships with others through conducting certain behaviors, such as gift-giving or ask for help [10, 21]. Trivers [25] has suggested altruism to be the user's desire to conduct reciprocal behaviors with others on the basis of trust. Altruists indirectly contribute to their fitness through reciprocation with others.[10]In the context of collaborative storytelling websites, support for gift-giving and charity are the most popular altruistic behaviours. Specifically, altruism is also considered as a strategy to attract new users.[10, 21] For instance, users may receive a gift from someone that pulls them into the game, and then they're incented to send gifts to friends, eventually creating a acquisition loop.

4.2.3 Role-playing

Group identification. Group identification represents user's affective and cognitive loyalty to the group as users participate together.[10, 26-28] Users with higher group identification are often willing to remain in group permanently and to strive toward the goals, obey the guild managers' commands, and devote themselves to group affairs.[29] At present the gamification design mechanics of collaborative storytelling websites are self- organized quest teams or members' family.

Self-expression. Self-expression refers to users' desire to express their autonomy and originality, which shapes their unique personalities.[10, 21] User's self-expression involves the user's feeling of social toleration, life satisfaction, public expression, and an aspiration to liberty. Gee [30] conducted a study on digital game based learning, also considered assisting users to build their self-identity in virtual world can facilitate user' involvement. To show off user's uniqueness on collaborative storytelling websites, the gamification design mechanics of self-expression are virtual goods, spaces, and avatars.[10, 19]

Time pressure. Time pressure means giving users time limits to conduct certain behaviors in order to encourage them to interact heavily during this period [5, 21]. For users, creating time pressure can produce more emotional feedback and encourage greater participation as the time pressure is connected to their goals. For example, some mobile applications set a 5 second time limit to find the targets, which encourages the user to interact with application heavily during this period. As a player fails, a new game automatically starts 5 seconds later. The gamification design mechanics of collaborative storytelling websites employed to create a sense of time pressure include countdown timers, time bars, and check points.[10]

4.3 Identifying gamification features for collaborative storytelling websites

A focus group interview was conducted with the purpose of identifying the gamification features of collaborative storytelling websites. Materials, subjects, and results of interview are described below.

4.3.1 Materials

Three websites including Protagonize.com, Storybird.com, and Flickspin.com were used in this study. These three websites are representative collaborative storytelling service providers, with a myriads of users worldwide.

4.3.2 Participants and Procedures

The survey was advertised on several strorytelling forums to recruit volunteers to participate. Eighteen experts, consisting of nine male and nine female story website users, were selected for the interview. All of them are frequent story creators and have at least five years story writing experience. All users were asked to identify and discuss gamification features based on the proposed systematic gamification framework..

4.3.3 Results

To improve the features, three human-computer interaction experts were invited to examine the framework. These experts reviewed all features of the framework, considering the significance and rationality. Finally, thirty-five gamification features were developed following the in-depth interviews, as shown in Appendix 1.

4.4 Determining the relative attractiveness of gamification features

This study asked collaborative storytelling website users to identify the 35 proposed gamification features. Following this, a fuzzy-AHP methodology was applied to determine the relative attractiveness of the various gamfication features.

4.4.1 Questionnaire design and data collection

A questionnaire was developed for the present study to gather collaborative storytelling website user's assessments of the relative attractiveness of the different gamification features in a pair-wise comparison data input format based on the hierarchical structure (see Fig. 1) and gamification features described above. The questionnaire used a nine-point rating scale which assessed therelative attractiveness of each gamification feature, for example, as equally attractive, moderately attractive, strongly attractive, very strongly attractive and extremely attractive, as suggested by Saaty[31] (see Appendix 2 for an example of the Fuzzy AHP questionnaire). To validate the instrument, the questionnaire was first pilot tested with thirty evaluators. All evaluators had more than 3 years' experience using collaborative story telling websites. They were asked to comment on the relevance, clarity, and meaningfulness of the criteria. Therefore, the questionnaire has confirmed content validity. After this we administered the questionnaire through an internet survey and recruited 6333 users who had used collaborative storytelling websites. After primary data analysis, we deleted incomplete questionnaires and outlier data, leaving us with 5566 valid samples (87.9 %) for use in this study. The gender distribution of participants was 2639 (47.4%) males and 2927 (52.6%) females. The age range was included 21-30 (34.7%), 31-40 (39.2%), 41-50 (10.6%), 51-60 (10.1%), 61 and above (5.4%). Additionally, 12.7% of the same had experience using collaborative storytelling websites for less than a year, 31.4% had experience for 1–2 years, and 55.9 % had experience of more than two years.

4.4.2 Data Analysis

There were seven steps in our proposed fuzzy-AHP approach. We first used triangular fuzzy numbers to construct the fuzzy comparison matrix. Second, we integrated the collected user's assessments of each gamification features design factor and design components using the fuzzy average method proposed by Buckley[32]. Third, we computed the fuzzy weight of each gamification feature using the Approximation Method introduced by Buckley[32]. Fourth, the Center of Gravity Method, a defuzzifying method proposed by Tzeng and Teng [33], was performed to defuzzify the weight of each gamification feature. Fifth, we normalized the weights of all gamification features. Sixth, we aggregated each level of the proposed gamification framework and calculated the relative attractive value of the fuzzy weight for each feature at factor levels. Finally, we computed the consistency index (CI) and consistency ratio (CR) for each fuzzy comparison matrix. The detailed process of data collection and the proposed fuzzy-AHP model are described in Appendix 3.

4.4.3 Results

Among the 35 fun gamification features, the top 10 most attractive features, listed in Table 1, account for more than 50% (57.47%) of gamification attractiveness.

Table 4.1. Top 10 attractive gamification features for collaborative storytelling websites

Gamification features	*Contribution (%)*	*Accumulative contribution (%)*
GF2: The relationship between action and reward is clear.	9.30	9.30
GF35: The types of time pressure are unpredictable.	7.66	16.96
GF18: Instruction is easy to learn.	7.25	24.22
GF27: Building groups with other users to accomplish a story is helpful.	6.00	30.22
GF8: Badges types are diverse and interesting.	5.81	36.02
GF20: Instructions presented within the websites are not too complex.	5.23	41.26
GF21: Types of Leaderboard are diverse.	4.95	46.21
GF1: Points can be accumulated easily.	4.17	50.38
GF33: Behaviors are quick and based on well-timed responses to changes in the situation	3.64	54.01
GF24: Gifts are creative.	3.46	57.47

4.5 Discussion

4.5.1 General Discussion

For the purpose of this chapter, the top five attractive gamification features are discussed below.

The most attractive gamification feature is "the relationship between action and reward is clear". It means the collaborative storytelling website users pay more attention to feedback after conducting certain behaviors. Users prefer to know the immediate consequences of his or her behavior. It also reflects the websites' need to assist users map their behaviors with rewards intuitively. This finding is consistent with previous studies. Norman [34] considers that natural mapping provides users with immediate feedback on their controls because it reduces user's effort and memory load. In addition, Ducheneaut and Moore[18], conducted a survey on Massively Multiplayer Role-Playing Games (MMORPGs), finding that a clear relationship between action and rewards can foster user's motivation, and drive users to engage in activities more.

The second most attractive gamification feature is that "the types of time pressure are unpredictable". This gamification feature makes users involved because they have to respond to various unexpected events within a collaborative storytelling website. The feature may be related to challenge, which is a basic intrinsic motivation of users. Users may be attracted by the challenges proposed by unpredictable time pressure. Surprisingly, this finding has not been revealed in the previous literature.

The third most attractive gamification feature is "instruction is easy to learn," which means that users emphasize the learnability or usability of websites' instructions. This finding is consistent with Crawford's study, [35] which found that good instructions enable users to master the system effectively, which increases their involvement.

"Building groups with other users to accomplish a story is helpful " is the fourth most attractive gamification feature. This feature reflects users need to be socialized or affiliated with groups as they write stories online. This finding is consistent with Gee's research, which stated that users constitute an "affinity group," in which they work together under the same goals.[30] Moreover, Hsu et al. (2009) also found that self-organized groups will form experience social bonding effect, which increase user's engagement with activities.

Finally, "Badge types are diverse and interesting" is the fifth most attractive feature, which suggests that players are attracted by badges and enjoy attempting to collect all of them. This finding is also consistent with previous studies. Law and his colleagues[36], conducted a study on the relationship between gamification and sustainability of mobile applications, and proposed that badge collection is an important enhancer of user's involvement. As users enjoy collecting different kinds of badges, they are more likely to engage in using mobile applications.

4.5.2 Design guideline for implementing gamification in collaborative story telling websites

The gamification features introduced in this study present some of the most attractiveness elements for users. Based on these features, the following guidelines were designed to enable website owners to attract more users.

Encourage social events and group activities

Websites could display information regarding upcoming social events or invitations to group activities as users log onto websites. Increased participation in social events translates into higher user engagement with the website.

Build rapid feedback cycles for users –

To improve usability, providing immediate feedback facilitiates users progressing to new tasks and new skill levels. Especially for new comers, websites should give users direct feedback as instructions in order to to assists in improving their story writing skills.

Adjust in-website tasks to skill levels

Like computer games always attract users since it allow users foreseen the success of game, website designers should design tasks with different levels adapted to user's different skill levels. Challenging tasks increase user's likelihood of stay longer, as opposed to frustrating tasks.

Assist users to improve their skills through social incentives

Users can receive recognition for writing achievements by peers helping users to develop their identity on the website. Social recognition also motivates users to improve their skills.

Motivate users to give others' reward or social recognition

In the game World of Warcraft (WoW), player groups often use a special scoring system called Dragon Kill Point (DKP) for promoting collaboration among members. DKP provides transparent information of each member's task allocation and involvement, which is the same as groupware in the real-world setting. In collaborative storytelling websites, users can get recognition and rewards for their participation with storytelling activities. Users also have to learn to reward other users in order to promote social bonding and a sense of belonging between user groups.

Enable website users to try as many new identities and roles as possible

In most online games, players can assume different identities and perform different roles. In collaborative storytelling websites, users can also be allowed to try different sides of themselves and gain a more immersive experience.

Encourage mutual competition among users to facilitate valuable behaviors

Website designers can design various challenges tailored to the user's level of writing skill, increasing the difficulty of these challenges as the users acquires new skills. Challenging tasks are also more fun for users and increase their engagement with the website.

4.6 Conclusion

This study aimed to identify attractive gamification features in the context of collaborative storytelling websites. Using an empirical method we propose 35 attractive gamification features of collaborative storytelling websites. Among these attractive gamification features, the feature of "the types of time pressure is unpredictable", was identified and was not yet revealed by previous studies. A reasonable explanation may be that users tend to enjoy something which is challenging and immerse.

This research has both theoretical and practical contributions. From a theoretical standpoint, this study presented a systematic framework for studying gamification in collaborative storytelling websites or similar environments. This study not only confirms but also extends the current line of research on gamification.

On the practical side, the findings can serve as a reference framework to assist in the design and development of collaborative storytelling. Also, the questionnaire used in the study can also be employed to evaluate attractiveness of specific gamification dimensions to improve their function and design.

Limitations of this research should be noted. We do not suggest that the factors we have discussed represent an exhaustive list, in that other possible gamification factors may not have been included in this study.

4.7 Areas for Future Research

Future research may wish to use different methodologies, such as longitudinal studies, focus groups, and ethnography approachs to identify other gamification factors for collaborative storytelling websites.

References

1. Cao Y, Klamma R, Martini A. Collaborative storytelling in the web 2.0. In: Proceeding of the first international workshop on story-telling and educational Games 2008.
2. Hourcade JP, Bederson BB, Druin A, Taxén G. KidPad: a Collaborative Storytelling Tool for Children. Extended Abstracts of Human Factors in Computing Systems 2002 (CHI 2002).ACM Press, 500–501.
3. Liu CC, Liu KP, Chen WH, Lin GD, Chen GD. Collaborative storytelling experiences in social media: Influence of peer-assistance mechanisms. Computers & Education; 57(3):1544-1556
4. Chuang SC, Tsai CC. Preferences toward the constructivist internet-based learning environments among high school students in Taiwan. Computers in Human Behavior 2005; 21(1):255–272.
5. Reeves B, Read JL (2009). Total Engagement: Using Games and Virtual Worlds to Change the Way People Work and Businesses Compete. Harvard Business Press.
6. Choe PC, Jang H, Song J. Roleplaying gamification to encourage social interactions at parties. In: CHI 2011, May 7–12, 2011, Vancouver, BC, Canada, ACM press.
7. Simões J, Redondo RD, Vilas BF. A social gamification framework for a K-6 learning platform. Computers in Human Behavior 2012; 29(3): 1557-1577.
8. Bajdor P, Dragolea L. The gamification as a tool to improve risk management in the enterprise. Annales Universitatis Apulensis Series Oeconomica 2011; 13(2):574-583.
9. McCALLUM S. Gamification and serious games for personalized health. In pHealth 2012: Proceedings of the 9th International Conference on Wearable Micro and Nano Technologies for Personalized Health 2012, IOS press, 85-96.

10. Bunchball. Gamification 101: An introduction to the use of game dynamics to influence behavior. White paper 2010.
11. Yee N. Motivations for Play in Online Games. Cyberpsychology, Behavior, and Social Networking 2006;9:772-775.
12. Choi D , Kim J. Why People Continue to Play Online Games: In Search of Critical Design Factors to Increase Customer Loyalty to Online Contents. CyberPsychology & Behavior 2004; 7: 11-24.
13. Chen CH, Sun CT, Hsieh J. Player guild dynamics and evolution in massively multiplayer online games. CyberPsychology & Behavior 2008; 11: 293-301.
14. Williams D., Ducheneaut N, Xiong L, Zhang Y, Yee N, Nickell E. From Tree House to Barracks: The Social Life of Guilds in World of Warcraft. Games and Culture 2006; 1: 338-361.
15. Jang Y, Ryu S. Exploring game experiences and game leadership in massively multiplayer online role-playing games. British Journal of Educational Technology 2011; 42 (1): 616 – 623.
16. Hou HT. Exploring the behavioral patterns of learners in an educational massively multiple online role-playing games (MMORPG). Computers & Education 2012; 58(4): 1225-1233.
17. Ryan RM, Deci EL. When paradigms clash: Comments on Cameron and Pierce's claim that rewards do not undermine intrinsic motivation, Review of Educational Research 1996; 66(1): 33-54.
18. Ducheneaut N, Moore RJ. The social side of gaming: a study of interaction patterns in a massively multiplayer online game. In: Proceedings of the ACM Conference on Computer-Supported Cooperative Work 2004 (CSCW 2004), Chicago, USA , ACM, 360-369.
19. Hsu SH, Wen MH, Wu MC. Exploring user experiences as predictors of MMORPG addiction. Computers & Education 2009; 53: 990-999.
20. Lin SC, Chang JN. Goal orientation and organizational commitment as explanatory factors of employees' mobility. Personnel Review 2005; 34 (3), 331 – 353
21. Antin J., Churchill EF. (2011). Badges in Social Media: A Social Psychological Perspective. Proceedings of the 2011 SIGCHI conference on Human Factors in computing In: CHI 2011, Vancouver, BC, Canada.
22. Tulathimutte T.Trust, Cooperation, and Reputation in Massively Multiplayer Online Games, Game Research (2006).
23. Wolf KD. Communities of Practice in MMORPGs: an entry point into addiction? In: Proceeding of the Third Communities and Technologies Conference 2000, Springer, London, 191-208.
24. Montola M, Nummenmaa T, Lucero A, Boberg M, Korhonen H. Applying game achievement systems to enhance user experience in a photo sharing service. In Proc. MindTrek 2009. ACM Press (2009), 94-97.
25. Trivers RL. (1971). The evolution of reciprocal altruism. The Quarterly Review of Biology, 46(1), p35-57.
26. Bergami M, Bagozzi RP. (2000). Self-categorization, affective commitment and group self-esteem as distinct aspects of social identity in the organization. British Journal of Social Psychology 2000; 39(4): 555-577.
27. Jo S, Moon J, Garrity E, Sanders GL. Massively Multiplayer Online Role-Playing Games (MMORPGs) and Commitment Behavior: An Integrated Model. In: Proceedings of Americas Conference on Information Systems 2007 (AMCIS 2007) (pp. 70).
28. Pisan Y.(2007). My guild, my people: role of guilds in massively multiplayer online games. In: IE '07 Proceedings of the 4th Australasian conference on Interactive entertainment of Conference. Melbourne, Australia: RMIT University.
29. Seay, AF, Jerome WJ, Lee KS, Kraut RE. Project Massive: A study of online gaming communities. In: Conference on human factors in computing systems 2004 (CHI 2004). Vienna, Austria: ACM.
30. Gee JP. (2004). What video games have to teach us about learning and literacy? Palgrave Macmillan, London, U.K.

31. Saaty TL. How to Make a Decision: The Analytic Hierarchy Process, European Journal of Operational Research 1990; 48(1): 9-26.
32. Buckley JJ. Fuzzy hierarchical analysis. Fuzzy Sets and Systems 1985; 17(3):233-247.
33. Tzeng GH, Teng Y. Transportation investment project selection with fuzzy multi-objectives, Transportation Planning and Technology 1993; 17(2): 91-112.
34. Norman D. (1990).The Design of Everyday Things. Doubleday, New York.
35. Crawford C. (1982). The Art of Computer Game Design. Amazon Digital Services, Inc., Seattle, Washington, U.S.
36. Law FL, Kasirun ZM, Gan CK. Gamification towards Sustainable Mobile Application. In: 2011 5th Malaysian Conference in Software Engineering (MySEC).

APPENDIX 1. GAMIFICATION FEATURES

Rewards
GF1: Points can be accumulated easily. GF2: The
relationship between act and rewards is clear. GF3:
Rewards varies with events. GF4: Rewards is
adequate. GF5: Rewards
that are more deeply immersed in the situation.

Goal Setting
GF6: Publish writing awards on their personal profile. GF7:
Expose the progress bar of stories publicly. GF8:
Badges types are diverse and interesting. GF9:
Progress bar is clear. GF10:
An obvious over-riding goal of collaborative storytelling at the beginning.

Reputation
GF11: Reputation rule is clear. GF12:
Reputation can be accumulated. GF13:
Give users specific titles based on their reputation level.

Status
GF14: Automatic notification of other users' level-up and comment.
GF15: Statistics about authors' story progress and writing experience are retrievable.
GF16: Enable recognition of users' progress by peers.

Instruction
GF17: Provide instruction suits the event. GF18:
Instruction is easy to learn. GF19:
All instructions are retrievable. GF20:
Instruction presented within the websites not too complex.

Competition
GF21: Types of Leaderboard are diverse. GF22:
High score user board can be viewed.

Altruism
GF23: Gifts are varying. GF24:
Gifts are creative. GF25:

Gifts are looking-real GF26:
Charity types vary with events

Group identification
GF27: Building groups with other users to accomplish a story is helpful
GF28: Inviting other users to perform a story chain is easy

Self-expression
GF29: Personalized user profile GF30:
Animated web page component and icons GF31:
Virtual goods are diverse GF32:
Style of space is similar to mine

Time pressure
GF33: Behaviors are quick and well-timed responses to changes in the situation
GF34: The types of time pressure are varying GF35:
The types of time pressure are unpredictable

APPENDIX 2.
A FUZZY-AHP APPROACH FOR DETERMINING RELATIVE ATTRACTIVENESS OF COLLABORATIVE STORYTELLING GAMIFICATION FEATURES

Step 1. Constructing the fuzzy comparison matrix

Triangular fuzzy numbers $\widetilde{M}_{ij}$ from $\tilde{1}$ to $\tilde{9}$ were employed to represent the results of users' assessments of the pair-wise comparisons between each of the design features (see Table 1) by constructing a fuzzy positive reciprocal matrix M. The proposed fuzzy comparison matrix was defined as follows:

$M = [\widetilde{M}_{ij}]$
M: fuzzy positive reciprocal matrix

$$\widetilde{M}_{ij} = (L_{ij}, M_{ij}, R_{ij})$$

L_{ij}: the left value of the fuzzy membership function of the collected subject assessments of design feature j of decision element i
M_{ij}: the middle value of the fuzzy membership function of the collected subject assessments of design feature j of decision element i
R_{i}: the right value of the fuzzy membership function of the collected subject assessments of design feature j of decision element i

$$\widetilde{M}_{ij} = 1 / \widetilde{M}_{ji}, \forall i, j = 1, 2, \ldots, n$$

Table 1. Membership function and definitions of fuzzy numbers

Fuzzy Number	Membership Function	Definition
$\tilde{1}$	(1,1,2)	equally attractive
$\tilde{2}$	(1,2,3)	between equally and moderately attractive
$\tilde{3}$	(2,3,4)	moderately attractive
$\tilde{4}$	(3,4,5)	between moderately and strongly attractive
$\tilde{5}$	(4,5,6)	strongly attractive
$\tilde{6}$	(5,6,7)	between strongly and very strongly attractive
$\tilde{7}$	(6,7,8)	very strongly attractive
$\tilde{8}$	(7,8,9)	between very strongly and extremely attractive
$\tilde{9}$	(8,9,10)	extremely attractive

Step 2. Integration of the collected subjects' assessments of each decision element
There are many possible approaches to integrating subject assessments when calculating the triangular fuzzy number. In contrast to some studies that apply statistical parameters such as the minimum, maximum, mean, and mode to represent the fuzzy numbers, this study applied the geometric mean method proposed by Buckley [59]. The computing process is defined as follows:

$$\tilde{m}_{ij} = \left(1/n\right) \otimes \left(\tilde{m}_{ij}^{1} \oplus \tilde{m}_{ij}^{2} \oplus \cdots \oplus \tilde{m}_{ij}^{n}\right)$$

$\tilde{m}_{ij}$: Integrated triangular fuzzy numbers

$\tilde{m}_{ij}^{N}$: The value of the pair comparison of the collected subject assessments of design feature j of decision factor i
n: The number of subjects

Step 3. Computation of fuzzy weight
After integrating the collected data and calculating the corresponding triangular fuzzy numbers, we used the Approximation Method proposed by Buckley [59] to compute the fuzzy weight. The formula of the Approximation Method for computing the fuzzy weights is defined as follows:

$$\tilde{Z}_i = \left(\tilde{a}_{i1} \otimes \tilde{a}_{i2} \otimes \cdots \otimes \tilde{a}_{in}\right)^{1/n}, \forall i = 1,2,\ldots,n$$

$$\tilde{W}_i = \tilde{Z}_i \otimes \left(\tilde{Z}_1 \oplus \tilde{Z}_2 \oplus \cdots \oplus \tilde{Z}_n\right)^{-1}$$

$\tilde{Z}_i$: The geometric mean value of the triangular fuzzy number

$\tilde{a}_{ij}$: The triangular fuzzy number of row i and column j in the fuzzy positive reciprocal matrix

$\tilde{W}_i$: The fuzzy weight of each row of the fuzzy positive reciprocal matrix

Step 4. Defuzzification of decision elements
The weights of the decision elements were represented by fuzzy values. The defuzzification process assigned a distinct number to each of the decision elements. We then used the Center of Gravity Method of defuzzification to calculate the center of gravity of the triangular fuzzy number. Given a triangular fuzzy number and its three sides, denoted by $\tilde{A} = (L_{ij}, M_{ij}, R_{ij})$, the defuzzified weight DF_{ij} was calculated using the following formula:

$$DF_{ij} = [(R_{ij} - L_{ij}) + (M_{ij} - L_{ij})]/3 + L_{ij}$$

Step 5. Normalization of defuzzified weights

To compare the importance of different decision elements at different levels, we first normalized the defuzzified weights. The definition of the normalized weights (NW_i) of each decision dimension at each level can be defined as follows:

$$NW_i = DF_{ij} / \sum DF_{ij}$$

Step 6. Calculation of the synthesized weight for each element at each level

We calculated the normalized weights of each element at each level after step 5. However, to determine the priority of each feature, it was still necessary to synthesize weights for each decision element at each decision level. The larger the value of the synthesized weight, the higher the priority of the dimension. The definition of synthesized weights of each decision element at each level was defined as follows:

$$NW_K = NW_i \times NW_{ij} \times NW_{ijk}$$

Step 7. Checking for consistency

Consistency Index (CI) was employed to designate overall inconsistency for the proposed hierarchy and for each decision dimension. Consistency Ratio (CR) was also calculated to describe the consistency of the pair-wise comparisons. The equations for calculating CI and CR for each decision were:

$$Consistency\ \ Index\ \ (CI) = \frac{\lambda_{Max} - n}{n-1}$$

where λ_{max} is the maximum eigenvalue, and n the number of the decision component

$$Consistency\ \ Ratio\ \ (CR) = \frac{CI}{RI}$$

RI is the average index for randomly generated weights obtained from a table of random consistency indices. To judge the consistency of the pair-wise outputs, if CR was ≤ 0.1, then the output of the pair-wise comparison was sufficiently consistent. On the other hand, if CR was > 0.1, then the results of the pair-wise comparison was inconsistent.

Jose A. Carmona, Adolfo J. Cangas, Roberto Zarate, Ari Ucar, Alvaro I. Langer

5 Assessment Of Risk Behaviors Related To Substance Use, Bullying and Alterations in Body Image in Adolescents Through a 3D Simulation Program

Abstract: Currently, the expansion and use of new technologies has occured not only in the field of entertainment and communication, but also in applied professional contexts. In this sense, the development of virtual reality (VR) environments has proved to be a fruitful field for the development and implementation of various programs for the treatment of different psychopathological disorders. In this sense, it is not strange that diverse authors have recently pointed out the great impact that VR environments could have on human interaction and on their consciousness; this is why they have become a deeply appealing kind of technology for people nowadays. In this regard, Blaschovich & Bailenson (2011) in their book Infinite Reality brilliantly address the question of the affinity and attraction that VR environments produce in human beings. Thus, it is interesting to notice that as VR environments are more widely accepted and integrated into our daily lives, they will be used in some environments as a replacement for the natural or physical world. In such cases, as for example when using VR environments in psychotherapy, the question arises as to what is real and what is not, but the fact is that we do get immersed in such virtual environments, and react within them as though we were in the "real" world.

In this chapter, the importance and application of VR will be addressed in three areas of great relevance in Psychology for the study of risk behaviors in young people. In particular, drug use behaviors, bullying among pupils at school, and the alterations of body image commonly present in people with eating disorders. To begin with, in the first section we will discuss the distinctive characteristics of VR, such as its main definitions, the existing types of VR, and the main advantages that this sort of technology would present. Then, some of the most important developments of VR applied to the treatment and assessment of problematic behaviors appearing at school ages will be described. Lastly, we will discuss the features of a new desktop VR computer program named MySchool4web aimed at the detection of problematic behaviors in young people at school ages as well as its main outcomes.

5.1 Definition of virtual reality

There have been several attempts at defining VR over time, as such we will first present the most relevant characteristics. Virtual reality implies a new sort of human-computer interaction, being that the users are not only external observers of images on a computer, but active participants in the frame of a three-dimensional computer-generated world (Riva, 1997). As can be deduced from this description, VR would imply the use of computers as much for its development as its application. At the same time, it is important to emphasize that VR would be a dynamic system of interaction between a computer and the person who uses it. In this sense, VR systems wouldn't be passive devices, such as TVs – they imply real interaction, allowing the person to participate in the simulated context.. Continuing with the characteristics of VR, this technology would fall somewhere between a TV and a computer, making it possible for us to watch, hear, and feel in a three-dimensional graphically created world and to interact with it, facilitating in the participant a surrounding experience, which would lead the person to feel and believe they are really there (Perpiñá, Botella, & Baños, 2003).

In a similar way, other authors have defined VR as an advanced type of contact (interface) between a human being and a computer, which would allow the user to both interact and become immersed in a computer generated environment in a natural way (Adams, Finn, Moes, Flannery, & Rizzo 2009). For instance, this interaction could happen through the use of tracking devices that make it feasible to determine both the position and the orientation of the person's head in space and to use this information in order to change the image that is being virtually presented. In addition, this sort of contact between the person and the virtual environment brings about a different way of showing information, generating the feeling of immersion, which is a perceptual and psychological sensation of being present in the digital environment. Being-present and immersion experiences are the two main features that would distinguish virtual reality systems from other computer applications (McLellan, 2001).

In conclusion, VR systems would imply at least the following basic distinctive characteristics (Carmona, 2012):

i. The use of computer systems for its development and application.
ii. The simulation of environments (mainly three-dimensional) that would appropriately recreate both real life and imaginary situations.
iii. The possibility of interaction between the computer and the person who uses it.
iv. The person as subject of the presence and immersion experiences generated by the virtual environments and the machine-person interaction.

5.1.1 Types of virtual reality

Nowadays, several classifications of virtual reality exist. Brill (1993, 1994) differentiated seven categories or types of VR, these include: (i) Immersive first-person with HMD, (ii) desktop VR, (iii) mirror world, (iv) Waldo world, (v) CAVE o chamber world, (vi) cab simulator environment and (vii) cyberSpace. As McLellan (2001) pointed out, there would be three more types of VR, that is: (viii) augmented reality, (ix) VisionDome y (x) Experience Learning System. Next, a brief description of each of these VY types will be presented.

i. Immersive first-person with HMD. The most widely accepted VR, it would be mainly characterized by using devices such as VR glasses, best known as head-mounted display (HMD), fiber-optic-wired gloves, position-tracking devices, and audio systems providing 3-D (binaural) sound as well as olfactory stimuli. The HMD device mainly contains screens inside of the goggles through which virtual reality images are presented. At the same time, a sensor attached to the helmet and a movement-tracker allow the participant to change the vision of the virtual world consistently with the motion of the head in the real world - in such a way that movement made in real life would produce this same movement in the virtual world.
ii. Desktop VR. This form of VR introduces a three-dimensional world generated virtually that is watched through the screen of a conventional computer. As a consequence, the user interacts with such an environment through devices usually used in normal personal computers (PC), such as a keyboard, mouse, or a control pad similar to those used in videogames. This type of VR is not considered as immersive as those with HMD. Nevertheless, desktop VR would have significantly fewer technical and economic requirements than immersive first-person VR using HMD systems.
iii. Mirror world. This system provides a second-person experience projecting virtual realities by using a video camera. However, the person is able to interact and communicate with objects and people, although this interaction is always done outside of the virtual world. At the same time, the image of the person who participates could be either superimposed on the simulated virtual image or mixed with the virtual world through the projected video image. A digitizer is used with the purpose of processing the user's images and features, such as the position, movement or number of fingers in the scene.
iv. Waldo world. Also known as virtual animation, this sort of VR device consists of real-time computer animation in which user's motion is digitally detected using a electronic mask or body armor equipped with sensors. Therefore, it is possible to generate a real-time virtual animation of the person's motion on a screen or in a robot.
v. CAVE or chamber world. This is actually a version of the immersive virtual reality with HMD. Nevertheless, the virtual simulation system called CAVE (cave automatic virtual environment) allows us to cause an even greater sensation of immersion in

the participant thanks to the possibility of projecting the virtual world using several computers that generate images which are then projected on a cubicle of 4 or 6 walls. These images can be seen in three dimensions through the use of HMD.

vi. Cab simulator environment. Conceived as a way to realistically recreate the cab of a vehicle (a plane, car, etc.), this VR system manages to produce an experience of immersion though virtual environments that use additional components, such as visual elements that are bigger than the field of view and three-dimensional sound inputs.

vii. Cyberspace. This term encompasses all those nets and databases generated and maintained by computers creating an artificial global reality. It can be visited simultaneously by many people through connected computers making up a net.

viii. Augmented reality. The main characteristic of this system is that it uses both virtual stimuli generated by a computer and real world stimuli. In this regard, augmented reality uses computer generated items that are superimposed over the real world to highlight certain features. VR items can be displayed by VR glasses such as HMD but also using a desktop monitor or a hand held display.

ix. VisionDome. This is a VR system similar to CAVE, with the exception that it is not necessary to use any VR device (goggles, helmet, etc.) to watch the simulation. Here, the users are immersed in a VR system that generates three-dimensional models using a 180 degrees screen inside a hemispheric structure. This results in a total experience of being immersed in 360 degrees by a 180 degrees virtual environment thanks to the synchronization of that structure with the motion of the participant.

x. Experience Learning System. This system has been designed in the context of the military industry in order to provide the Army with highly realistic training simulations that rely on advances in virtual reality, artificial intelligence, and other cutting-edge technologies. At the same time, the developed systems are aimed to produce immersive environments for simulations, ranging from better head-mounted displays and force-feedback devices to surround-sound audio systems and computer networks that allow the simultaneous participation of troops all over the world in real-time simulations.

5.1.2 Advantages of virtual reality

As many other researchers in the field of Virtual Reality have mentioned, the use of this type of technology would have some advantages compared with traditional treatment and evaluation procedures. In this regard, some of the most relevant are (Scozzary & Gamberini, 2011; Botella, García-Palacios, Baños, & Quero, 2007; Adams et al., 2009; Perpiñá et al., 2003):

a) Experiences similar to real life. The main characteristic of this technology is that it allows a person to experience something similar to what they might in the real world if they were in that context. Thus, VR can cause the same emotions, thoughts, and behavioral responses as if the person were exposed to the real context.

b) Safety of the virtual world. VR are presented as a safe context where the person is not exposed to the risks that they would face in the real world. In this sense, the person immersed in the virtual world can experience emotions, thoughts, and react knowing that nothing in the virtual environment that really frightens them can cause any harm, which allows the context of therapy to be perceived by the person as a safe environment where they can behave freely and without any risk.

c) Simulation of real world situations. As we all know, the use of 3D simulation allows any situation in the real world to be realistically recreated. This characteristic is especially relevant in both evaluation and intervention, since it allows the person to be submerged in a virtual world with characteristics similar to those in the real world, where their responses in certain conflictive contexts can be studied, and which could, in turn, improve the ecological validity of measures using VR instruments over the usual procedures.

d) Control of scenes presented. The use of VR systems allows the therapist greater control over the presented stimuli . Certain parameters in the scene can be manipulated, for example the intensity of the stimuli. In fact it makes evaluation and treatment more flexible and adaptable to each person, as well as to the demands of the therapist or researcher.

e) Presenting situations at any moment. Therapists often struggle with the fact that they cannot control what the patient experiences outside of therapy. Using VR as a supplement to existing therapy, however, helps to overcome this limitation, as it permits the therapist to present to the client, at any moment during the therapeutic process, key situations or stimuli as often as needed

f) Confidentiality. The use of VR environments inside the office of the therapist safeguards the privacy and confidentiality of the client's answers without it being necessary to expose the person to real contexts.

5.2 Virtual reality applications in psychology: drug use, bullying and alterations in body image

This current paper is not aimed at making a detailed review of the existing VR developments, which is beyond the scope of this chapter Instead this section will show those elements that are associated with the contents of the different scenes included in the MySchool4web simulation program (which will be described in section 3). We will focus on the work carried out by the principal research groups that have studied the use of VR in three common phenomena in adolescence, that is: drug use, bullying and alterations in body image. Nevertheless, for a more comprehensive outlook on the multiple VR applications developed so far there are several books which have focused on this topic. In this regard, one which is very much recommended is the book entitled

Advanced Computational Intelligence Paradigms in Healthcare 6 (Brahnam & Jain, 2011), which focuses on the use of VR in psychotherapy, rehabilitation and assessment. This book offers an extensive picture of the multiple applications developed so far in the field of psychological interventions, assessment, and healthcare rehabilitation. In addition to this, we think the book edited by Christiane Eichenberg (2012) can provide a wider perspective of the state-of-the-art technology in the field of VR applications, applied not only to psychotherapeutic contexts, but also to pedagogical and medical contexts.

5.2.1 Virtual reality and drug use

In the field of addictive behaviors, similar to exposure therapy in specific phobias, repeatedly showing cues of alcohol, tobacco, or other drugs not followed by substance-administration should lead to the extinction of craving responses, therefore removing the motivation or desire to continue using drugs. Specifically, VR environments have focused on the recreation of situations related to the consumption of different drugs, mainly tobacco and alcoholic drinks, but also marihuana, cocaine, amphetamines, and opiates (Scozzari & Gamberini, 2011). Through this sort of procedure, the person is exposed to virtual contexts explicitly related to the consumption of different drugs in order to reduce or eliminate their craving responses by means of extinction. Thus, drugs and objects directly related to substance use (paraphernalia) are presented. At the same time, rituals of consumption are simulated; that is, people, behaviors, and common interactions that usually happen when consumers are in this sort of contexts. To sum up, we try to introduce through the use of VR those places related to consumption of drugs, along with all those stimuli which are usually present.

The information obtained after the exposition to the contexts associated with drug consumption and the subsequent generation of craving responses, are then used in the treatment of addictions throughout the therapeutic process. This is used as a therapeutic technique aimed at the reduction or extinction of craving answers when these behaviors have been shown as a maladapted pattern. In the frame of interventions that use this sort of technology, VR scenes have been developed as valid exposition strategies inside the virtual reality exposure therapy (VRET).

With regard to the efficacy of VR environments to generate craving, several studies have shown the effectiveness of this technology when provoking craving responses for all the drugs assessed. At this regard, there would be enough evidence to support the use of VR environments as a therapeutic tool for the treatment of people with drug use problems (Bordnick, Graap, Copp, Brooks, Mirtha, & Ferrer, 2005; Bordnick et al., 2008; Bordnick et al., 2009; Lee et al., 2003, 2008; Saladin, Brady, Graap, & Rothbaum, 2006; Scozzari & Gamberini, 2011).

5.2.2 Virtual reality and bullying

At present, as part of the efforts aimed at diminishing the problems related to the dynamics of bullying at schools, we found the ECircus European project (Education through Characters with emotional-Intelligence and Role-playing Capabilities that Understand Social interaction), which created a tool called "FearNot!" (Fun with Empathic Agents to Reach Novel Outcomes in Teaching). Developed to be applied on children at school ages. "FearNot!" is a software that simulates a virtual school in which several avatars (pupils) interact autonomously. The scene simulated in "FearNot!" shows a narrativesequence, in which bullying episodes follow a coherent and established structure similar to real life. Firstly, the participant is witness (from a distance, without getting involved) to a bullying situation between characters inside the school. Then, the victim moves on to ask the participant for advice as to the management of bullying situations. The participant then has to give the victim advice about in what manner to react in order to cope. In terms of this advice, the participant can choose among several coping answers predefined by the program. Next, the victim who is asking for help modifies his/her behavior depending on the advice given by the participant (Zoll, Enz, Schaub, Aylett, & Paiva, 2006). Lastly, depending on the advice given and its functionality, a final scene is simulated in which the participant would watch the consequences of their advice. At this point, the participant receives feedback on the appropriateness of his or her advice to solve the bullying problem appropriately.

The purpose of involving the pupil in this sort of interaction is to move him or her to empathy; that is, that he or she gets to feel the emotional state of the victim, their feelings, emotions, and thoughts. As the program's authors pointed out, the promotion of empathy with regard to victims of bullying through the interactions in "FearNot!" would result in a reduction of the probability of participants becoming bullies. However, this research group hasn't published any results with regard to the efficacy or validity of this anti-bullying program so far.

5.2.3 Virtual reality and eating disorders

Different research groups have shown interest in both the characteristics of the answers given by people with eating disorders immersed in VR contexts and the therapeutic possibilities of VR as an assessment and treatment tool. The real effect of exposure to meaningful stimuli in people with eating disorders has been recently evaluated in three experimental conditions: virtual, real world, and photos. People diagnosed with anorexia and bulimia, and people without any psychological disorder participated in this study (Gorini, Griez, Petrova, & Riva, 2010). Findings from the study found that virtual situations were able to generate anxiety. In particular, the main outcomes showed a significant principal effect in the interaction of groups and the type of exposure in regard to anxiety. Post-hoc analysis revealed that both anorexia and bulimia groups showed significantly higher levels of anxiety than those shown by the group without any diagnostic (control group). Furthermore, the anxiety and bulimia groups showed high levels of anxiety when they were exposed to real and virtual food compared to these same stimuli in photos. In conclusion, this study demonstrates that exposure to virtual stimuli, such as different sorts of food, hotel trade situations, etc., would be as effective as the exposition to these stimuli in real life and more effective than in photos (Gorini et al., 2010).

If we focus on the VR environments developed, Riva and collaborators created the Virtual Environment for Body Image Modification (VEBIM) (Riva, 1998), aimed at the treatment of body image distortions and dissatisfaction that is usually associated with eating disorders. With regard to the outcomes, the application of the VR program in conjunction with a cognitive-behavioral psychological intervention was useful in reducing body dissatisfaction increasing the body awareness in individuals with anorexia (Riva, Bacchetta, Baruffi, Rinaldi, & Molinari, 1999). At the same time, in people with obesity and binge-eating disorders, researchers not only found a reduction of the dissatisfaction with their own body, but also a positive change in their behavior. In particular, the quality of social relationships improved and the use of dresses to hide their body and their worries about social judgments decreased (Riva, Bacchetta, Baruffi, Rinaldi, Vincelli, & Molinari, 2000). Furthermore, the intervention with VR jointly applied with cognitive-behavioral therapy was more effective in the short term than this treatment alone without VR expositions with regard to the improvement in the satisfaction with their own bodies, the reduction of their anxiety levels and binges (Riva, Bacchetta, Baruffi, & Molinari, 2002). It is also important to emphasize the work done by Perpiñá and collaborators (Perpiñá, Botella, Baños, Marco, Alcañiz, & Quero, 1999; Perpiñá, Botella, & Baños, 2002), who, using similar VR environments to those used by Riva (1998), also demonstrated the efficacy of VR in treating alterations in body image. Once again, the intervention using VR and the usual treatment jointly proved to have the same effectiveness at least as the usual treatment alone (without VR). Nevertheless, those people exposed to VR environments showed a meaningful improvement in general psychopathology measures, specifically in anxiety, and a bigger satisfaction with their own bodies in social situations. In addition, they showed less negative thoughts and attitudes toward their own body, and less fear in increasing their weight to become healthier. Furthermore, the VR group showed less withdrawal rates than the cognitive-behavioral group (Perpiñá et al., 1999). In the follow-up, these positive outcomes even improved after one year (Perpiñá, Marco, Botella, & Baños, 2004).

Finally, we think it is important to note that there are also VR environments developed to be used in conventional computers (desktop VR), without having to use any devices such as HMD, which would facilitate use through increased accessibility. Letosa-Porta, Ferrer-García, & Gutiérrez-Maldonado (2005) developed a program called The Body Image Assessment Software (BIAS). As these authors point out,

BIAS would permit the modeling of the avatar's body proportions more freely than in previous programs. At the same time, BIAS would allow us to modify specific parts of the virtual body while keeping a holistic vision of the avatar. The program was valid in differentiating people at risk of having an eating disorder from those who are not and those who had a clinic history of such disorders (Ferrer-García & Gutiérrez-Maldonado, 2008). Subsequent studies showed the effectiveness of VR environments used in personal computers (desktop VR) which were able to produce emotional responses in people with a diagnosis of eating disorders and in people without any disorder diagnosed. The evaluation of people with or without an eating disorder diagnostic who were immersed in VR scenarios showed the existence of a significant effect on anxiety and depression (Ferrer-García, Gutiérrez-Maldonado, Caqueo-Urízar, & Moreno, 2009).

5.3 MySchool4web: Detection of drug use, bullying and alterations in body image through a virtual reality desktop program

Designed to be used in personal computers, the recently developed program named MySchool4web recreates scenes related to drug use, bullying, and alterations in body image using three-dimensional environments. In particular, this would be the first program designed to detect these sorts of behaviors, which arecommonly present in school settings.. In fact, MySchool4web is the improved and up-to-date version of the Mii-School simulation program, which was previously developed by the same research team (Carmona, Espínola, Cangas, & Iribarne, 2010a).

In particular, MySchool4web consists of a total of 12 scenes in which situations regarding drug use, bullying, and social situations related to body image distortions are presented. The final objective of the computer program is to be used as a screening tool to detect pupils that were drug users or at risk of being implicated in bullying. In addition, the program is also aimed at the detection of young people at risk of having problems with their body image. Given the relationship between the alterations of body image and the presence of an eating disorder, such us anorexia and bulimia, the program allows for the early detection of these sorts of disorders.

Generally speaking, MySchool4web consists of the 3D presentation of different close-to-real-life scenes in which the participant has to point out how they would react in the specific simulated situation. Once the scene is presented, the program also simulates the different answer options available for each specific scene. Then, a static screen is presented displaying the possible answers. Lastly, through the use of a mouse the participant chooses how they would react.

With the intention of giving the reader a more specific idea as to the content assessed by MySchool4web, next we will describe the main characteristics of the different scenes in the program. In total, six scenes are aimed at assessing drug use in young people. Five of them allude to the consumption of drugs, and a sixth scene is related to parental behavior with regard to the participant. In particular, the drug scenes assess the consumption of tobacco, alcoholic drinks, marihuana, cocaine (stimulants), and MDMA (ecstasy). If we have a look at the context in which drugs are used in MySchool4web, tobacco and marijuana simulations take place in a park. In this scene, two friends are sitting on a bench smoking. The interior of a house has been recreated for the alcoholic drinks scene. There, a group of young people are enjoying a party in which they are dancing and drinking while other are sitting down on couches speaking. For the MDMA (ecstasy) the interior of a pub has been simulated in which young people can be seen dancing excitedly while others offer the participant substances. On the other hand, the cocaine consumption scene occurs in the toilets of this same pub, where it is possible to observe how this substance is consumed. Finally, is also the situation in which the familiar dynamic with the parents of the participant is evaluated. In this scene the participant arrives home late at night; here it is the reaction of the parents to her son's or daughter's disobedience that is being assessed.

Figure 5.1. Drug use scene of the MySchool4web program

In all the situations described before, the participant is offered each one of the drugs. We think it is important to note that we have tried to assess the consumption of each drug by simulating the natural contexts in which the consumption of these drugs occur most commonly at young ages. Thus, in MySchool4web we emphasize the realism of the scenes simulated and the interaction among avatars.

With regard to bullying, three scenes were created. The courtyard of a high school was simulated in the first bullying situation. In particular, some bullies surround the participant while aggressively insulting and threatening them. In the second bullying scene the participant is sitting down in the classroom. Again, some bullies surround him, threatening and even beating the participant while they remain still. The last bullying scene assesses the participant's social relationship with his or her peers. Thus, the character of the participant is shown different situations in order to assess if he or she is usually alone, in a group, or even if he or she feels different from others or is nervous and afraid when he or she is in a group.

Figure 5.2. Bullying scene of the MySchool4web program

It is important to emphasize that in all bullying scenes we were especially careful about the animation of the avatars (aggressiveness, fear, bravery, etc.). In this sense, the aggressive and intimidating attitudes of the bullies are easy to perceive if we examine the facial and body gestures of the avatars involved.

Last but not least, a group of three scenes are aimed at the detection of people with body image problems. One of the situations assesses the participant's response to a social situation which takes place in a park. In this simulation a group of people can be seen chatting around a bench. The participant has to point out how he or she would act when they are looking at him or her. In a second scene, the interior of a room in a house is simulated. The participant is watching their own body reflected in a big mirror. Then, the attitude toward his or her own body is assessed. The last scene is related to eating disorders, and involves a situation in which the participant's attitude toward an extremely thin person is assessed. In particular, in this scene the participant can be seen with a friend in the hall of a high school. They are observing an extremely thin person who is passing by. Then, the participant is asked about how they reacted after having seen this person.

Figure 5.3. Body image scene of the MySchool4web program

In essence, through the simulation of alterations in body image related scenes we aim at detecting people who could be at risk of developing an eating disorder.

The MySchool4web program has been designed to be applied online, without the handicap of using any sort of extra device, such as a CD or DVD. In this regard, a virtual platform has been created through which any person interested in the use of the program can make a request and get permission to use it by using the following link: http://www.myschool4web.com.

Furthermore, there are several versions of the MySchool4web program translated into different languages so far. As well as the Spanish version, the program has been translated into English, German, Italian, and a Spanish dialect spoken in Chile.

5.4 Evaluation of the MySchool4web properties: preliminary results

Once virtual environments have been developed in order to be applied throughout assessment and treatment processes in psychology, it is of utmost importance to assess the validity of these VR environments when used as effective support tools for the treatment or assessment of different mental disorders. In other words, there is little point in creating attractive VR environments if they will not show their validity in the context of the psychological interventions for which they were created.

For this reason, we carried out a number of studies in order to assess the MySchool4web program in detecting young people at risk of problematic behaviors.

As such, in this section we will show the psychometric properties related to the reliability and validity of the MySchool4web program when trying to detect drug use, bullying, and alterations in body image. In this regard, there have been two studies aimed at the evaluation of the validity and reliability of the MySchool4web program so far.

In a first study (Cangas, Gallego, Aguilar-Parra, Salinas, Zárate, & Roith, 2013) the construct validity and internal reliability of the MySchool4web scenes were evaluated. Based on the outcomes obtained, with regard to the validity analysis of the program, an exploratory factorial analysis with the principal components method and VARIMAX rotation (with KAISER normalization) was carried out. The outcomes revealed the existence of a 4-factor structure, which explained the 64.07% of the total variance. In particular, these 4 factors would gather three clearly differentiated dimensions, that is: drug use, bullying, and body image. Specifically, as to drug use dimension, one of the factors would gather the situations of tobacco, alcoholic drinks, and marihuana consumption. That is, drugs with the highest frequency and prevalence compared to others (European Monitoring Centre for Drugs and Drugs Addiction, 2007); therefore, their use would be more disseminated and socially accepted than other drugs. The second factor would gather those situations in which drugs used are less disseminated in the general population, in particular cocaine and MDMA (ecstasy). The third factor would gather bullying situations, both as bully or victim in this context. Finally, a fourth factor would gather those situations related to the assessment of body image.

The reliability analysis of this same study showed the internal consistency of the MySchool4web situations or items to have a Cronbach's alpha index of .688 for the drug use dimension and of .822 for the bullying dimension. The body image dimension was not analyzed due to the different nature of the scenes and as such the scoring of the different answer options wouldn't be equivalent (Cangas et al., 2013). In conclusion, taking into account that Cronbach's alpha is usually used as a sign of the global reliability of a tool (Busch, 2002), these results would show MySchool4web as a reliable instrument for the detection of those risk behaviors the program is aimed toward.

The second study was focused on analyzing whether the program was able to detect and differentiate between young people at risk of drug use, bullying, and alterations in body image and those who are not (Cangas, Gallego, Aguilar, Carmona, & Langer, 2013). In other words, we tried to analyze the criterion validity of the program for the detection of these behaviors. With regard to the criterion validity statistical analysis, the answers that pupils gave to the different simulated scenes in MySchool4web were compared to the answers obtained from three paper-and-pencil questionnaires, which were used as external criterions of comparison.

First, it is important to emphasize that the total of 12 scenes included in MySchool4web have passed the specified significance value $p < .05$ as to its relationship with drug use, bullying, and alterations in body image. Thus, the total of the simulated scenes in MySchool4web would be valid to detect these sort of risk behaviors. In addition, we found significant relationships between specific answers of the computer program and the use of drugs, being a bully or victim of bullying, and having problems in body image. These results are similar to those obtained in the previous version of the program (Carmona, Espínola, Cangas, & Iribarne, 2010b). To sum up, thanks to the analysis of the answers obtained through the MySchool4web program, specific answer profiles have been found that would differentiate between young people at risk and those who are not at risk of presenting these sorts of conflictive behaviors.

Thus, drug users answer in MySchool4web situations with use and trying the substances, whereas no-users react by rejecting the offer, giving advice about the risk of using the drug, and even leaving the place in which people are using drugs. In addition, as to the family situation, people who don't comsume alcoholic drinks point out that they have parents who are not indifferent in the situation in which the youngster disobeys them by arriving late at night. Instead, they claim to have understanding parents who get angry when they disobey them in this situation. On the contrary, marihuana users point out that they have parents who remain indifferent to this sort of disobedience, whereas those who are not users of marihuana answers that they have understanding parents.

With regard to the different bullying scenes of the MySchool4web program, bullies answered with indecision to threats, whereas those who are not bullies reacted with irony and insults. If we have a look at the profile of victims of bullying, these answered with shame, whereas those who are not victims would react aggressively, showing indecision when coping with threats. At the same time, victims stated that they usually remain alone when they are on a break at school and that they feel different from others. On the contrary, young people who are not victims of bullying point out that they usually stay in group.

Finally, if we focus on those with body image problems, they answer in the MySchool4web scenes with leaving the place and hiding themselves as a way to avoid others staring or even seeing their own bodies. At the same time, they place importance on having an extremely thin body similar tothe characters displayed in the simulation. On the contrary, those who wouldn't be at risk of having body image disorders answer in a manner that is accepting of their own body. In addition, they are indifferent to the presence of an extremely thin person and wouldn't like to look like him or her.

In conclusion, based on the results obtained in the two described studies, we could affirm that the MySchool4web computer program would not only be valid at detecting the presence of pupils at risk of being drug users, bullies, victims of bullying, and presenting body image problems, but also to demonstrate the specific coping answers that young people need when they are in conflictive situations. Therefore, MySchool4web allow us to obtain risk profiles associated with having these sorts of problematic behaviors.

5.5 Discussion

In the current chapter we have tried to demonstrate the relevance and importance that VR environments have in the field of applied psychology. Specifically, the MySchool4web program has been presented. In particular, this computer desktop program uses 3D simulation environments to detect pupils at risk of being involved in drug use, bullying, and problems with their own body image. As was described previously in this chapter, MySchool4web is the improved and up-to-date version of the Mii-School simulation program (Carmona et al., 2010a), also developed by the same research team. In this regard, MySchool4web presents considerable upgrades compared with its predecessor. Mainly:

i. The graphical environment has been notably improved in regard to the recreated scenes, the avatars interactions, and the physical and facial features of them - such as expressions, emotions, etc. Overall, the new desktop VR program simulates situations and interactions in a much more realistic way.

ii. The process to get permission and use the program has been simplified, with it now being possible to use it online on any PC and operative system without the need to use any extra or external hardware or device.

We think social networking within the educative system could take advantage of the utilities that this sort of program presents, particularly because of the importance and implications that drug use behaviors, bullying, and eating disorders can have when they appear at school ages. Furthermore, it is in school contexts that young people usually spend the most of their daily time, and that the problematic behaviors mentioned before appear. Therefore, the school context may become a powerful field from which to start working on both prevention and intervention in order to reduce the possible risks associated with these sorts of conflictive behaviors.

In conclusion, the MySchool4web program would join the existing VR programs applied in psychology. In particular, this program has proved to be a valid and reliable screening tool to detect young people at risk of being drug users, bullies or victims of bullying, and having body image problems. However, it is important to emphasize that while the MySchool4web program is a valid procedure, it is not to be used in isolation, but as detection tool used in combination with other assessment tests that confirm or reject what is suggested by the program. In other words, the use of MySchool4web is conceived by its authors as a valid screening VR tool to be applied in large populations and aimed at the detection of the possible existence of pupils at risk. Therefore, once the program is used, other assessment procedures are needed in order to start a subsequent intervention.

Overall the program also has a number of positive aspects. Initially one of the advantages that desktop VR programs would have in general, and MySchool4web in particular, is that they can be applied directly through the internet using a regular PC, without the need to acquire special high-cost equipment, something that would complicate their use. At the same time, we think it is also important that a unique tool assesses all three of the most relevant types of problematic behaviors within school context, that is, drug use, bullying, and problems with body image that are associated with eating disorders. In this regard, MySchool4web is a tool that can be easily applied in the school environment, with the aim of the intervention and prevention of the problems associated with specific risk behaviors that appear during school ages.

Acknowledgment: This work was funded by the Regional Government of Andalusia, Spain (Excellence Research Projects SEJ-7204) awarded to the second author. Alvaro I. Langer was supported by the Chilean National Fund for Scientific and Technological Development, CONICYT/PAI, Project N° 82130055 and the Chilean Millennium Scientific Initiative, Project N°. NS100018.

References

Adams, R., Finn, P., Moes, E., Flannery, K., & Rizzo, A.S. (2009). Distractibility in Attention/Deficit/ Hyperactivity Disorcer (ADHD): The Virtual Reality Classroom. Child Neuropsychology, Vol.15, No.2, (March 2009), pp. 120-135, ISSN 1744-4136

Blaschovich, J., & Bailenson, J. (2011). Infinite reality. Avatars, eternal life, new worlds, and the dawn of virtual revolution. New York, EEUU: William Morrow.

Bordnick, P. S., Copp, H. L., Traylor, A., Graap, K. M., Carter, B. L., Walton, A., & Ferrer, M. (2009). Reactivity to cannabis cues in virtual reality environments. Journal of Psychoactive Drugs, 41, 105-112. Recuperado de http://www.tandf.co.uk/journals/ujpd

Bordnick, P.S., Graap, K.M., Copp, H., Brooks, J., Mirtha, F., & Ferrer, B. F. A. (2005). Virtual reality cue reactivity assessment in cigarette smokers. CyberPsychology & Behavior, 8, 487-492. doi:10.1089/cpb.2005.8.487

Bordnick, P. S., Traylor, A., Copp, H. L., Graap, K. M., Carter, B., Ferrer, M., & Walton, A. P. (2008). Assessing reactivity to virtual reality alcohol based cues. Addictive Behaviors, 33, 743-756. doi:10.1016/j.addbeh.2007.12.010

Botella, C., García-Palacios, A., Baños, R. M., & Quero, S. (2007). Realidad virtual y tratamientos psicológicos. Virtual reality and psychological treatments. Cuadernos de Medicina Psicosomática y Psiquiatría de enlace, 82, 17-31.

Brahnam, S., & Jain, L. C. (Eds.). (2011). Advanced computational intelligence paradigms in healthcare 6. Virtual reality in psychotherapy, rehabilitation, and assessment. Berlin Heidelberg, Germany: Springer-Verlag. doi:10.1007/978-3-642-17824-5

Brill, L. (1993). Metaphors for the travalling cybernau. Virtual Reality World, 1, q-s.

Brill, L. (1994). Metaphors for the traveling cybernaut-Part II. Virtual Reality World, 2, 30-33.

Busch, A. B. (2002). Validity, reliability, and other key concepts in outcome assessment and services research. In W.W. IsHak, T. Burt, & L.I. Sederer, (Eds.), Outcome Measurement in Psychiatry: a Critical Review (pp.35-55). Washington DC, United States: American Psychiatric Publishing, Inc.

Cangas, A. J., Gallego, J., Aguilar, J. M., Carmona, J. A., & Langer, A.I. (2013). Risk answers of drug use, bullying and alterations in body image in a 3D simulation computer program. Manuscript submitted for publication.

Cangas, A. J., Gallego, J., Aguilar-Parra, J. M., Salinas, M., Zárate, R., & Roith, C. (2013). Propiedades psicométricas de My-School4web: programa informático de simulación 3D encaminado a la detección de consumo de sustancias, acoso escolar y alteraciones de la imagen corporal.

International Journal of Psychology and Psychological Therapy, 13, 307-315. Retrieved from http://www.ijpsy.com/volumen13/num3/363.html

Carmona, J. A. (2012) Aplicaciones de la simulación tridimensional para la detección precoz de consumo de sustancias y violencia escolar en ámbitos educativos: desarrollo y validación de una herramienta informática para su detección (Doctoral thesis, University of Almería, Spain). Retrieved from http://repositorio.ual.es/jspui/handle/10835/1775

Carmona, J. A., Espínola, M., Cangas, A.J., & Iribarne, L. (2010a). Mii School: New 3D Technologies Applied in Education to Detect Drug Abuses and Bullying in Adolescents. In Lytras, M., Ordoñez, P., Avison, D., Sipior, J., Jin, Q., Leal, W., Uden, L., Thomas, M., Cervai, S., & Horner, D. (Eds.). Technology Enhanced Learning: Quality of Teaching and Educational Reform (pp. 65-72). Heidelberg, Germany: Springer.

Carmona, J. A., Espínola, M., Cangas, A.J., & Iribarne, L. (2010b). Detecting Drug Use in Adolescents Using a 3D Simulation Program. Psychology, Society, & Education, 2, 143-153.

Eichenberg, C. (Ed.). (2012). Virtual reality in psychological, medical and pedagogical applications. Rijeka, Croatia: Intech. Doi:10.5772/2607

European Monitoring Centre for Drugs and Drugs Addiction (2007). The 2007 ESPAD Report. Substance Use Among Students in 35 European Countries. Luxemburg: The Swedish Council for Information on Alcohol and other Drugs.

Ferrer-García, M., & Gutiérrez-Maldonado, J. (2008). Body image assessment software: Psychometric data. Behavior Research Methods, 40, 394-407. doi:10.3758/BRM.40.2.394

Ferrer-García, M., Gutiérrez-Maldonado, J., Caqueo-Urízar, A., & Moreno, E. (2009). The validity of virtual environments for eliciting emotional responses in patients with eating disorders and in controls. Behavior Modification, 33, 830-854. doi:10.1177/0145445509348056

Gorini, A., Griez, E., Petrova, A., & Riva, G. (2010). Assessment of the emotional responses produced by exposure to real food, virtual ffod and photographs of food in patients affected by eating disorders. Annals of General Psychiatry, 9, 1-10. Retrieved from http://www.annals-general-psychiatry.com/

Lee, J. H., Ku, J., Kim, K., Kim, B., Kim, I. Y., Yang, B., . . . Kim, S. I. (2003). Experimental application of virtual reality for nicotine craving through cue exposure. CyberPsychology & Behavior, 6, 275-280. Recuperado de http://www.liebertpub.com/overview/cyberpsychology-behavior-and-social-networking/10/

Lee, S. J., Namkoong, K., Ku, J., Cho, S., Park, J. Y., Choi, Y. K., . . . Jung, Y. C. (2008). Social pressure-induced craving in patients with alcohol dependence: Application of virtual reality to coping skills training. Psychiatry Investigation, 5, 239-243. Recuperado de http://www.psychiatryin-vestigation.org/index_pc.asp

Letosa-Porta, A., Ferrer-García, M., & Gutiérrez-Maldonado, J. (2005). A program for assessing body image disturbance using adjustable partial image distortion. Behavior Research Methods, 37, 638-643. Retrieved from http://www.springer.com/psychology/cognitive+psychology/journal/13428

McLellan, H. (2001). Virtual realities. Retrieved from http://www.aect.org/edtech/ed1 /17.pdf

Perpiñá, C., Botella, C., & Baños, R. M. (Eds.). (2002). Body image in eating disorders: Virtual reality assessment and treatment. Valencia, España: Promolibro.

Perpiñá, C., Botella, C., & Baños, R.M. (2003). Virtual Reality in Eating Disorders. European Eating Disorders Review, Vol.11, No.3, (May/June 2003), pp. 261-278, ISSN 1099-0968

Perpiñá, C., Botella, C., Baños, R. M., Marco, J. H., Alcañiz, M., & Quero, S. (1999). Body Image and Virtual Reality in Eating Disorders: Exposure by Virtual Reality is More Effective that the Classical Body Image Treatment? CyberPsychology & Behavior, 2, 149-159. doi:10.1089/cpb.1999.2.149

Perpiñá, C., Marco, J.H., Botella, C. & Baños, R. (2004). Tratamiento de la Imagen Corporal en los Trastornos Alimentarios Mediante Tratamiento Cognitivo-Comportamental Apoyado con

Realidad Virtual: Resultados al Año de Seguimiento. Psicología Conductual, 12, 519-537. Retrieved from http://www.behavioralpsycho.com/

Riva, G. (1997). Virtual reality as assessment tool in psychology. In G. Riva (Ed.), Virtual Reality in Neuro-Psycho-Physiology. Cognitive, Clinical and Methodological Issues in Assessment and Rehabilitation (pp. 71-79). Amsterdam, The Netherlands: IOS press.

Riva, G. (1998). Virtual environment for body image modification: virtual reality system for the treatment of body image disturbances. Computers in Human Behavior, 14, 477-490.

Riva, G., Bacchetta, M., Baruffi, M., & Molinari, E. (2002). Virtual-reality-based multidimensional therapy for the treatment of body image disturbances in binge eating disorders: A preliminary controlled study. IEEE Transactions on Information Technology in Biomedicine, 6, 224-234. Retrieved from http://ieeexplore.ieee.org/xpl /RecentIssue.jsp?reload=true&punumber=4233

Riva, G., Bacchetta, M., Baruffi, M., Rinaldi, S., & Molinari, E. (1999). Virtual Reality Based Experiential Cognitive Treatment of Anorexia Nervosa. Journal of Behavior Therapy and Experimental Psychiatry, 30, 221-230. Retrieved from http://www.journals.elsevier.com/journal-of-behavior-therapy-and-experimental-psychiatry/

Riva, G., Bacchetta, M., Baruffi, M., Rinaldi, S.,Vincelli, F., & Molinari, E. (2000). Virtual reality-based experimental cognitive treatment of obesity and binge-eating disorders. Clinical Psychology and Psychotherapy, 7, 209-219. Recuperado de http://onlinelibrary.wiley.com/journal/10.1002/%28ISSN%291099-0879

Saladin, M. E., Brady, K., Graap, K., & Rothbaum, B. O. (2006). A preliminary reporto n the use of virtual reality technology to elicit craving and cue reactivity in cocaine dependent individuals. Addictive Behaviors, 31, 1881-1894. doi:10.1016/j.addbeh.2006.01.004

Scozzari, S., & Gamberini, L. (2011). Virtual Reality as a tool for Cognitive Behavioral Therapy. In S. Brahnam & L.C. Jain (Eds.), Advanced computational intelligence paradigms in healthcare 6. Virtual reality in psychotherapy, rehabilitation, and assessment, (pp. 63-108). Berlin Heidelberg, Germany: Springer-Verlag. doi:10.1007/978-3-642-17824-5

Zoll, C., Enz, S., Schaub, H., Aylett, R., & Paiva, A. (2006, April). Fighting bullying with the help of autonomous agents in a virtual school environment. The 7th International Conference on Cognitive Modeling, Trieste, Italia. Retrieved from http://www.macs.hw.ac.uk/EcircusWeb/Publications/Psychology /ICCM%202006%20Proceedings.pdf

Chun-Chia Lee, Jen-Wei Chang

6 Play With My Team— Modeling Online Game Players' Teamwork Model in Massively Multiplier Online Role Playing Games (MMORPGs)

Abstract: The need for teamwork has grown significantly in today's online community. Especially for online game players, teamwork is an important means of engagement because many difficult missions require players to play with teams. This study attempts to investigate the impacts of trust on players' teamwork with affective commitment and normative commitment as mediators. Furthermore, this research includes team experience as a moderator to compare the difference between different player groups. A model was proposed and tested on 296 online game players' data using structural equation modeling. Findings revealed that team experience moderated the relationship between trust and teamwork. The results indicated that trust promotes teamwork for players with high experience through affective commitment compared to those with low experience. Following this, we conducted a focus group interview to develop several design recommendations that facilitate teamwork in MMORPGs. The proposed recommendations were organized as a honey comb which regards how online community should develop strategies for monitoring, understanding, and responding to different players' teamwork situation.

6.1 Introduction

Teamwork, working collaboratively with a group of people in order to achieve a goal, is identified as an effective, system-based intervention that has broad implications for all organizations.[1] Teamwork is the basis for the organization development today, since the increasing complexity of projects and has made them unachievable for individuals. Especially for online game communities, teamwork plays a critical role because prior studies have proposed that teamwork is highly correlated with players' motivation to engage in game playing.[2] Teamwork also brings numerous benefits for online game players, such as giving players more control and decision making power in groups, resolving member's conflicts, providing greater opportunities to engage in interactive learning activities, and peer tutoring, which refers to allowing players to practice and clarify game skills through other's assistance.[3,4] More importantly, teamwork is proven to assist players in improving their playing performance compared to those who learn on his or her on. Consequently, these benefits attract more online game players to input more time and contribute to the success of games.[4, 5] Thus, to understand and cultivate teamwork is becoming more and more important for both game practitioners and scholars.

Manser[6] reviewing the literature on teamwork, summed up trust, shared mental models, coordination, communication, and leadership as factors affecting teamwork. Among these factors, prior study highlighted trust as the most important factor contributing to successful teamwork because trust leads to a set of behavioral expectations among player.[6-8] Trust refers to the confidence that they will not be harmed or put at risk by the actions of the other party.[9] Trust allows player to manage the uncertainty or risk associated with the interaction, which leads players to jointly optimize the gains that will foster more teamwork behavior.[10]

Despite the importance of trust in teamwork, previous research also reported that organizational teamwork is fragile for most online teams because of team dynamics.[11] The purpose of this work is to establish a stringent understanding as to the formation and mediators of teamwork, in order to help understand the formation of teamwork in online game settings. Some of the emerging ideas in the literature that suggest that introducing online games in the workplace might improve employees' teamwork.[12] For instance, a recent survey reported that IBM managers used lessons learned from online game to promote teamwork in their real jobs.[12] Compared to other types of online communities, learning teamwork in an online game is often essential and quite different from other forms of teamwork. Online games often have aguild system to teach users about interpersonal and intercultural communication skills.[12, 13]Online games also provide an in-game shared space to alleviate the social isolation caused by lack of face-to-face interaction.[12, 14] Foremost, online games motivate users to engage in teamwork situations through an engagement cycle comprising motivating emotion, player re-engagement, social call to action, and visible progress/reward.[13] Therefore, along with the trend of gamification, studying teamwork in online game settings can bring some helpful ideas for both the researchers and practitioners.

This work differs from previous research in three important ways. First, this study aims to examine the effect of trust on teamwork in a gaming context. The issues related to the influence of trust on teamwork have been examined for real world teams in some previous research,[12-14] but in contrast, it is still uncertain whether the findings of previous research can be applied in various online teamwork environments.

Second, prior studies considered the influence of trust on teamwork to be mediated by several factors comprising of cognitive ability, emotional intelligence, mental model, and organizational commitment.[15-18] Among these factors, organizational commitment comprising affective commitment and normative commitment is applied herein, because it helps explain various social relationships that are critical for collaboration and interactions among players.[15]Affective commitment refers to team member's emotional attachment to, identification with, and involvement in a team, while normative commitment reflects member's sense of obligation to remain in a team.[15]

Team experience will also be assessed as a critical moderator during the formation of teamwork. Even though experience is an important variable in the context of consumer behavior (e.g. Yoon [20]), and it has been rarely studied in the context of teamwork. Therefore, this research includes team experience as moderator to compare the differences between different player groups.

6.2 Modeling the teamwork mechanism in game

The research model displayed in Figure 1 illustrates trust affect teamwork through the meditation of affective commitment and normative commitment. This study extends the commitment theory model proposed by Meyer and Allen, [15] and believes it can be utilized to explain the relationship between trust and teamwork in this study. More specifically, in the proposed model team experience operates as moderator to compare the difference between different groups.

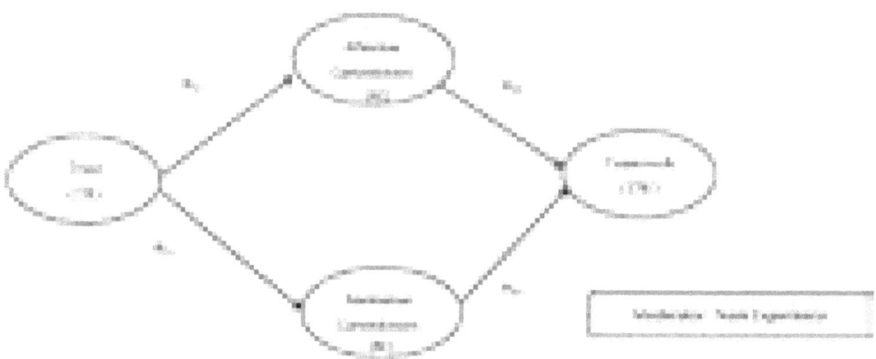

Figure 6.1. Proposed conceptual model

We consider the level of team experience as a potential moderating variable because a review of the literature reveals that players with a high level of experience are different from those with a low level of experience in terms of knowledge structure.[21, 22] Hernandez Maestro and colleagues[23] indicated that differences in knowledge structure are reflected in varying cognitive behaviors related to information processing, such as problem solving, reasoning and induction, forming opinions, and recalling and recognizing information. Specifically, many studies have highlighted the importance of experience on players' behavior and intention. For instance, Bennett et al.[24] conducted a study on business-to-business brand commitment and found that use experience is the critical moderator for managers' decision making. Yoon[20] also investigated the antecedents of customer satisfaction with Internet banking service in China and explored how experience operates as the moderator on user's satisfaction and commitment. He found that users with a high level of use experience perceived a different level of commitment compared with those with a low level of use experience. Many game studies have also suggested that use experience is critical to players' social interaction behavior and intention.[25–27] These observations imply that players may perceive teamwork differently depending on their team experience.

To optimize gaming achievement, online game players utilize a reciprocal relationship with other team members if they need items, weapons, and equipment. This reciprocal relationship operates between players based on the foundation of mutual trust.[28] Mutual trust provides a sense of belonging within a group and comfort in supporting team members, which facilitates team members' affective attachment to organizations. Moreover, mutual trust is considered an important factor in the long-term stability of the organization and the well-being of its members.[29] Fukuyama[30] also found that higher levels of trust fulfill members' social needs and sense of belonging, which drive experienced team members to implement organizational tasks and missions spontaneously. Steinauer et al.[31] surveyed organizational trust issues in an e-commerce environment and found that high levels oftrust not only motivated member's organizational citizen behavior but also facilitated member's sense of obligation. Thus, this study hypothesizes that trust will increase experienced members' affective commitment and normative commitment to teams. Two hypotheses of this study are as follows:

H_{1a}: The relationship between trust and affective commitment is moderated by experience, and the relationship is stronger among college players with high levels of experience than among those with low levels of experience

H_{1b}: The relationship between trust and normative commitment is moderated by experience, and the relationship is stronger among college players with high levels of experience than among those with low levels of experience

Adebanjo and Kehoe [17] conducted a study on employee teamwork in organizations, and found experienced employee's affective commitment is highly correlated with group member's teamwork. He found that affiliating needs within the workplace would increase members' attitude to work with others. Silos[32] identified that the key to Japanese efficiency was teamwork and concluded that affective commitment is the predictor of experienced members' teamwork. Moreover, teamwork increases overall organizational performance by enhancing synergy and coordinated efforts, which increases members' sense of obligation within an organization.[33, 34] Therefore, based on above literature we propose the following hypothesis:

H_{2a}: The relationship between affective commitment and teamwork is moderated by experience, and the relationship is stronger among college players with high levels of experience than among those with low levels of experience

H_{2b}: The relationship between normative commitment and teamwork is moderated by experience, and the relationship is stronger among college players with high levels of experience than among those with low levels of experience

6.3 Investigate the impacts of trust on players' teamwork

6.3.1 Subjects

To gain a clear understanding of player's team experience in-game, a participative observation was first conducted with ten World of Warcraft (WOW) players (five male and five female). We observed and collected data from these players' team play behaviors and player to player interaction. Based on the collected information, we found 20 teamplay-per-week is the median of team play frequency among all participants. The result was also supported by extensive reviews of reference artifacts such as documents, communication logs, news and development's updates, and posts in WOW main forums. Therefore, we adopted 20 teamplay-per-week as the cut-off point for high and low experience groups.

An online survey was then advertised on course websites and bulletin board systems (BBS) to recruit WOW players to participate in the study. After excluding volunteers with incomplete data, 296 college student's data was collected for the study. Table 1 summarizes the demographic data of all subjects. At this stage, we partitioned all subjects into two groups: 155 players with more than twenty team play per month (high-experience group), and all the rest (low-experience group).

Table 6.1. Study Participants: High Experienced Players (N=155) and Low Experienced Players (N=141)

	Participants(*N*=296)	*N*	%	*High (%)*	*Low (%)*
College level	First year	77	26.01%	51.95%	48.05%
	Second year	62	20.95%	51.61%	48.39%
	Third year	37	12.50%	54.05%	45.95%
	Forth year	28	9.46%	42.86%	57.14%
	Graduates	92	31.08%	55.43%	44.57%
Sex	Male	231	78.04%	54.98%	45.02%
	Female	65	21.96%	43.08%	56.92%
Guild participation experience	1-12Months	87	29.39%	49.43%	50.57%
	12-36months	105	35.47%	56.19%	43.81%
	>36 months	104	35.14%	50.96%	49.04%
No. of Friend list	<10	54	18.24%	55.56%	44.44%
	10-25	116	39.19%	50.86%	49.14%
	25-40	91	30.74%	51.65%	48.35%
	>40	35	11.82%	54.29%	45.71%
Team Experience	20 times team play per month	155	52.36%		
	< 20 times team play per month	141	47.64%		
Average age	20.02 years old (*Std.* = 3.11).				

6.3.2 Measures

The questionnaire used for data collection contained scales to measure the various constructs of the research model. The measurements were adapted from studies by DeRosa et al.[8], Hsu et al. [27], Bateman, et al. [35], Meyer and Allen, [15] and McCallum. [36] A pilot test was, therefore, conducted with university players to validate the measurement items. The wording of the survey items was modified based on the results of the pilot test and the advice of game study experts. Individuals indicated their agreement or disagreement with the survey items using a seven-point scale. Data analysis proceeded in two stages. First, a validity test on the research measurements was conducted by confirmatory factor analysis (CFA). Second, an analysis of the structural multi-group model was used to test the associations in the research model.

6.3.3 Reliability and validity of measurement items

As shown in Table 2, Cronbach's α for all constructs was above 0.7. Accordingly, the questionnaire meets the requirement of inter reliability. [37] The factor loading value of all items was larger than 0.5, and the CRs of all constructs greater than the 0.7, which met the requirement of convergent validity [38, 39] (see Table 2). Discriminant validity was also very high because each construct's square root value of the average variance extracted (AVE) was higher than the others in corresponding rows [38] (see Table 2).

Table 6.2. Square root of AVE, inter-construct correlations and composite reliability

Construct	No. of items	*Mean*	*SD*	*CR*	*AVE*	*α*	1	2	3	4
Trust	4	5.04	1.18	0.905	0.761	0.840	**0.825**			
Affective commitment	6	5.04	1.05	0.864	0.768	0.847	0.669	**0.748**		
Normative commitment	6	4.00	1.08	0.914	0.810	0.800	0.401	0.311	**0.797**	
Teamwork	3	5.15	1.07	0.881	0.776	0.839	0.519	0.474	0.217	**0.831**

Note. Square root of AVE is on the diagonal in bold.

6.3.4 Structural model testing

To build the teamwork model, we employed the partial least squares (PLS) approach to perform structural equation modeling (SEM) analysis. The analysis was implemented using the PLS software—SmartPLS 2.0. Our research adopted one-tailed testing (t-value >1.645, $p<0.05$)[40] and sets the re-sampling number at 500.

6.3.5 Result

To validate the hypothesized effects of the structural multi-group analysis, we examined the coefficients of the causal relationships between constructs. Figure 2 illustrates the paths and their significance on the structural model. In high experience group, as shown in Figure 2, trust explains 51.7% variance of affective commitment ($R^2=0.517$) and 46.7 % variance of normative commitment ($R^2=0.467$), and finally explains 45.7% teamwork ($R^2=0.457$). In low experience group, trust influences teamwork significantly with normative commitment as mediator, explain 45.5% normative commitment ($R^2=0.455$), and explains 47.2% teamwork ($R^2=0.472$).

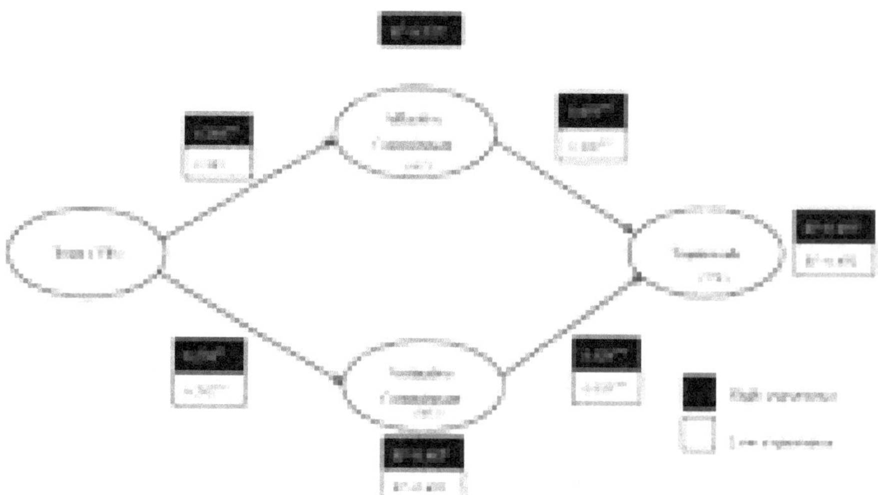

Figure 6.2. SEM result

Based on the entire sample (see Table 3), two hypotheses are significant, withH_{1a} and H_{2a} being supported. Regarding the moderating effects of experience, the influence of trust on affective commitment is stronger for players with high experience than for those with low experience (H_{1a} is supported); however, the influence of trust on normative commitment is not stronger for players with high experience than for those with low experience (H_{1b} is not supported). Consequently, the influence of affective commitment on teamwork is stronger for players with high experience than for those with low experience (H_{2a} is supported); while the influence of normative commitment on teamwork is not stronger for players with high experience than for those with low experience (H_{2b} is not supported).

Table 6.3. Comparison of the path coefficients in both samples

Hypothesis		**High Experience(n_1=155)**		**Low Experience(n_2=141)**		***t-Value* comparing the two group**	**High experience V.S. Low experience**	**Conclusion**
		Coefficient	**stand error**	**Coefficient**	**stand error**			
H1a	TR->AC	0.28	0.096	0.081	0.076	19.64**	H>L	Supported
H1b	TR->NC	0.274	0.041	0.292	0.055	-3.21*	H<L	Not supported
H2a	AC->TW	0.477	0.115	0.3	0.074	15.58**	H>L	Supported
H2b	NC->TW	0.329	0.123	0.633	0.071	-25.71**	H<L	Not supported

*p < 0.05 level. **p < 0.01 level*Significant at the 0.05 significance level.

$$s_p^2 = \frac{(n_1-1)s_1^2 + (n_2-1)s_2^2}{n_1+n_2-2}$$ **Significant at the 0.01 significance level.

$$t_{(n_1+n_2-2)} = \frac{(\bar{x}_1-\bar{x}_2)-(\mu_1-\mu_2)}{\sqrt{s_p^2(1/n_1+1/n_2)}}$$ = High Experience group

n_2 = Low Experience group

TR= Trust

AC=Affective commitment

NC=Normative commitment

TW=Teamwork

Further analysis of indirect and direct effects was performed as shown in Table 4 and Table 5. For high experience group, the decomposition first indicates that the mediated effect of trust on teamwork through affective commitment (50.54%) is substantially stronger than that through normative commitment (49.46%).

Table 6.4. Analysis of indirect effects in high experience group

	Indirect path				
Path	**Affective Commitment**		**Normative commitment**		**Total Effects**
Trust->Teamwork	0.280	50.54%	0.274	49.46%	0.554

For low experience group, the decomposition in Table 5 also indicates that the mediated effect of trust on teamwork is through normative commitment (100%) rather than that on affective commitment (0%).

Table 6.5. Analysis of indirect effects in low experience group

		Indirect path		
Path	Affective Commitment	Normative commitment		Total Effects
Trust->Teamwork	–	0.292	100%	0.292

Finally, in order to compare the path coefficients of hypothesis testing as well as the moderating effect, hypotheses were examined by comparing the path coefficients referencing Chin.[38] Therefore, this study performs standard error estimates from each re-sampling in a parametric sense via t-tests. All t-values comparing the two groups are significant above the 0.05 level and are showed in Table 3. As shown as Figure 3, the slope means the affective commitment varies more for players with high experience group, while Figure 4 means the normative commitment varies more for players with low experience group.

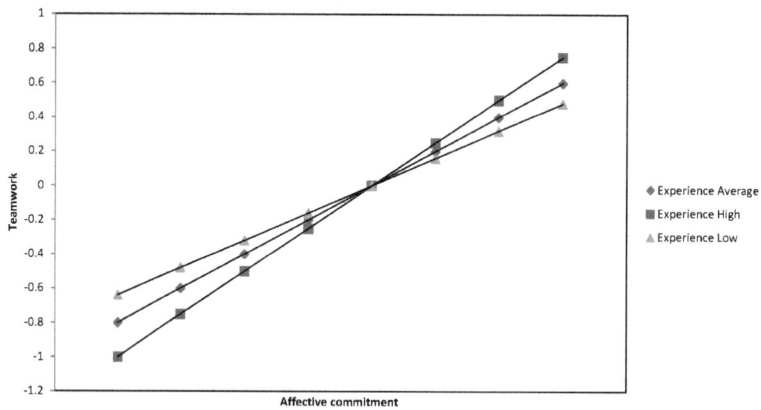

Figure 6.3. Interaction between teamwork and affective commitment.

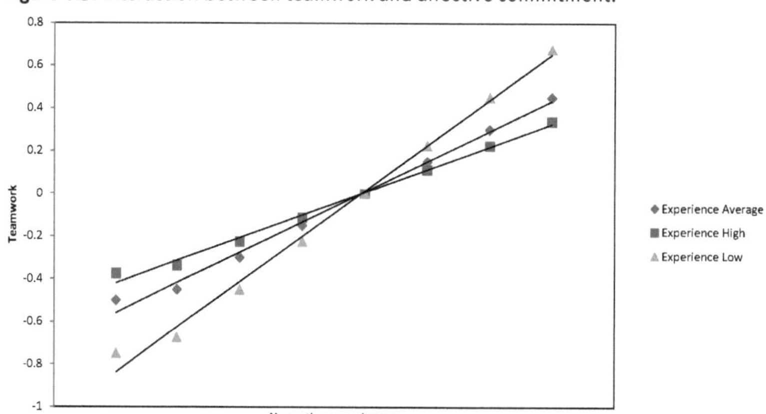

Figure 6.4. Interaction between teamwork and normative commitment.

6.4 Developing several design recommendations that facilitate teamwork in MMORPGs

6.4.1 Subjects and Procedures.

Five male and five female MMORPG guild leaders, participated in the interview. All of them are frequent team leaders and have at least five years team-play experience, with the size of their guilds ranging from 330 to 500. All users were asked to identify and discuss teamwork recommendations based on their prior experience in-game. Finally, several teamwork recommendations were developed following the interviews.

6.4.2 Results

Design recommendations that facilitate teamwork in MMORPGs are as follows:
- Shared space called guild territory.
- Mentor system to promote social learning.
- Off-world communication system to improve negotiation and communication.
- Player-guild recommendation mechanisms.
- Guild uniforms to increase guild members' sense of belonging.
- Reward distribution mechanisms to promote teamwork behaviors.
- Guild forums to increase the guilds' sociability and social capital.

6.5 Discussion and Implication

To our best knowledge, this study is the first study to theoretically specify or empirically test the impacts of trust on online game player's teamwork with affective commitment and normative commitment as mediators. The results indicated that trust only promotes more teamwork for players with high experience through affective commitment in comparison to those with low experience. This finding is partially consistent with the previous research indicating that team experience offers a possible basis for effective teams.[1, 12-14, 34] For example, Antin and Churchill [34] proposed the gamification design for social media users and also suggested that design elements such as badges can actively increase user's sense of trust, which results in more teamwork.

Based on the results of this study, it turns out that low teamwork is likely attributed to a lack of trust based on affective commitment or normative commitment. Thus, we may discover a few theoretical, managerial, educational implications as follows.

From the theoretical perspective, this article contributes to the literature on commitment and teamwork in several ways. First, it extends research of Meyer and Allen's [15] organizational commitment theory by examining trust and teamwork for players. Previous research considering attachment from a multidimensional perspective used commitment to organizational entities as independent variables and examined their relationships with various teamwork outcomes. This research focused on evaluating the influence of trust on teamwork, with affective commitment and normative commitment serving as mediators. By doing so, we identified relationships that could help explain how members with different level of experience employ teamwork in organizations. Also, this study found team experience is valuable in constructing theory about the nature of team structures and coordinative mechanisms that are needed to support interpersonal social systems in the online environment.

From managerial standpoint, prior study [12, 14, 36] has considered MMORPGs as effective tools to support group formation, maintenance, and coordination. The significant influence of affective commitment and normative commitment (i.e., mediators) on user's perception of teamwork suggests that both mediators should be taken as checking points for monitoring how trust affects teamwork in the virtual work environment. Business managers should know that employees are very sensitive to any confusion about business activities in which their affective and normative commitment is weakened. As managers detect employees' low trust in the organization, they should further fortify affective and normative commitment by transcribing business activities and verifying such activities as corporate culture to the employees in order to win their trust. Also, when forming different project teams, managers can use prior team experience for selecting employees to promote teamwork and reduce potential conflicts.

In terms of education, this study explored the role of affective commitment and normative commitment in strengthening participants' teamwork. This result represents the development of effective social bonds, which may promote the emergence of an online community of practice. Through this community of practice, all members can form a joint team with a mutual engagement to develop a shared repertoire of knowledge and competences together. Also, this result may increase the understanding of learner-to-learner interaction in the situated learning context. For instance, the result implied that participants with high experience are more sensitive to such an influence, and they will display greater willingness to conduct teamwork with other team participants. Instructors may accordingly assist learners to maintain long term affective relationships, such as online learning families, to enhance teamwork.

Some limitations of this research should be noted. First, the research design was non-experimental. Regardless of the sophistication of the statistical techniques, causal inferences must be treated with extreme caution when using non-experimental designs. Although the results are consistent with prior research and the hypothesized model, causal inferences should be withheld. Second, the respondents were mostly male (78%). Differences in how men and women are socialized may affect the team environment experiences and the willingness to commit to teams or organizations.

6.6 Conclusion

The need for teamwork has grown significantly in today's organizations. Based on the theoretical framework of teamwork and organizational commitment theory, a conceptual model was proposed in this study to examine the impacts of trust on players' teamwork via affective commitment and normative commitment. Results showed trust only facilitates more teamwork for players with high experience through affective commitment compared to those with low experience. To increase personal commitment, the community leader should provide high-level emotional support to each member, such as encouraging reciprocal behaviors, care culture, and mentor systems. This finding implies that organizations should check and redesign their community-environment components (e.g., sense of belonging, team-tasks design, and communication system) to facilitate members' teamwork. Todays' organizations should identify and overcome potential situational constraints in organizational learning processes that may be decrease members' teamwork efficacy.

6.7 Areas for Future Research

Future studies may examine the influence of regional and national cultures on players' teamwork behaviors, because online game players can be found throughout the world. Finally, further studies should address the broad applicability of these findings and should test the effect of the teamwork design recommended herein.

References

1. Hale N. A computer supported teamwork project for people with a visual impairment. British Journal of Educational Technology 2000; 31:246–250.
2. Yee N. Motivations for play in online games. Cyberpsychology, Behavior, and Social Networking 2006; 9:772–775.
3. Goodlad S, Hirst B. (1989) Peer tutoring: a guide to learning by teaching. London: Kogan Page.
4. Chen CH, Sun CT, Hsieh J. Player guild dynamics and evolution in massively multiplayer online games. CyberPsychology & Behavior 2008; 11:293–301.
5. Seay AF, Jerome WJ, Lee KS, Kraut RE. (2004) Project mas- sive: a study of online gaming communities. In Conference on Human Factors in Computing Systems (CHI 2004). Vienna, Austria: ACM Press.
6. Manser T. Teamwork and patient safety in dynamic domains of healthcare: a review of the literature. Acta Anaesthesiologica Scandinavica 2009; 53:143–151.
7. Barrett J, Gifford C, Morey J, et al. Enhancing patient safety through teamwork training Journal of Healthcare Risk Management 2001; 21:61–69.
8. DeRosa D, Hantula D, Kock N, D'Arcy J. Trust and leader-ship in virtual teamwork: a media naturalness perspective. Human Resource Management 2004; 43:219–232.
9. Bateson P. (1988) The biological evolution of cooperation and trust. In Gambetta D, ed. Trust: making a breaking coop- erative relations. Oxford: Blackwell, pp. 14–30.

10. Jones GR, George JM. The experience and evolution of trust: implications for cooperation and teamwork. Academy of Management Review 1998; 23:531–546.
11. Jarvenpaa SL, Leidner DE. Communication and trust in global virtual teams. Journal of Computer Mediated Communication 1999; 3:544–579.
12. Reeves B, Read JL. (2009) Total engagement: using games and virtual worlds to change the way people work and businesses compete. Boston, MA: Harvard Business Press.
13. Zichermann G, Cunningham C. (2011) Gamification by design: implementing game mechanics in Web and mobile apps. Sebastopol, CA: O'Reilly.
14. Simo˜ es J, Redondo RD, Vilas BF. A social gamification framework for a K-6 learning platform. Computers in Human Behavior 2012; 29:1557–1577.
15. Meyer JP, Allen NJ. A three-component conceptualization of organizational commitment. Human Resource Management Review 1991; 1:61–89.
16. Entin E, MacMillan J, Serfaty D. Analysis of organizational processes in adaptive command and control architectures. Systems, Man, and Cybernetics 1998; 4:3664–3668.
17. Adebanjo D, Kehoe D. An evaluation of factors influencing teamwork and customer focus. Managing Service Quality 2001; 1:49–56.
18. Sue-Chan C, Latham GP. The situational interview as a predictor of academic and team performance: a study of the mediating effects of cognitive ability and emotional intelli- gence. International Journal of Selection and Assessment 2004; 12:312–320.
19. Choi D, Kim J. Why people continue to play online games: in search of critical design factors to increase customer loyalty to online contents. CyberPsychology & Behavior 2004; 7:11–24.
20. Yoon C. Antecedents of customer satisfaction with online banking in China: the effects of experience. Computers in Human Behavior 2010; 26:1296–1304.
21. Mitchell AA, Dacin PA. The assessment of alternative mea- sures of consumer expertise. The Journal of Consumer Re- search 1996; 23:219–239.
22. So¨ derlund M. Customer familiarity and its effects on satis- faction and behavioral intentions. Psychology & Marketing
2002; 19:861–879.
23. Hernandez Maestro RM, Munoz Gallego PA, Santos Re- quejo L. The moderating role of familiarity in rural tourism in Spain. Tourism Management 2007; 28:951–964.
24. Bennett R, Ha¨ rtel CEJ, McColl-Kennedy JR. Experience as a moderator of involvement and satisfaction on brand loyalty in a business-to-business setting. Industrial Marketing Management 2004; 34:97–107.
25. Hsu CL, Lu HP. Consumer behavior in online game com- munities: a motivational factor perspective. Computers in Human Behavior 2007; 23:1642–1659.
26. Salas E, Dickinson TL, Converse S, Tannenbaum SI. (1992) Toward an understanding of team performance and training. In Swezey RW, Salas E, eds. Teams: their training and performance. New York: Ablex Publishing, pp. 3–29.
27. Hsu SH, Wen MH, Wu MC. Exploring user experiences as predictors of MMORPG addiction. Computers & Education 2009; 53:990–999.
28. Mui L, Mohtashemi M, Halberstadt A. (2002) A computational model of trust and reputation. In Proceedings of the 35th Annual Hawaii International Conference on System Sciences, Hawaii.
29. Cook J, Wall T. New work attitude measures of trust, or- ganizational commitment and personal need non-fulfilment. Journal of Occupational Psychology 1980; 53:39–52.
30. Fukuyama F. (1995) Trust: social virtues and the creation of prosperity. New York: Free Press.
31. Steinauer DD, Wakid SA, Rasberry S. Trust and traceability in electronic commerce. Standard View 1997; 5:118–125.
32. Silos IM. Employee involvement–a component of total quality management. Production and Inventory Manage- ment Journal 1999; 40:56–65.

33. Pisan Y. (2007) My guild, my people: role of guilds in massively multiplayer online games. In IE '07 Proceedings of the 4th Australasian conference on Interactive entertainment. Melbourne, Australia: RMIT University.
34. Antin J, Churchill EF. (2011) Badges in social media: a social
psychological perspective. In Proceedings of the 2011 SIGCHI Conference on Human Factors in Computing Systems (CHI)
2011. Vancouver, BC, Canada.
35. Bateman P, Gray PH, Butler BS. (2006) Community com- mitment: how affect, obligation, and necessity drive online behaviors. In International Conference on Information Systems (ICIS). Milwaukee: Citeseer.
36. McCallum S. Gamification and serious games for personal- ized health. In pHealth 2012: Proceedings of the 9th Interna- tional Conference on Wearable Micro and Nano Technologies for Personalized Health 2012. Washington, DC: IOS Press, pp. 85–96.
37. Hair JF, Black WC, Babin BJ, et al. (1998) Multivariate data analysis. Upper Saddle River, NJ: Prentice Hall.
38. Fornell C, Larcker DF. Structural equation models with unobservable variables and measurement error: algebra and statistics. Journal of Marketing Research 1981; 18:382–388.
39. Teo HH, Wei KK, Benbasat I. Predicting intention to adopt interorganizational perspective. MIS Quarterly 2003; 27: 19–49.

Biosketch

CHUN-CHIA LEE (chunchia.derek@gmail.com) received a Ph.D. in human factors from the Department of Industrial Engineering and Management, National Chiao-Tung University, Taiwan. He is also an assistant professor of Information Management at Fooyin University, Taiwan. His research areas include human factors engineering, and human–computer interaction, organizational behaviour in the online game environment.

JEN-WEI CHANG (jenweichangnctu@gmail.com) received a Ph.D. in human factors from the Department of Industrial Engineering and Management, National Chiao-Tung University, Taiwan. Now he is a postdoctoral fellowship of Department of Electrical Engineering, National Taiwan University, Taiwan. His current research focuses on gamification, sociability design, game based learning, cyber-social relationship, and on-line game community issues.

Lina Gega, Richard White, Andrew O'Neill, David Fowler

7 Virtual Environments With Chroma-Keying Video Capture In Psychological Therapy

Abstract: A novel system of virtual environments (VEs) was developed and evaluated in the context of cognitive behaviour therapy (CBT) for socially anxious patients recovering from psychosis. The system uses chroma-keying video-capture to allow the person to see a life-size projection of their self interacting with specially-scripted and digitally-edited filmed environments played in real time on a screen in front of them. Two feasibility studies collected self-reported ratings of anxiety and paranoia along with narrative feedback from 32 patients before and after using three non-interactive VEs. Six patients also used a variety of interactive VEs to carry out exposure-type behavioural experiments during a single therapy session. About two-thirds of patients found that the VEs variably evoked responses that were similar to real life. These types of VEs can potentially be used as a therapy tool to help patients understand psychological processes, practise social skills, and gain the impetus to carry out real life behavioural experiments. Patients experience VEs in different ways - albeit as surreal, strange, or weird - depending on what is relevant and meaningful to them, what extraneous factors they find stressful or distracting (e.g. the presence of the researcher in the room or using the equipment), whether they perceive the VEs as realistic or immersive, and whether they use safety behaviours and avoidance strategies while in the VEs to control anxiety or paranoia.

7.1 Introduction

Effective psychological therapies, particularly cognitive behaviour therapy (CBT) for anxiety disorders, require that patients carry out repeated and prolonged exposure to anxiety-provoking situations either in real-life (in-vivo exposure) or in imagination (imaginal exposure) (Scholing & Emmelkamp, 1993; Feske & Chambless, 1995). In-vivo exposure is very effective but can be time-consuming or impractical to do due to logistical or safety issues in finding appropriate situations. Also, it may be difficult to contain or control live exposure situations to suit patient needs because real life is unpredictable. Using imaginal exposure, such as going over a script or running images in one's mind, lacks realism and intensity because most people are not able to hold-on to images for long enough and can easily disengage from them when they become distressed. Also, patients often find it difficult to progress from practising exposure in imagination to doing exposure tasks in real life. To overcome some of these limitations, virtual environments which simulate appropriate exposure conditions (in virtuo exposure) have been used effectively as part of CBT (reviews by Powers & Emmelkamp, 2008; Marks, Cavanagh & Gega, 2007).

Virtual environments (VEs) are artificially generated scenes or objects which are presented or conveyed through visual, tactile, motion, and/or auditory media. One type of VE is Virtual Reality (VR) which uses a head-mounted display system (like a pair of goggles) to present three-dimensional computer-generated graphics including virtual characters (avatars). VR systems have been used as part of CBT for post-traumatic stress disorder by simulating exposure conditions such as helicopter flying and jungle clearing in Vietnam (Rothbaum, Hodges, Ready, Graap & Alarcon, 2001), earthquakes (Salcioglu & Basoglu, 2010), and the World Trade Centre attack (Difede & Hoffman, 2002). VR has also been used in the treatment of the fear of flying (Rothbaum et al, 2000) and social phobia (Klinger, Bouchard, Légeron, Roy, Lauer, Chemin & Nugues, 2005).

Another use of VR has been to influence psychological processes, such as the perception of pain, rather than as a means to deliver therapy for mental health problems. An example is “Snow World”, a VR system which is reported to act as a non-pharmacological analgesic during burns wound-dressing. Patients are immersed into scenes of flying through an icy canyon filled with rivers and waterfalls, as snowflakes drift down, and shoot snowballs into the scene and hear them splash into the river (Hoffman, Chambers, Meyer, Arceneaux, Russell, Seibel et al 2011). The VR works by distracting patients and by creating a stimulus which evokes the opposite sensation (cold) to the trigger of pain (fire).

In the field of psychosis, a VR system showed promise for understanding delusional beliefs such as paranoia (Freeman, 2008; Fornells-Ambrojo, Barker, Swapp, Slater, Antley & Freeman, 2008). Researchers used this VE system to compare paranoid beliefs across people with low paranoia, high non-clinical paranoia, and delusional beliefs (Freeman, Pugh, Vorontsova, Antley & Slater, 2010). The assessment of paranoia is an inherently difficult process because both interview and questionnaire-based measures rely on retrospective recall of events and cannot rule out the possibility of paranoid thoughts being based in reality. VR allows access to live thinking processes and ensures strict experimental control but has not yet been used in the delivery of psychological therapy for psychosis.

Another type of VE which has lent itself well to CBT can be described as visual display (VD) systems. These systems use two-dimensional computer-generated scenes similar to computer games. The person who uses the VD system guides an on-screen character through the virtual environment. VD systems have been used in the context of psychological therapy for agoraphobia (Chandler, Burck & Sampson, 1986) and obsessive-compulsive disorder (Clark, Kirkby, Daniels & Marks, 1998). These systems lack the immersive qualities of VR but are still engaging because of their interactivity and the users’ identification with a character on the screen.

By definition, all different types of VEs comprise two elements: first, the technological media and equipment which convey the artificial scene or object, and second, the experience of the scene or object itself. The use of VEs requires the user to interpret the artificial world as real and respond to it in a manner true to real life. One way of conceptualising the quality of this experience is through the idea of "virtualisation". Virtualisation refers to an individual's conviction that the artificial environment is real. This is important on the basis that the more realistic the artificial environment feels, the more natural the individual's reactions to that environment would be.

A marker of virtualisation is having a sense of 'presence' in the VE; this could be either a "physical presence", when the individual feels that they are physically "there" in the VE, or a "functional presence", which refers to the individual's ability to respond to the VE in the same way as they would have done in real life. Presence, whether physical or functional, can be influenced by factors either external or internal to the individual who uses the VE. External factors include the immersive qualities of the VE equipment, its ability to match the conditions of the real life environment, and its interactivity, vividness, and reproduction of accurate and quick feedback information to the user. Internal factors which may influence presence in the VE relate to the user's idiosyncratic interpretations, feelings, and reactions because of their personal experiences, personality traits, or mental state.

Presence in virtual reality has been suggested as a necessary ingredient for successful exposure therapy (Price & Andersson, 2007; Wiederhold & Wiederhold, 2005), though not all studies have supported this (Krijn, Emmelkamp, Biemond et al, 2004). This comes back to distinguishing physical from functional presence and identifying which of these two types makes more sense to evaluate in the context of psychological therapy. The literature seems to suggest that the value of VEs in a therapeutic context lies in their ability to induce the feelings, thoughts, and behaviours that an individual would have if they encountered the real-life alternative (e.g. Difede & Hoffman, 2002; Klinger et al., 2005).

7.2 Virtual Environments With Chroma-Keying Video Capture

7.2.1 System Description

To use the system, the person goes into a 1.5 x 1.5 meter portable booth within which are enclosed a video-processing unit with a camera linked to a computer and video-recorder, a screen-monitor, and an adjustable sitting stool. The user sits in the booth facing the screen with the camera pointing to them at a half-profile angle. There is a grey screen (illuminated by a green light) in the booth which provides a background to the user. Real-time chromo-keying technology is used to separate the image of the participant from the background and to combine the person's image with the pre-filmed scene and then display it on a video- screen in front of them. This chromo-keying technology allows users to simultaneously observe the scene and view themselves interacting with the characters of the film. The system automatically creates digital recordings of the person's interactions in the VEs which the person can take away with them and watch retrospectively.

Users can experience scenes selected from a library of specially scripted video-clips that last 2-10 minutes. Non-interactive scenes depict familiar environments, such as a city centre, a bus route, and local cafes. Interactive scenes include characters who could be hostile (e.g. a fellow customer at a bar who insists to be served first), rude (e.g. a medical secretary with a condescending tone of voice who speaks on the phone and ignores the patient), neutral (e.g. a waitress taking an order), or friendly (e.g. a helpful bus driver). Some characters ask innocuous questions (e.g. at a job interview or a street survey) and other ask personal or intrusive questions (e.g. during speed-dating or a medical survey). In some environments, the patients have to initiate conversations which could vary from "safe" to highly embarrassing (e.g. asking the shopkeeper of a local shop for products such as washing powder, toilet roll, or condoms).

7.2.2 Use of video clips and chroma keying video-capture in VEs

The VE system discussed here has two main differences from conventional VR or VD systems. First, it does not use a head-mounted display or computer-generated graphics with avatars but uses custom-scripted and digitally-edited filmed environments played onto a screen. Second, it uses chroma-keying technology to capture the person's image and superimpose it onto the virtual scene. The person sees a life-size projection of themselves (an inverse and not a mirror image) observing and verbally interacting with people in the environments played in real time on a screen in front of them.

Video-clips or photographs rather than computer-generated graphics have been used in other VR or VD systems, for example to recreate virtual audiences to help with fear of public speaking (Anderson, Rothbaum & Hodges, 2003; Lee, Ku, Jang, Kim, Choi, Kim & Kim, 2002).; however, these systems did not include the user within the scene. Video-capture and motion-capture systems have also been used to treat phantom-limb pain (Cole, Crowle, Austwick & Henderson, 2009) and in the rehabilitation of stroke patients (Jack et al., 2001; Merians et al, 2002); however, these systems involved either artificially re-created parts of the body or avatars rather than real-time capture and projection of the user themselves.

7.2.3 An "Out-of-Body" Experience?

The VE system described here offers a "self-observation" view, similar to an out-of-body experience, because the person sees a life-size projection of themselves interacting with an on-screen environment (third-person perspective). This is neither the first person perspective of conventional VR systems (watching the environment through goggles) nor the vicarious experience of computer games (identifying with a small avatar on the screen). It is also different from a mirror image because the person sees an inversed image of their back in an over-the-shoulder shot rather than a face-on picture (fig 1). Researchers in the field of psychology have previously used this projected image to create an "out-of-body" experience, like the "rubber hand illusion" (Botvinick & Cohen, 1998) but not within a therapeutic context and without placing the person in an interactive environment.

Figure 7.1. Representation of Virtual Environment with Chroma-Keying Video-Capture

7.3 Feasibility Studies With Social Anxiety & Paranoia

7.3.1 Design

Two feasibility case series explored the use of this novel VE system as part of CBT with patients who had been recovering from psychosis and also had social anxiety. This is a particularly complex, vulnerable, and socially disabled group of patients who is usually difficult to engage in therapy and has received little attention in research. The first study used three non-interactive standardised VEs at baseline (before the patients began CBT). The second study used several VEs tailored to the patients' specific feared triggers as part of a single therapy session half-way through a 12-week CBT programme (Gega, White, Clarke, Turner & Fowler, 2013).

The reason for using non-interactive standardised VEs in the first study was to exercise caution and prevent our patients from becoming overwhelmed at baseline (we had assumed that the more interactive and tailored the VEs had been, the stronger the emotional responses they would have evoked). Interactive and tailored VEs were used as part of therapy in the second study because the patients had already experienced the non-interactive VEs at baseline and developed a trusting relationship with their therapists.

7.3.2 Objectives

The two feasibility studies aimed to generate hypotheses about the potential value of VEs with chroma-keying video-capture as a psychological therapy tool. They also explored patient experiences of these VEs specific to a clinical population with social anxiety and paranoia. The studies addressed four questions:

1. Can the VEs evoke emotional, cognitive, and behavioural responses which are similar to their "real-life" alternatives?
2. What factors may influence patients' emotional, cognitive, and behavioural responses to the VEs?
3. What do patients "learn" while using VEs in the context of psychological therapy?
4. How do patients feel about seeing themselves projected and interacting live on a screen?

7.3.3 Participants

Patients who had received treatment for an acute psychotic episode and reported symptoms of social anxiety were assessed for eligibility for the study at a community psychiatric service where they routinely received follow-up care. Patients were eligible to participate in the study if: a) they scored a minimum of 30 on the Social Interaction Anxiety Scale (SIAS; Mattick & Clarke, 1998) denoting the presence of clinical social anxiety and b) their residual positive psychotic symptoms were mild-to-moderate (not scoring more than 4 on the positive symptoms sub-scale of the Positive and Negative Syndrome Scale (PANSS; Kay, Oplar, & Lindenmayer, 1987). A distinctive feature of social anxiety in patients with a history of psychosis is their self-perception of being vulnerable and their view of the world as threatening, partly due to the stigma and social disability associated with psychosis, and partly due to residual positive psychotic symptoms such as paranoia (Birchwood, 2006; Fowler, 2006).

7.3.4 Intervention

Three standardised non-interactive VEs were used at baseline before patients started therapy: a) a street scene which featured a crowded cityscape with the point of view as if you were sat outside a shop on the main road, b) a drinks party, which was recorded at a local college during a display of artwork with people engaging one another in conversation in small groups; and c) a bus trip in which the vantage point was from the top floor of the bus having a view of the seats opposite as well as outside.

As part of a therapy session, several interactive VEs were used including travelling on the bus where a young woman sits opposite the patient and makes friendly conversation, sitting at a bar and having to order a drink while another customer gives his turn to order, being at a drinks party where two different people initiate small talk and ask personal questions, and others.

Therapy was based on a CBT approach for social anxiety (Butler et al, 2007) and the VE system was used as part of a behavioural experiment to: explore patients' thoughts and feared outcomes in social situations; demonstrate the role of their safety behaviours in maintaining anxiety; modify unhelpful responses to other people during social interactions. A researcher (assistant psychologist) was in the room but did not interact with the patient whilst using the VE.

7.3.5 Data Collection

Patients were assessed at baseline using a structured clinical interview and a battery of psychometric tests, including the Social Interaction Anxiety Scale (SIAS; Mattick & Clarke, 1998) and the Green et al. Paranoid Thought Scales (GPTS, Green et al, 2008). The SIAS is a 20-item scale assessing symptoms of anxiety in a range of social situations on a five-point (0-4) scale; the total score range is 0-80 with higher scores indicating higher levels of social anxiety. The GPTS comprises 2 x 16-item sub-scales assessing ideas of social reference and persecution, each rated on five-point scale from 1 (not at all) to 5 (totally). The aggregate range of scores for both sub-scales is 32-160 with higher scores denoting higher levels of paranoia.

Before and immediately after participants used each of the three VEs at baseline, they self-rated their situational anxiety and paranoia on a visual analogue scale presented to them with two questions: "on a scale of 0-100, how anxious do you currently feel?" and "on a scale of 0-100, how paranoid do you currently feel (having thoughts or worries that others are trying to harm you)?". When the VEs were used as part of the therapy session, narrative and numerical data were collected via behavioural experiment forms and from therapist field notes detailing which VE scenes were used, how they were used within the context of CBT, and what patients said during their VE therapy session.

7.3.6 Analysis

We tabulated qualitative and quantitative data into a template that included the patients' narrative feedback on the use of each VE and of the equipment overall, along with their paranoia and anxiety scores before and after using each VE. No personal identifiers (apart from gender and age) have been used in order to protect patient identities. Thematic analysis of patients' narrative feedback looked for evidence of virtualisation, e.g. if patients described the VEs by using words such as "immersive" and "realistic", if they demonstrated or expressed strong emotional responses to the VEs, etc. Visual inspection of individual anxiety and paranoia scores in the context of the received narrative feedback explored how virtualisation and other factors influenced patients' emotional, cognitive, and behavioural responses to the VEs.

7.3.7 Findings

7.3.7.1 Sample characteristics

Thirty two patients gave informed consent to use the VE system at baseline. Of those, five patients consented to also use the system half-way through therapy and an additional sixth patient, who was too nervous to try it at baseline, gave consent to use it as part of therapy. The sample of 32 participants who used the VEs at baseline included 21 men and 11 women. They were all White British with a mean age of 25 years (sd=6, range=17-36). A few participants were in full-time education (n=3) or employment (n=7), while the rest spent their days at home doing activities such as watching television, browsing the internet, or reading. Mean SIAS and GPTS scores at baseline were 51 (sd=13) and 85 (sd=32) respectively, which denoted high levels of social anxiety and moderate levels of paranoia in our sample.

7.3.7.2 Can the VEs evoke emotional, cognitive and behavioural responses which are similar to their "real-life" alternatives?

Out of the 32 participants, 4 gave no feedback about the system and 8 thought that the system was "not very interesting", "did not feel real", and "was more like watching TV". Participant no. 39 commented: "The drinks party felt like watching a YouTube video clip. I was expecting something to happen, like something to jump into view like in a horror movie...".

About two-thirds of the participants (n=20) showed or reported strong responses of either anxiety or paranoia to at least some of the environments: "I started to breathe heavily like when I get anxious in real life" (no. 35); "There were young people laughing, were they laughing about me?" (no. 34); "I thought other people were talking about me and saying negative things" (no. 54); "I felt anxious and paranoid in the scene and thought 'who is behind me? What are my escape routes?'"(no. 17).

Interestingly, some participants did not report anxiety or paranoia in response to the virtual environments or reported a reduction in their symptoms; this was representative of their "real" life responses: "I found [the street scene] relaxing, it is something I would do normally" (no. 43), "I don't get anxious on the bus in real life...I was looking at the scenery" (no. 53).

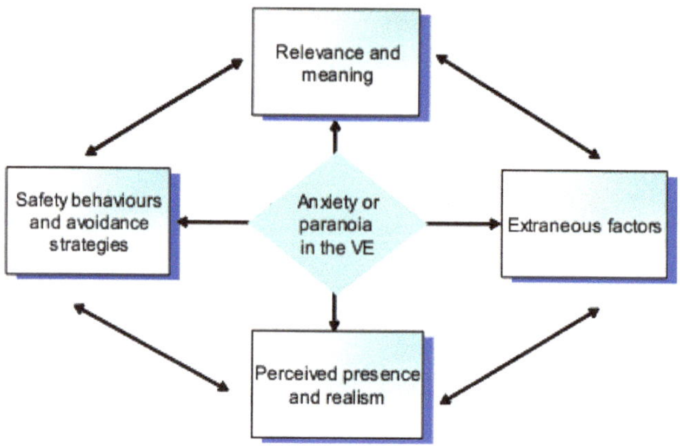

Figure 7.2. Factors influencing responses to virtual enviroments (VEs) in therapy

7.3.7.3 What factors may influence patients' emotional responses to the VEs?

Figure 2 illustrates the four main factors that we observed influencing anxiety and paranoia ratings of different patients about the same VE and of each patient about different VEs: relevance and meaning of the VE, using or refraining from safety behaviours and avoidance strategies while in the VE, patients' perceived presence in and realism of the VE, and extraneous factors relating to the use of the VE but not the VE per

The first factor, relevance and meaning of the VEs, is associated with the fact that an individual's anxiety or paranoia may be triggered by different situations and driven by different fears; therefore, the more relevant and meaningful a specific VE is in terms of an individual's fears and circumstances, the more likely the individual is to have an emotional response to that VE. Indicative quotes are: "The bus felt horrible as I hate using the bus" (no. 9); "I was less anxious on the bus but felt a bit more paranoid because I wasn't able to see the people that were talking in the background. It was a bit like the voices I sometimes hear due to my illness" (no. 48).

The second factor relates to the safety behaviours and avoidance strategies that participants may instinctively use while in the VEs such as reassuring themselves that the environments were not real, or looking away from the screen. The use of safety behaviours and avoidance strategies may dampen the level of anxiety or paranoia evoked by the VE experience: "The [street scene] was easier as I was thinking 'it's not real life... you know the people aren't real'" (no.21). "I would look away when I started to feel anxious" (no. 9). On occasions when the VEs made it impossible for patients to use avoidance strategies, anxiety increased: "On the bus I felt anxious... I didn't feel that I had control... in real life I could get off" (no. 44); "[Street scene] I felt anxious, I watched people to see if I recognised any of them. In real life I would have been with someone or rolling a cigarette which would lessen my anxiety" (no. 53).

The third factor of perceived presence in and realism of the VEs meant that the more realistic a VE felt the stronger the resemblance of an individual's emotional response to real life, or the greater the magnitude of emotional change pre-post VE. Participant no. 35 showed an increase in anxiety and paranoia scores from 0 to 30% at the drinks party scene: "[it] felt a lot like being there. I started to breathe heavily like when I get anxious in real life". Participant no. 34 showed high levels of both anxiety (pre-post VE: 80-90%) and paranoia (pre-post VE: 60-70%) while experiencing the street scene: "[the street] was unnerving – I didn't like the idea of people walking behind me. It felt very realistic and I am familiar with [the street]". On the contrary, no 47, whose anxiety and paranoia scores pre-post VE were 0-10% commented on the lack of perceived realism and presence: "It didn't feel like any of the scenes were realistic, it was like watching myself on TV".

Finally, several extraneous factors influenced anxiety in anticipation of, or in response to, using the VE, including the presence of the researcher in the room, the technological equipment per se, or seeing oneself on screen. The influence of extraneous factors tended to wear off with time: "The equipment made me feel anxious... I was worried what you [researcher] were thinking" (no. 22); "The equipment was initially daunting but I didn't notice it by the third clip" (no. 39); "Watching myself on a camera made me feel self-conscious and was not pleasant... it was easier after the start (no. 32); "The equipment was ok but a bit weird at first" (no. 35). Some patients' also reported a reduction in anxiety at the end of a clip because of their task finishing rather than because of the VE per se.

7.3.7.4 What do patients "learn" while using VEs in the context of psychological therapy?

Patients' feedback about using the VEs as part of their therapy was that the system offered a safe stage for them to correct unhelpful safety behaviours, such as looking at the floor or looking out for trouble, and to practise helpful social skills, such as making eye contact and small talk. Patients also reported that using the system helped them gain impetus to go to crowded public places and engage in social interactions in real life. The VEs were conducive to challenging patients' anxiety/paranoia-driven misperceptions about themselves and others, for example by realising that they looked/spoke better than they thought or expected, and that they could feel threatened without actual threat being there. Repeated rehearsal of social skills while in the VEs (e.g. making small talk) made the point of 'practice makes perfect' and that anxiety subsides with time. Case examples under each key learning point are outlined on table 1.

Table 7.1. Key learning points from using VEs in psychological therapy

Key learning point	Participant	Use of the VE system
"Even if someone or something feels threatening, it does not mean that it is actually threatening"	No.17 male 30 years SIAS=63 GPTS=83	The participant had the strong feeling that someone on the screen was "looking at him funny", which made him feel anxious and scared. Talking about the virtual experience afterwards, he said that, as he knew it was artificial, the person on the screen could not have been looking at him with bad intentions, so it must have been his own mind creating the threat or blowing things out of proportion.
"Having rehearsed something in the virtual world, makes it easier to do it in the real world".	No.15 Male 30 years SIAS=66 GPTS=121	The participant used a virtual environment to engage in polite conversation and make eye contact with a young woman, whom he perceived was flirting with him, whilst both were travelling on a bus. Encouraged by his achievement of facing up to his two worst fears in a virtual environment (public transport and young women), the patient decided to go into "real-life" social situations that he would otherwise have avoided: he used public transport and he waited at the job centre despite feeling nervous and uncomfortable when a young woman sat opposite him.
Things are better than expected and get easier with time and practice	No. 13 Male 27 years SIAS=60 GPTS=32	The participant used four virtual environments (talking with a young woman while travelling on the bus, ordering at a bar and interacting with a fellow-customer, making small talk at a drinks party) to test his belief that he might stutter or not know what to say. The participant's anxiety response, a 'stomach feeling', was at its worse at the beginning of his first virtual small-talk, but it improved the longer he spent in the each environment and having rehearsed what to say to the characters on the screen. Even when he felt at his worst, the participant said that he did not do as bad as he thought he would.
Safety behaviours make anxiety about social situations worse	No. 18 Male 31 years, SIAS=76 GPTS=95	To demonstrate that the safety behaviour of looking at the floor rather than at eye-level when meeting people maintained social anxiety, we conducted a behavioural experiment with a participant alternating between looking at the ground and then deliberately making eye contact in three virtual environments (standing in a supermarket, at an arts exhibition, and at a busy street in the middle of the city). The participant reported that he surprisingly felt less anxious when he was looking up and making eye contact rather than when he was looking at the floor; he also said that he wouldn't have dared test this in real life.

7.3.7.5 How do patients feel about seeing themselves projected and interacting live on a screen?

Several patients commended that the system felt "weird" and "surreal": "I thought the angle I was sat at on the bus was unusual. It was weird to watch myself" (no. 32). Other patients found that seeing themselves on screen helped them shift their attention focus from themselves to the environment: "Because I could see myself I was thinking more about what other people were doing" (no. 39).

7.4 Discussion

A novel VE system, which uses specially-scripted and digitally-edited video clips and real-time chroma-keying video-capture of the patient's image, was evaluated in two feasibility case series as part of a CBT intervention for patients with social anxiety and paranoia. The VEs evoked the same responses as the real life alternatives for at least for two-thirds of the patients who used them. The case series suggest that everyone experiences the system in a different way and that several factors may influence users' responses to it. Researchers and clinicians who may use and evaluate the system in different clinical settings or with different clinical populations need to:

- Select VEs that are tailored to each patient's fears and triggers by asking patients how anxious/paranoid they would have felt if they had to experience similar scenarios in real life.
- Monitor patients' safety behaviours and avoidance strategies while in the VE by asking them what they do, or avoid doing, or say to themselves to feel better or less anxious/paranoid about using the VE.
- Control for extraneous factors, such as technological anxiety, by helping patients get used to the equipment through non-threatening or relaxing VEs at first.
- Use standardised measures of presence and immersion to assess whether the VE system feels real and absorbing to patients.

Our case series also suggests that a simple way of evaluating the VE system is to ask patients whether they felt in the VE the same as, or better/worse than (e.g. as anxious as or less/more anxious than), they would have felt in a similar situation in real life. This is more helpful than simply measuring state anxiety or paranoia in the VE because of all the different confounding factors that may influence emotional responses to the VE. Any discrepancies between the VE and real life could be further explored, e.g. feeling less anxious in the VE than would be expected in the real life alternative may be because the system was not perceived as realistic/immersive enough or because patients used safety behaviours while in the VE.

Some patients in our studies perceived the virtual environments as "not real" but this was not necessarily a disadvantage. Given that an artificial environment still evoked anxiety or paranoia, maintaining a certain degree of control in the knowledge that the situation was indeed artificial proved helpful for some patients for two reasons. First, it made patients more willing to take "risks", i.e. face up to the worse case scenario and drop safety behaviours. Second, it helped patients challenge their paranoid or anxious interpretations of social situations, e.g. realising that an artificial character cannot possibly intend to harm the patient or think badly of them, so there must be an alternative explanation as to why the patient felt threatened.

A major difference between VEs and real life is that VEs are standardised and constant, whereas real life is unpredictable and varied. These case series have not explored whether the repetitive and standardised interactions of the VEs helped reduce anxiety because patients knew what the characters would say. Although this is helpful for social skills training, having slight variations in the virtual characters' reactions may be more helpful as a transferable "relationship" skill that would lend itself better to the unpredictability of real life. An interesting question is how patients relate to the virtual characters and whether they can develop a relationship with them as they would do with real people.

A pertinent question for future research is whether having a "self-observation" view by watching a full-sized image of oneself interact live on-screen may resemble an out-of-body experience. The projection of self in the VEs can be confused with depersonalisation (Sierra, 2009) which in itself can be a symptom of anxiety or psychosis; however, in depersonalisation one feels detached from themselves, whereas in the VE one identifies with their projected image. We do not know whether, in the context of CBT with patients who have both conditions, inducing such as feeling could be helpful in the context of exposure therapy.

An additional research question following from this is whether it is important that the patient sees himself or herself in real-time (chroma-keying) or whether a recording of the scenario played back to them (retrospective feedback) is sufficient to achieve the same results. Some studies support the use of video in the treatment of social anxiety, though others have demonstrated that video-feedback has an added value to CBT only if it is combined with cognitive preparation (patients make predictions prior to using the video) (Harvey et al, 2000) and cognitive review (therapists follow up the video with restructuring of patients' unhelpful beliefs) (Orr & Moscovitch, 2010). An interesting objective for future research is to compare patients' emotional responses when they see themselves on screen versus when they interact with the VE without being present in the scene versus when they see only part of their body (e.g. an arm or a leg).

Future research needs to test whether the added value of the VEs, over and above real life or imagination, is in engaging difficult-to-reach or difficult-to-treat populations, in speeding up therapy because of opportunities for mass practice, or in there being less need for therapist-assisted in-vivo exposure and quicker transition between a clinical setting and "real life". Completion of self-efficacy measures and standardised real-life behavioural tests is necessary to test whether patients feel more confident to confront their feared social situations "in-vivo" after doing it "in-virtuo".

7.5 Conclusion

Virtual environments (VEs) using video clips and chroma-keying video-capture can evoke emotional, behavioural, and cognitive responses that are similar to those of real life. VEs can potentially be used as a therapy tool to help patients understand psychological process, practise social skills, and gain the impetus to carry out real life behavioural experiments. Patients experience VEs in different ways - albeit as surreal, strange or weird - depending on what is relevant and meaningful to them, what extraneous factors they find stressful or distracting (e.g. the presence of the researcher in the room or using the equipment), whether they perceive the VEs as realistic or immersive, and whether they use safety behaviours and avoidance strategies while in the VEs to control anxiety or paranoia.

Author Disclosure Statement No competing financial interests exist.

Acknowledgements: We are grateful to the participants of this study. We thank Mr Paul Strickland of Xenodu Virtual Environments, the University of East Anglia (UEA), U.K, and the Norfolk and Suffolk National Health Service (NHS) Foundation Trust, UK.

References

Anderson, P., Rothbaum, B.O. & Hodges, L.F. (2003). Virtual reality exposure in the treatment of social anxiety. Cognitive and Behavioral Practice, 10(3), 240-247.

Birchwood, M., Trower, P., Brunet, K., Gilbert, P., Iqbal, Z., & Jackson, C. (2006). Social anxiety and the shame of psychosis: a study in first episode psychosis. Behaviour Research & Therapy, 45, 1025-37.

Botvinick, M., & Cohen, J. (1998). Rubber hands "feel" touch that eyes see. Nature, 391, 756.

Butler, G. (2007). Overcoming Social Anxiety and Shyness Self-help Course (3 Parts): A 3-part Programme Based on Cognitive Behavioural Techniques. London: Robinson.

Chandler, G.M., Burck, H.D. & Sampson, J. (1986). Generic computer program for systematic desensitization: Description, construction and case study. Journal of Behavior Therapy and Experimental Psychiatry, 17, 171-174.

Clark, A., Kirkby, K.C., Daniels, B.A., and Marks, I.M. (1998). A pilot study of computer-aided vicarious exposure for OCD. Australian & New Zealand Journal of Psychiatry, 32, 268-275.

Clark, D.M. (1999) Anxiety disorders: Why they persist and how to treat them. Behaviour Research and Therapy; 37:S5-S27.

Cole, J., Crowle, S., Austwick, G., & Slater, D. H. (2009). Exploratory findings with virtual reality for phantom limb pain; from stump motion to agency and analgesia. Disability and Rehabilitation, 31(10): 846-854

Difede, J. & Hoffman, H.G. (2002). VR exposure therapy for World Trade Center posttraumatic stress disorder: Case report. Cyberpsychology & Behavior, 5(6), 529-535.

Feske, U. & Chambless, D. L. (1995). Cognitive Behavioral Versus Exposure Only Treatment for Social Phobia: A Meta-Analysis. Behavior Therapy, 26, 695-720.

Fornells-Ambrojo, M., Barker, C., Swapp, D., Slater, M., Antley, A. & Freeman, D. (2008) Virtual reality and persecutory delusions: safety and feasibility. Schizophrenia Research, 104, 228-36.
Freeman, D. (2008). Studying and treating schizophrenia using virtual reality: a new paradigm. Schizophrenia Bulletin, 34(4), 605-10.
Freeman, D., Pugh, K., Vorontsova, N., Antley, A. & Slater, M. (2010). Testing the continuum of delusional beliefs: an experimental study using virtual reality. Journal of Abnormal Psychology, 119, 83–92.
Gega, L., White, R., Clarke, T., Turner, R. & Fowler, D. (2013) Virtual Environments using Video-Capture for Social Phobia with Psychosis. Cyberpsychology, Behavior, and Social Networking, 16(6): 473-479.
Green, C. E. L., Freeman, D., Kuipers, E., Bebbington, P., Fowler, D., Dunn, G. and Garety, P. A. (2008). Measuring ideas of persecution and social reference: the Green et al. Paranoid Thought Scales (GPTS). Psychological Medicine, 38, 101–111.
Harvey, A.G., Clark, D.M., Ehlers, A., Rapee, R.M. (2000). Social anxiety and self-impression: cognitive preparation enhances the beneficial effects of video feedback following a stressful social task. Behaviour Research & Therapy, 38(12), 1183-92.
Hoffman, H.G., Chambers, G.T., Meyer, W.J. 3rd, Arceneaux, L.L., Russell, W.J., Seibel, E.J., Richards, T.L., Sharar, S.R. & Patterson, D.R. (2011) Virtual reality as an adjunctive non-pharmacologic analgesic for acute burn pain during medical procedures. Annals of Behavioral Medicine, 41(2):183-91.
Jack, D., Boian, R., Merians, A.S., & Tremaine, M. (2001). Virtual reality-enhanced stroke rehabilitation. Neural Systems and Rehabilitation Engineering, 9 (3), 308-318
Kay, S. R., Oplar, L. A., & Lindenmayer, J. P. (1987). Reliability and validity of the positive and negative syndrome scale for schizophrenics. Psychiatry Research, 23, 111–114.
Klinger E., Bouchard S, Légeron P, Roy S, Lauer F, Chemin I, Nugues P. (2005). Virtual reality therapy versus cognitive behavior therapy for social phobia: a preliminary controlled study. Cyberpsychology & Behavior, 8(1), 76-88.
Krijn, M., Emmelkamp, P.M.G. Biemond, R. de Wilde de Ligny, C., Schuemie, M.J., van der Mast, C.A.P.G (2004) Treatment of acrophobia in virtual reality: The role of immersion and presence. Behaviour Research and Therapy, 42(2), 229-239.
Lee, J.M., Ku, J.H., Jang, D.P., Kim, D.H., Choi, Y.H., Kim, I.Y. & Kim, S.I. (2002) Virtual reality system for treatment of the fear of public speaking using image-based rendering and moving pictures. Cyberpsychology & Behavior, 5(3), 191-5.
Marks, I.M., Kavanagh, K. & Gega, L. (2007) Hands-on Help: Computer-aided Psychotherapy. Maudsley Monograph – No. 49. Hove, UK: Psychology Press.
Mattick, R. P., & Clarke, J. C. (1998). Development and validation of measures of social phobia, scrutiny fear and social interaction anxiety. Behaviour Research and Therapy, 36, 455-470.
Merians, A. S., Jack, D., Boian, R., Tremaine, M., Burdea, G.C., Adamovich, S.V., Recce, M. & Poizner, H. (2002). Virtual Reality–Augmented Rehabilitation for Patients Following Stroke. Physical Therapy. 82(9), 898-915
Orr, E.M., Moscovitch, D.A. (2010) Learning to re-appraise the self during video feedback for social anxiety: Does depth of processing matter? Behaviour Research & Therapy, 48(8), 728-37.
Powers, M.B. & Emmelkamp, P.M.G. (2008) Virtual reality exposure therapy for anxiety disorders: A meta-analysis. Journal of Anxiety Disorders, 22, 561–569.
Price, M. & Anderson, P. (2007) The role of presence in virtual reality exposure therapy. Journal of Anxiety Disorders, 21, 742–75.
Rodebaugh TL, Holaway RM, Heimberg RG (2004) The treatment of social anxiety disorder. Clinical Psychology Review; 24:883-908.

Rothbaum, B.O., Hodges, L., Ready, D., Graap, K., and Alarcon, R.D. (2001). Virtual reality exposure therapy for Vietnam veterans with posttraumatic stress disorder. Journal of Clinical Psychiatry, 62, 617-622.

Rothbaum, B.O., Hodges, L., Smith, S., and Lee, J.H. (2000). A controlled study of virtual reality exposure therapy for the fear of flying. Journal of Consulting Clinical Psychology, 68, 1020-1026.

Salcioglu E & Basoglu M. (2010) Control focused behavioral treatment of earthquake survivors using live exposure to conditioned and simulated unconditioned stimuli. CyberPsychology, Behavior, and Social Networking, 13, 13-19.

Scholing A. & Emmelkamp, P.M.G. (1993) Exposure with and without cognitive therapy for generalized social phobia: effects of individual and group treatment. Behaviour Research & Therapy, 31(7), 667-681.

Sierra, M. (2009). Depersonalization: A New Look at a Neglected Syndrome. Cambridge, UK: Cambridge University Press.

Wiederhold, B. K., & Wiederhold, M. D. (2005). The effect of presence on virtual reality treatment. In: B. K. Wiederhold, & M. D. Wiederhold (Eds.), Virtual reality therapy for anxiety disorders: advances in evaluation and treatment (pp. 77–86). Washington, C: American Psychological Association.

Elizabeth Sillence

8 Sharing personal experiences and offering advice within online health-based social networks

Abstract: Online personal experiences (PEx) are becoming increasingly available to patients and provide an important resource for people to learn more about different aspects of a disease or treatment. Despite the availability of such patient stories, questions remain about whether or not they are beneficial to health decision making. Access to experiential information and advice can empower people to take control of their own health but can also leave patients feeling overwhelmed or isolated. One consequence of this rise in peer-to-peer healthcare is an increase in online advice exchange (i.e. asking for and offering advice to fellow patients). The process of advice exchange within online social networks is interesting, not least because it raises issues associated with trust, expertise, and disclosure. In practical terms clinicians have queried the usefulness of peer support in offline settings and raised concerns that health information exchanged online might be incomplete or inaccurate. In this chapter we review some of the key issues associated with online PEx and advice exchange. Drawing on the social and psychological literature we explore notions surrounding experience, expertise, and advice and provide illustrations from our own research. Using detailed online analyses we present findings from a study exploring advice exchange within an online breast cancer support group and in particular highlight the importance of personal experience as a form of advice giving. The implications for using online advice in health care decision making are considered along with a discussion of the issues surrounding this research method.

8.1 Introduction

Access to other peoples' online accounts of their health and wellbeing now provides patients and carers with a major resource for health information and advice (Ziebland & Wyke, 2012).Whilst studies have documented the social and emotional support these websites offer through their exchanges, there has been little attention given to the way in which people use these sites to exchange advice. How do people decide to trust one person's advice over another? What types of advice are people offered online and how does the advice translate into behaviour? This chapter aims to explore the notion of advice exchange within online forums and is organised as follows: In the next section we discuss the role of the Internet in the context of health information and advice, focussing on the role of personal accounts or narratives as a resource for health information. In Section 3 we examine the context of advice within narratives and illustrate the concepts of expertise and experience with examples from our own research. Section 4 presents findings from a detailed study exploring advice exchange with an online breast cancer community. This section details the way in which advice exchange can be embedded within personal experiences. Section 5 draws together the literature and the results of the work to present some conclusions and considerations for future research.

8.2 Online Health Information

The Internet offers access to experiential information for people across a wide range of health issues including HIV/AIDS (Mo & Coulson, 2008), asthma (Sillence, Hardy, Briggs & Harris, 2012); antenatal diagnostic testing (France, Wyke, Ziebland, Entwistle, & Hunt, 2011) and informal caregiving (Hughes, Locock & Ziebland, 2013). Patients are increasingly the first source of information and advice for other patients in a new peer-to-peer process where patients are turning to others like themselves for advice and support and where detailed patient experiences (PEx) are offered online and used to inform health decisions (France et al, 2011; Entwistle, France, Wyke, Jepson, Hunt, Ziebland, & Thompson, 2011). This process of sharing information and advice appears to vary across different social networks according to, amongst other things, the types and frequency of the peer-to-peer exchanges they contain. Some social networks exchange more instrumental messages whilst others may contain more messages of social and emotional support (Mo, Malik & Coulson, 2009). These differences may reflect the nature of the health condition, the gender of the contributing members (see Mo et al., 2009 for a review) or the underlying ethos of the community (Lamerichs, 2003; Sillence, 2010).

The process of advice exchange also varies across different online settings, with some studies indicating that it forms a key constituent of a particular online social network (Kouper, 2010) and others reporting that advice exchange is not seen as central to the community's functioning (Lamerichs, 2003). At a practical level advice exchange has the potential to influence treatment decisions. Because of this potential influence, clinicians have queried the usefulness of peer support in offline settings (Steginga, Smith, Pinnock, Gardiner & Dunn, 2007), and with there being little control over the accuracy of information and feedback provided on the web there have been concerns that health information exchanged online might be incomplete or inaccurate. The picture here is mixed (Braithwaite, Waldron & Finn, 1999; Esquivel Meric-Bernstam & Bernstam, 2006; Hoch, Norris, Lester, & Marcus, 1999; Sillence & Mo, 2012) suggesting that the notion of how information and advice is exchanged within such settings may be more complex than first thought. Narratives or personal stories are one way in which people convey information about their health and wellbeing and are readily available on the Internet, on social media sites, and in patient decision support tools. Narratives can be seen as consisting of different content types as people, for example, share the outcome of a treatment, explain the process behind their decision making, or provide details of their experiences (Shaffer & Zikmund-Fisher, 2013). Work on narratives within patient decision support tools settings has highlighted the fact that different narrative content types differentially affect outcomes and responses in terms of decision making (Shaffer, Hulsey & Zikmund-Fisher, 2013) so narratives containing process content (i.e. explanations of how the patient made his or her decision) appear to guide information search whereas narratives containing experiences, for example of treatments or side effects, improve evaluations of the decision process in an experimental setting. This suggests that the framing of the advice exchange (i.e. the way in which advice is both sought and subsequently offered) may affect readers subsequent search behaviour and decision making around the area, although this remains to be seen in more realistic settings.

8.3 Advice Exchange

The process of advice exchange within online social networks is interesting not least because it raises issues associated with trust, expertise, and disclosure. Expertise is not straightforward within peer settings (Lamerichs, 2003), unlike traditional health settings in which there is one expert advisor (i.e. the medic and one lay advice seeker, the patient), online support groups are by their nature a community of supposedly equal peers and so issues of expertise and credibility in such settings may prove more difficult. Advice has been defined as 'opinions or counsel given by people who perceive themselves as knowledgeable, and/or who the advice seeker may think are credible, trustworthy, and reliable' DeCapua & Dunham, 1993, p519). This definition highlights the difficulties involved for both parties in managing the interaction. For the advice seeker, asking for advice is in a way undermining their identity as a competent person, playing down their own knowledge and abilities, whilst the advice giver has to demonstrate they are worthy of offering advice. Advice givers also have to pay attention to the cues of the advice seeker. They have to be sensitive to their needs, even recognising that advice is being sought. The way in which that advice is presented is crucial if the giver is to succeed in passing on his or her way of thinking on the topic. The context may require that the advice giving is mitigated. Locher & Hoffman (2006) suggest that such mitigation occurs in the form of humour or through the use of lexical hedges such as 'maybe' or perhaps'.

The literature on expert advice giving has mainly concentrated on face-to-face settings or written expert advice, often in the form of personal problem pages in newspapers, magazines, or online (e.g. Locher & Hoffman, 2006; Silverman, 1997), however the structural and pragmatic features of the advice exchange process are one indicator of its value within the online community (Kouper, 2010). These features can include the ways in which advice is solicited and the degree of directness of advice mapping onto the look and feel of the community – its ethos. Kouper (2010), for example, notes that advice requests can be embedded within narrative structures which typically include long elaborations on the background and advice seekers tend to justify their requests. In replying to the messages, Kouper (2010) notes contributors dealt with the potentially difficult issue of 'being an expert' by using personal experiences to encapsulate advice rather than using direct advice messages such as "You should do x". Richardson (2003) noted that members who respond to requests for advice use a number of warranting strategies to indicate their credibility and suitability for the task. These include presenting their own history and experiences through their profiles and their message posts, presenting their own key statistics and making reference to other websites and sources of information.

Our own work has shown how expertise in online health forums is managed through the adoption of quasi-medical conventions in which more senior posters display the technicalities of their conditions in medical short hand. They also request this form of patient notation from each new patient asking for advice before they offer any advice response (Sillence, 2010). Other studies within a health context have noted the importance of politeness strategies (e.g. mitigated suggestions in the form of questions and stories or the use of positioning statements) which allow the advice seekers to set the parameters by which they wish to receive advice (Harrison & Barlow, 2009; Sillence, 2010).

8.4 A study of advice exchange within an online breast cancer forum

Breast cancer patients make use of online health resources in a number of ways including increasing their sense of social support, (Fogel, Albert, Schnabel, Ditkoff & Neugut, 2002) gathering information and helping them make sense of the experience of cancer (Rozmovits & Ziebland, 2004). Advice exchange within breast cancer forums may not be restricted to treatment options and side effects but may also encompass advice about day-to-day living with breast cancer or interactions with doctors, friends, and family (Setoyama, Yamazaki, Nakayama, 2011).

8.4.1 Method

Data for the study were collected between January and February 2011 and consisted of one month's posts and comments to a breast cancer support site. The site was chosen because it was publically accessible (i.e. the messages on the site were publicly posted with no membership or password required for access) and because it appeared to be active (i.e. the site contained at least 100 members with at least 50 messages posted within the last 30 days).

8.4.1.1 Analysis

The data analysis consisted of three stages: Assessment of posting activity; analysis of advice solicitations and analysis of advice giving. The general assessment of posting activity consisted of producing descriptive statistics such as numbers of posts with and without advice and number of comments. A qualitative examination of the messages in terms of advice solicitations was carried out using a modified version of Goldsmith's (2000) typology. The typology consists of four advice solicitation types which vary in their directness and transparency: request for advice, request for opinion or information, announcement of a plan of action. The fifth advice pattern (Same boat) was added to Goldsmith's typology (Table 1) after a preliminary examination of the messages. As increasing numbers of appeals to 'people in the same boat as me' were identified it became apparent that this could be considered a distinctive type of advice solicitation.

Table 8.1. Types of advice solicitation

No.	Advice pattern	Description
1	Request for advice	Explicit solicitation of advice using the following phrases: a) "I need your advice"; b) What should I do?"; c) " Should I do X?"
2	Request for opinion or information	Questions such as "What do you think?" or What do you think of X?" that can often generate advice responses even though they may be ambiguous about whether the posters wants to solve a problem or get emotional support.
3	Problem disclosure	Also potentially ambiguous as it can be interpreted as a request for advice, sympathy, solidarity etc.
4	Announcement of a plan of action	The poster may receive advice after announcing their intentions.
5	Anyone in the same boat?	The poster asks specifically to hear from anyone in the same boat as themselves or who is going through the same experience.

To address the issue of reliably differentiating among the categories, a small subsample (10%) of messages were coded again by the author two weeks after the original coding exercise. The coding produced identical results for both sessions indicating that the categories in Tables 1 and 2 could reliably be differentiated by the researcher. Pieces of advice posted in comments in response to the original advice solicitation were examined for their degree of directness. The degree of directness is interesting to examine because of the tension that exists between showing support and appearing to impose. Advice seekers and givers have to make choices about the way in which they exchange advice and this impacts upon the ethos of the community. In this respect the following categories were used in the analysis. These categories (see Table 2) are based on those reported by Kouper (2010).

Table 8.2. Levels of directness of advice

No.	Type of advice	Description
1	Direct advice	Any comment that included imperatives or the modal verb *should.*
2	Hedged advice	Any comment that contained explicit hedges or hedging devices e.g. "I think," "it seems," or "why don't you?"
3	Indirect advice	Any comment that lacked explicit or hedged advice but had enough information to act upon it e.g. 'here's one possibility' or 'there are a number of options'.
4	Description of personal experience	An account of how the personal dealt with the situation the advice seeker had described.

8.4.1.2 Findings

During January and February 2011, 425 original messages were posted (for more details on the message corpus see (Sillence, 2013). The analysis of the advice messages focused on both the ways in which advice was sought and the ways in which advice was offered. In this chapter we focus on two main findings: the search for advice from someone in the same boat and the offering of advice within the structure of a personal narrative.

Asking for advice

Members asked for advice under a number of different headings including treatment topics, after treatment has finished, living with breast cancer, and employment issues. The frequency of different types of advice solicitation is presented in Table 3. Looking at the pattern of advice solicitations it is clear that few messages contained direct requests for advice. The majority of advice solicitations took the form of opinion/information requests or problem disclosures.

Table 8.3. Frequency of advice solicitation types within the forum

Type of advice solicitation	Frequency (%)
	Breast Cancer forum
Request for advice	26 (9%)
Request for opinion or information	103 (34%)
Problem disclosure	106 (35%)
Announcement of a plan of action	3 (1%)
Same boat	61 (20%)
Total	299

Very few posters sought direct advice from other posters. Members of the social network typically welcomed 'any comments or advice' from readers without including a specific invitation to provide counsel. As such messages containing the word 'advice' were more often coded as requests for opinion or information. In cases where advice was sought directly it was typically accompanied by two possible options for the advice giver to comment upon rather than leaving it more open ended. In this way online peers may act as conversational 'sounding boards'.

> My step-daughter to be has a family history of bc. So far, she herself and her father brush it under the carpet and do not want to discuss it at all. Should I back off or should I try to encourage them to do something?

Within the social network a typical advice solicitation took the form of a narrative containing a number of different structures. In addition to the advice solicitations, narratives contained background and justification structures as well. The message below typifies this kind of narrative form and highlights the period of orientation to the circumstances of the poster.

> Was treated for triple negative BC in 2003 and next month will reach the magic eight years post diagnosis so have much to celebrate and am very grateful to still be here. However for the past few months I have felt so tired and generally unwell that I am finding life a real struggle at the moment. My energy levels never returned to their previous levels following treatment but I have managed to continue working full time and get on with life pretty well until fairly recently. I'm just wondering if anybody has any tips on how to deal with this horrendous lack of energy - any advice would be very gratefully received.

Within the narrative structure a new type of advice solicitation was seen. This typically contained a problem disclosure followed by a call "is there anyone in the same boat as me?" in order to reach a specific set of people within the community. 20% of messages in the forum contained an advice solicitation which was built upon the specific desire to hear from people in the same position as themselves or from people who had experienced the same issues.

> I've been given the usual advice, one big op better than two and better cosmetic outcome, but the nearer this gets the more panicky I get as I can't imagine what it will be like having both front and back operated on. So would love to hear from anyone who's had this done.

Interestingly the types of messages containing the 'same boat' advice solicitation were more frequently those under the treatment headings on the website. Where treatment decisions are being considered it appears that women are drilling down through the resources on offer within the community to find advice from very specific people, namely those that match their own medical experience as closely as possible.

Offering advice

Advice was offered through comments posted in response to the original message. Most comments contained one piece of advice but others contained more. Members used all four strategies for providing advice with direct advice and descriptions of personal experience being the most popular forms (see Table 4).

Table 8.4. Frequency of advice directness responses within the forum

Directness of advice in comments	Frequency (%)
	Breast Cancer forum
Direct	133 (21%)
Hedged	128 (21%)
Indirect	58 (9%)
Personal experience	303 (49%)
Total	622

The direct advice in the forum typically called for posters to seek medical assistance or to start or stop a behaviour immediately. Posters were told, for example, "you should go to see your doctor". Nearly half of the advice comments posted under the sub heading 'have I got breast cancer' were examples of direct advice.

Of course you should mention anything that is worrying you when you go to your appt. They'll ask anyway but don't keep schtum.

It is interesting to note that nearly half of the advice offered on this forum was offered through personal experiences. This kind of advice giving was particularly noticeable when members were responding to advice requests concerning breast reconstruction, living with breast cancer, and treatment options and less so when the advice pertained to, for example, employment rights. The use of personal experience allows the poster to emphasize the importance of making one's own decision whilst recognising these kinds of messages can be useful to readers "hope this helps".

I had LD Flap immediate recon last November. ....I have to say, I am delighted with the results. It was the right decision for me to go to sleep with 2 breasts and wake up with 2 and I was amazed at how it looked immediately after surgery. The surgery itself was a long op and I spent 6 days in hospital and I did feel like I'd been run over for the first few days. I'd say I was feeling good 4 weeks later and off the painkillers....Hope this helps a bit. Take your time in making your decision though, don't feel rushed.

Personal experience messages offer the advice seeker an insight into the choices and thought processes of a 'similar' person. The reader can then evaluate the experience in terms of their own preferences and biases and decide whether or not to use the experience as advice. As a further step we examined the extent to which these personal experiences contained a variety of content types (see Shaffer & Zikmund-Fisher, 2013). To explore this we took those advice messages given in response to queries under the forum sub-heading 'reconstructive surgery'. There were a total of 31 responses containing personal experiences as a vehicle for offering advice. These responses were broken down into Outcome (5) Process (3) Experience (7) Outcome and Experience (7) Outcome and Process (4) and finally Outcome, Process and Experience (5). Responses that related more directly to decision making contained more process content (i.e. explanations of the process by which people had arrived at their decisions). This was in comparison to advice, for example, about how long to wear a particular piece of supportive clothing or what to take into hospital. Overall the narrative content type of 'experience' was the most prevalent with more than half the messages containing an experience narrative.

8.5 Discussion

The findings from the study presented here add to our knowledge about the prevalence and characteristics of advice exchange within an online breast cancer support group but also point to the wider issues concerning advice exchange within online social networks. Using this form of research methodallows the subtleties and complexities of advice exchange to be examined in more detail. In terms of this specific forum it is apparent that advice exchange is a key function of the social network. People expect to be able to ask for and receive advice. Advice solicitations appear to be recognised as such and dealt with appropriately. This exchange involves effort on the part of community members but involvement in this form is important both on the individual level in terms of relationship development (Parks & Floyd, 1996) and to the community's maintenance as a whole. As is common in online communities there are different levels of contribution. Many members take the time to respond to advice requests with some members playing particularly central roles or adopting a 'caretaker' participatory stance (Jones et al, 2011). Advice exchange may seem an obvious function within a community in which people 'new' to the subject are struggling to deal with unfamiliar terminology, but in other domains the attitude towards newcomers asking often basic and repetitious questions can be very different (Raymond, 1991). Likewise this forum goes beyond what is often referred to as social Q&As (Shah, Oh & Oh, 2012) in that it offers a safe space for advice exchange, discussion, and social and emotional support.

The subtle range of ways in which members sought advice highlights the struggle they face in terms of mitigating potential power issues and displaying expertise against the backdrop of reduced cues, identity, and time flexibility (Suler, 2004). In addition this network (as seen in other health communities (e.g. Sillence, 2010) plays to the notion of active decision making and individual choice within the health forum.

Our work in the lab has established similar patterns of advice exchange within other health communities including prostate cancer (PCa) although subtle variations exist between social networks, with PCa forums demonstrating a preference for more direct advice exchange.

The study reported in section 4 identifies a novel type of advice solicitation - that of 'being in the same boat'. This format makes clear the kind of person someone wants to hear from. Advice responses are limited to those with very similar experiences (Sillence, 2010) and we know that people are more likely to adopt the advice offered when the source is more homophilous (i.e. when there is a high degree of perceived similarity between receiver and message source) (Wang, Walther, Pingree & Hawkins, 2008). Entwistle et al., (2011) also note that participants only find experiential information relevant if it is derived from people with whom they share other key characteristics such as age, gender, or health experiences, or if they have other reasons to identify with the account.

In keeping with previous research (e.g. Klemm, Hurst, Dearholt & Trone, 1999) sharing personal experiences was evident on the site. People often act as scientists testing out their own experiences and attitudes against the information they read online (Sillence, Briggs, Fishwick & Harris, 2007). Having an active community with multiple members posting their personal experiences ensures readers are exposed to a range of advice perspectives. Although people report that they do not automatically rely on any single personal experience they read online (Entwistle et al, 2011), indeed, they are selective in the advice and experiences they choose to engage with (DeCapua & Dunham, 1993). By seeking out people in the 'same boat' readers are trying to encourage and select the most appropriate people to offer them advice.

Lab based studies (e.g. Shaffer et al., 2013) have indicated that the type of content within personal stories may affect the readers' subsequent search behaviour and decision making. Our own work, focussing on more realistic settings, also suggests that the framing of advice exchanges is important. However, in such settings, the advice seeker appears to play a more active role in determining the type of content they receive. People faced with real health concerns and questions 'position themselves' for different types of advice (Sillence, 2010), making it clear which kinds of advice they are open to receiving. Offering personal experiences, typically in the form of narratives, allows posters to present enough information for the reader to assess how applicable the advice is in terms of its clinical compatibility and also its match for the reader's own point of view and biases. Within social networks these narratives often contain multiple content types with stories detailing outcomes, decision making processes, and experiential information. The results presented in section 4 do suggest that different types of message content are used in response to different types of advice requests, with experience content being prevalent. Other studies have indicated that people do provide more 'process' content (i.e. providing an explanation of their decision making reasoning if asked to by advice requesters) (Sillence & Mo, 2012). The proportion of content types within personal experiences may well vary depending on the nature of the community itself or be specific to a health domain, and these differences warrant further investigation. These findings suggest that the link between online advice and decision making behaviour is both subtle and complex and unpacking this relationship lies at the centre of our current research agenda.

8.6 Conclusions and implications

This chapter highlights that for some online social networks advice exchange remains an important function. Managing the process of advice is subtle and complex with members using a range of strategies both to ask for and present advice in an acceptable manner. In practice terms health care professionals should be aware that patients are using these forums in addition to offline sources of advice. As patients try to narrow down the advice they receive clinicians could support this process by ensuring that patients are given sufficient medical advice to be aware of which treatment options are suitable for them. This should assist in their selection of appropriate and useful advice from peer support groups. Using this form of research method allows some of the nuances of advice exchanges within social networks to be explored. Going forward we are keen to explore the mechanisms of decision making in more detail and investigate the factors that make personal experiences such a powerful resource for people in social networks.

References

1. Braithwaite D.O., Waldron V. R, Finn J. (1999). Communication of social support in computer-mediated groups for people with disabilities. Health Communication, 99 (11), 23-51.
2. DeCapua A, Dunham J. F. (1993). Strategies in the discourse of advice. Journal of Pragmatics, 20, 519–531.
3. Entwistle, V.A, France E, Wyke S, Jepson R, Hunt K, Ziebland S, Thompson A. (2011). How information about other people's personal experiences can help with healthcare decision making: a qualitative study. Patient Education and Counselling, 85, (3), e291-e298.
4. Esquivel, A., Meric-Bernstam, F., Bernstam, E.V. (2006). Accuracy and self correction of information received from an internet breast cancer list: content analysis. British Medical Journal, 332, 939-42.
5. Fogel, J., Albert S.M., Schnabel, F., Ditkoff, B. A., Neugut, A. I. (2002). Use of the Internet by Women with Breast Cancer. J Med Internet Res 4(2), e9.
6. France, E. F., Wyke, S., Ziebland, S., Entwistle, V. A, Hunt, K. (2011). How personal experiences feature in women's accounts of use of information for decisions about antenatal diagnostic testing for foetal abnormality. Soc Sci Med, 72 (5), 755-62.
7. Goldsmith, D. (2000). Soliciting advice: The role of sequential placement in mitigating face threat. Communication Monograph, 67, 1-19.
8. Harrison, S., Barlow, J. (2009). Politeness strategies and advice-giving in an online arthritis workshop. Journal of Politeness Research: Language, Behavior, Culture, 5, 93-111.

9. Hoch, D.B., Norris, D., Lester, J.E., Marcus, A.D. (1999). Information exchange in an epilepsy forum on the World Wide Web. Seizure, 8, 30-4.
10. Hughes, N., Locock, L., Ziebland, S. (2013). Personal identity and the role of 'carer' among relatives and friends of people with multiple sclerosis. Social Science & Medicine, 96, 78–85.
11. Jones, R., Sharkey, S., Smithson, J., Ford, T., Emmens, T., Hewis, E., Sheaves, B., Owens, C. (2011). Using Metrics to Describe the Participative Stances of Members Within Discussion Forums. J Med Internet Res,13(1):e3
12. Kendall, L. 'Noobs' and 'chicks' on Animutation Portal: power and status in a community of practice.(2008). International Journal of Web Based Communities, 4, 491-502.
13. Klemm, P., Hurst, M., Dearholt, S.L., Trone, S.R. (1999). Gender differences on Internet cancer support groups. Computers in Nursing, 17, 65-72.
14. Kouper, I. The Pragmatics of Peer Advice in a LiveJournal Community. (2010). Language@ Internet, 7, article 1.
15. Lamerichs, J. (2003). Discourse of Support. Exploring Online Discussions on Depression, PhD thesis. The Netherlands: Wageningen University.
16. Locher, M., Hoffmann, S. (2006). The emergence of the identity of a fictional expert advice-giver in an American Internet advice column. Text & Talk, 26, 69–106.
17. Locock, L., Brown, J. B. "All in the same boat"? (2010). Patient and carer attitudes to peer support and social comparison in Motor Neurone Disease (MND). Soc Sci Med, 71 (8), 1498-505.
18. Malik, S.H., Coulson, N.S. (2008). Computer-mediated infertility support groups: An exploratory study of online experiences. Patient Education and Counselling, 73, 105-113.
19. Mo, P. K. H., Coulson, N. S. (2008). Exploring the communication of social support within virtual communities: a content analysis of messages posted to an online HIV/AIDS support group. CyberPsychology & Behavior, 11, 371-374.
20. Mo, P.K.H, Malik, S.H., Coulson, N.S. (2009). Gender differences in computer-mediated communication: a systematic literature review of online health-related support groups. Patient Education and Counselling, 75, 16-24.
21. Parks, M.R., Floyd, K. (1996). Making friends in cyberspace. Journal of Computer Mediated Communication, 11 (4).
22. Raymond, E. (1991). The New Hacker's Dictionary. Cambridge, MA: The MIT Press.
23. Richardson, K. (2003). Health risks and the internet: establishing credibility online. Health, Risk and Society, 5 (2), 171-184
24. Rozmovits, L., Ziebland, S. (2004). What do patients with prostate or breast cancer want from an Internet site? A qualitative study of information needs. Patient Education and Counselling, 53 (1), 57-64.
25. Setoyama, S, Yamazaki Y, Nakayama K. (2011).Comparing support to breast cancer patients from online communities and face-to-face support groups. Patient Education and Counselling, 85 (2), e95-e100.
26. Shaffer, V. A., Zikmund-Fisher, B. J. (2013). All stories are not alike: A purpose, content and valence based taxonomy of patient narratives in decision aids. Med Decis Making, 33 (1) 4-13.
27. Shaffer, V. A., Hulsey, L., Zikmund-Fisher, B. J. (2013). The effects of process-focused versus experience-focused narratives in a breast cancer decision task. Patient Education and Counseling, 93 (2), 255-264
28. Shah, C., Oh, S., Oh, J-S. (2009). Research agenda for social Q&A research. Library and Information Science Research, 11(4), 205-209.
29. Sillence, E., Briggs, P., Harris, P.R., Fishwick, L. (2007). How do patients evaluate and make use of online health information? Social Science and Medicine, 64, 1853-1862.
30. Sillence, E. (2010). Seeking out very like-minded others: exploring trust and advice issues in an online health support group. International Journal of Web Based Communities, 6, 376-394.

31. Sillence, E., Mo, P. K. H. (2014). Communicating health decisions: an analysis of messages posted to online prostate cancer forums. Health Expectations, 17, 244–253,
32. Sillence, E. (2013). Giving and receiving peer advice in an online breast cancer support group. Cyberpsychology, Behavior and Social Networking, 16 (6), 480-485.
33. Sillence, E., Hardy, C., Briggs, P., Harris, P. R. (2013). How do people with asthma use Internet sites containing patient experiences? Patient Educ Couns, 93, 439-443.
34. Silverman, D. (1997). Discourses of counselling: HIV counselling as social interaction. London, UK: Sage Publications.
35. Steginga, S.K., Smith, D.P., Pinnock, C., Metcalfe, R., Gardiner, R.A., Dunn, J. (2007). Clinicians' attitudes to prostate cancer peer-support groups. BJU International, 99, 68-71.
36. Suler, J.R. (2004). The online disinhibition effect. CyberPsychology and Behavior, 7, 321-326.
37. Wang, Z., Walther, J.B., Pingree, S., Hawkins, R.P. (2008). Health Information, Credibility, Homophily, and Influence via the Internet: Web Sites versus Discussion Groups. Health Communication, 23 (4), 358-368.
38. Wood, J.T. (2000). Relational Communication (2nd Ed.). Belmont, CA: Wadsworth.

Ryan C. Martin, Lauren E. Vieaux

9 The Digital Rage: How Anger is Expressed Online

Abstract: Anger is expressed online through all sorts of different venues (e.g., Facebook, Twitter, discussion forums, email). Although such angry expressions are common, they also have potential to become highly problematic. It is not uncommon for people to indicate that they have behaved aggressively online through name-calling, rumor spreading, creating angry pages or events on Facebook, or even hacking into someone else's account to make inappropriate comments. Not surprisingly, such behavior can result in damaged relationships, regret, or other sorts of negative consequences.

Despite knowing that online anger is common and there can be serious consequences of such anger, relatively little research has been conducted on the subject. This is unfortunate as the few research projects there are point to online anger being an important phenomenon. For instance, Rui Fan and colleagues (2013) found that anger was shared more frequently on Weibo (a Twitter-like website in China) than other emotion. In fact, it was shared by both close connections and distant connections whereas an emotion like joy was shared mainly by close connections. Likewise, Martin and colleagues (2013) found that those who express their anger online via rant-sites (e.g., justrage.com) are more likely to experience maladaptive anger in other areas of their life.

The current chapter explores the limited research on online anger along with identifying psychological phenomena which makes online anger more likely (e.g., anonymity, impulsivity). Likewise, the chapter offers suggestions on how to minimize the frequency of expressing anger online, thus leading to fewer negative consequences.

9.1 The Digital Rage: How Anger is Expressed Online

Anger is expressed online through a variety of venues (e.g., Facebook, Twitter, discussion forums, email). Not only are such angry expressions common, they also have potential to become highly problematic. It is not uncommon for people to indicate that they have let their anger get the best of them and had it lead to them calling people names online, spreading rumors about people, creating angry pages or events on Facebook, or even hacking into someone else's account to make inappropriate comments. Not surprisingly, such behavior can result in damaged relationships, regret, or other sorts of negative consequences.

Despite knowing that online anger is common and there can be serious consequences of such anger, relatively little research has been conducted on the subject. In this chapter, we will explore the limited research on online anger along with identifying psychological phenomena which makes online anger more likely (e.g., anonymity, impulsivity). Likewise, we will offer suggestions on how to minimize the frequency of expressing anger online, thus leading to fewer negative consequences.

9.2 Challenges Surrounding Online Anger Research

As we said earlier, there is relatively little research on the subject of online anger. There are likely several reasons for this. For instance, because it is a relatively new phenomenon, researchers have likely not had time to begin studying it in depth. There are also fewer journal outlets available for such research, so authors may have difficulty finding a place to publish such research. However, what is likely the most significant reason for the slowness in publishing research on the topic has to do with the challenges associated with conducting such research.

There are three main obstacles to conducting research on online anger expression. First, the online community is a difficult population to assess. Unlike research conducted at universities or medical centers, there is no captured audience for a researcher to study. For the most part, we must try to gain access to willing participants through the websites they frequent (Twitter, discussion forums, YouTube, etc.). There is, not surprisingly, reluctance to be surveyed from such participants. They are posting online, often in an anonymous or semi-anonymous format, for a reason, and they are less likely to complete surveys because of their desire to remain anonymous. For instance, in one study that we tried to conduct, where we contacted randomly selected participants from Twitter and asked them to complete a survey for the potential to win a gift certificate, not only did we have almost no Twitter users elect to participate, we had a few of the selected users write us back with fierce criticism of our even contacting them in the first place.

There are a few potential solutions to this problem. However, none of them will address it fully. First, researchers could offer greater reward for participation (e.g., instead of a chance at a gift certificate, they could offer a gift certificate to each participant). One example of this might be to use Amazon Mechanical Turk, where participants would be paid a small fee for completing the survey. They could also utilize captured audiences who are active on social media and offer rewards to participants (e.g., students enrolled in a course who use Twitter could receive course credit for participation in the study). Finally, researchers could partner up with social media outlets to share data (e.g., researchers could work with Twitter/Facebook to exchange data on users).

A second hindrance is that it is sometimes difficult to infer emotional intent from written comments like tweets or Facebook posts. For instance, if someone were to tweet, "I can't believe this is happening," one could interpret them as angry, excited, devastated, overwhelmed, etc. Because tone of voice is so important to understanding emotional expressions, there can be a lack of clarity when trying to interpret the emotional intent of a post. This is particularly true when sarcasm may be involved. On the night of the 2012 United States Presidential Election, one of the tweets I came across read, "So Obama is the president for another 4 years. Good for you, America." You could easily interpret that as excitement or joy over the election results. However, when I looked at the user's other posts, what I found was a host of tweets in opposition to President Obama's policies, suggesting the real intent of the election night post was frustration being expressed through sarcasm.

One method people use to convey their emotions online is, of course, the emoticon, which people often use to mimic the nonverbal behavior they would use in an offline conversation (e.g., a smiley face instead of smiling, a sad face instead of frowning; Derks, Bos, & von Grumbkow, 2008a). Research on the use of emoticons reveals that people often use them to make the emotional display more clear or to demonstrate sarcasm (Derks, Bos, & von Grumbkow, 2008b).

While research on online anger could use emoticons as a means of classifying emotions, there are still problems with such an approach. First, people are unlikely to use them consistently (i.e., even frequent emoticon users are likely to post something sad without a sad face from time to time). For example, research has shown that males are more likely to use emoticons when interacting with females, particularly for teasing or sarcasm, and females are more likely to use emoticons when making a joke (Wolf, 2000). Consequently, while emoticons are one method for inferring emotion from written content, researchers cannot rely on them completely.

Related to emoticon usage in research, Fan and colleagues (2013) had an interesting solution to the problem of inferring emotions from written content by using a computer program to code emotions based on key words, emoticons, etc. While that does not eliminate the potential for error due to sarcasm or unclear intent, it does offer some consistency with regard to coding.

A final problem is that the technology associated with social networking changes very quickly and, sometimes it can make the research that has been conducted obsolete before it has been published. Facebook, for example, has been known to change its format often. Such changes likely influence how people express their emotions on the given website. Most notable, is that in January of 2013 Facebook added an option where you can explicitly indicate how you are feeling when you post a status update. Though many people do not use the "feeling..." option when they update their statuses, the fact that it exists allows for a different means of expressing yourself and changes the nature of online anger research. Another more recent example is that in November of 2013, Google announced a change in how comments would be displayed on YouTube and how they would no longer allow for anonymous comments. This was done as a direct result of anger and harassment online. It will likely have the effect of reducing anger and aggression online, as anonymity is one of the driving forces involved in internet anger, aggression, and bullying. There is no easy solution to this problem but for researchers and research outlets to work quickly in publishing results of studies.

9.3 Online Anger or Online Aggression

It is important to clarify the difference between online anger and online aggression. The two concepts are related, to be sure, but different enough as to warrant discussion. Anger is an emotion. It ranges from mild frustration someone might feel when they cannot find their car keys to the intense rage treated terribly by a friend or coworker (Spielberger, 1999). Aggression, meanwhile, is a behavior that can be expressed physically and verbally. Specifically, it is a behavior where the individual has the intent to harm someone or something (Graham et al., 2006). Hitting, kicking, or insulting someone are all examples of aggression. Although anger and aggression are related, they are separate, one obviously can be angry without being aggressive (e.g., anger control, anger suppression) and, though it is less common, one can be aggressive without being angry (hunting, boxing, etc.).

In the online environment, we see many examples of both anger and aggression. With regard to anger, it is not uncommon for people to vent online purely for the sake of venting. People will often use Twitter or Facebook to simply tell the world that they are angry about something. This is particularly true following nationally shared events like an election, a sporting event, or other controversial public experiences. In the wake of the Super Bowl, for example, it's common for people to tweet angrily about their team losing, perceived bad calls, or even their dislike of the halftime show.

People will also use social media as a means of aggressing against an individual or a group they dislike or want revenge against. Online aggression can take many forms; anything from name-calling, threatening, rumor spreading, or even hacking into social media accounts to disrupt social networks. Like most aggression, online aggression is typically motivated, in part, by anger. It is fair to say that online aggression is more problematic than online anger in the sense that it is likely to have more severe consequences. However, that does not diminish the seriousness of the potential consequences associated with online anger, like arguments, damaged relationships, or other common costs. It should also be noted that much, though not all, of online aggression is rooted in anger, so identifying ways to manage online anger will likely lead to a decrease in both anger and aggression.

A related topic that has gotten a lot of attention in the media is online bullying. Online bullying, or cyber-bullying, is an increasingly common form of aggression primarily associated with, but not limited to, social media use amongst school-age children and adolescents. Cyber-bullying, like online anger, is appealing to some for the social distance or even anonymity it allows; one can aggress and elicit harm without facing his or her targets or allowing them a chance to respond. Online bullying often has detrimental effects on the bully and the victim but is extremely difficult to curtail. Not surprisingly, online aggression and online bullying have received considerably more attention in the literature than online anger (Badaly, Kelly, Schwartz, & Dabney-Lieras, 2013; Runions, 2013)

9.4 Research on Online Anger

Given the difficulties associated with researching online anger, it is not surprising that there is scant literature in the area. There has been research exploring perceptions of those who express their anger online, especially in an aggressive way (Badaly et al., 2013; Teng, Tseng, Chen, & Wu, 2012). There has also been research exploring the emotions people have to shared events. For example, Lee (2012) looked at online emotional expressions following the death of Michael Jackson. Though the study looked at all emotional responses, and not just anger, Lee found that anger was the second most common emotion expressed online. However, very little research has explored anger directly rather than aggression or bullying.

Despite this, we have seen some research in the last few years that demonstrates the importance of understanding online anger and finding ways to minimize it. For instance, a recent study found that anger spread faster online than joy, disgust, or sadness (Fan, Zhao, Chen, & Xu, 2013). In other words, anger was more likely to be retweeted or favorited and was, therefore, more viral, than the other emotions they studied. The authors classified the emotions of more than 70 million tweets on Weibo (a social-networking site in China, similar to Twitter). They then looked to see which tweets were more likely to be retweeted or shared with others. They found that, while sad and disgusted tweets were not shared by many people, and joyful tweets were shared by those you were close to, angry tweets were shared by both close and distant relationships. The implication of this research is that anger is the most "viral" of all emotions.

Similar findings come from a previous study that looked at the "virality" of online stories and news (Berger & Milkman, 2012). It was found that how quickly a story spread, depended on both the content and the emotional foundation of what is shared. Although stories positive in nature were more likely to be shared than those negative in nature, stories with high arousal (e.g., angering) were more likely to be shared than those with low arousal (e.g., sadness).

Anger is not just quick to spread online, it is also problematic. In another recent study we explored the use of rant-sites (Martin, Coyier, Van Sistine, & Schroeder, 2013). Rant-sites are websites that provide people with an online space to rant, anonymously, on any topic they are angry about. Visitors post rants about politics, family members, coworkers, or even just situations that annoy them (e.g., being asked to install toolbars on their web browsers). There are rant sites for people to rant on general topics (e.g., http://www.justrage.com) whereas others are designed for rants on specific types of topics (e.g., offering service providers a place to vent about customers). Although clearly not as popular as social networking sites like Facebook or Twitter, they definitely see their share of internet traffic. Just one of these sites, Justrage, had more than 6,500 rants posted with more than 90,000 comments.

Our study surveyed rant site users to better understand why they visited rant-sites, why they posted on them, and how they felt after posting. We found that 100% of participants reported feeling calm and relaxed after posting and that the majority (66%) was hoping for comments from others on their posts. Some wanted validation or advice, and some were hoping for debate. We also surveyed participants on their general anger levels using the State-Trait Anger Expression Inventory-2 (STAXI-2; Spielberger, 1999) so we could compare them to the average as reported in the manual. We found that rant-site users were angrier than the average person and expressed their anger in more maladaptive ways. Finally, rant-site users reported many consequences as a result of their anger, including frequently feeling other negative emotions like sadness or fear, getting in physical or verbal fights, damaging property, or even having harmed themselves physically.

9.5 Problems With Expressing Anger Online

One of the most widespread misunderstandings involving anger expression is the catharsis myth; many people believe that releasing anger via venting, physical actions, or writing is a healthy coping mechanism, despite a wide array of research stating otherwise (Lohr, Olatunji, Baumeister, & Bushman, 2007; Bushman, Baumeister, & Phillips, 2001). Bushman (2002) showed that venting was actually counterproductive, as it caused people to further ruminate about their anger rather than move on. Similarly, one study showed that anger actually increased when those listening reinforced participants' venting behaviors, and decreased when the angering situation was reinterpreted by others (Parlamis, 2012). Additional research has shown that venting can be a healthy coping skill, but it must be used in a way that allows someone to release his or her anger and take a problem-solving approach to finding a solution for the cause of the anger. Nils & Rimé (2012) found that venting was only an effective coping method for dealing with anger when the person on the receiving end engaged in cognitive reframing directing the angered person toward problem-focused solutions.

The study on rant-sites described earlier (Martin et al., 2013) helps elucidate how online ranting reinforces the catharsis myth. All participants in the study reported feeling calm and relaxed after ranting. Although it may seem to the ranting person that their anger-reduction strategy has worked, that may not be the case. As pointed out by Olatuni and colleagues (2007), it is common for people to feel relaxed immediately after venting, which is why participants feel that venting their anger is worthwhile; they are immediately reinforced with feelings of calmness and relaxation. However, and consistent with the literature on catharsis outlined earlier, Olatunji and colleagues go on to argue that over the long term, people who vent in this way are angrier and suffer more maladaptive consequences as a result of their anger. This is consistent with Martin and colleagues (2013) finding that those who frequent rant-sites were angrier and expressed their anger in more maladaptive ways than the norm.

The fact that it makes one's anger worse is not the only problem with ranting online. There can be interpersonal consequences as well. This is especially true given the fact that much online aggression is rooted in online anger. In fact, recent research (Martin) surveyed participants on how often they become angry, how they express their anger, and what sorts of consequences they experience as a result of their anger. Regarding this last piece, anger consequences, we asked specifically about behaviors and consequences in online environments over the last month and found that a striking number of participants had behaved in angry and aggressive ways online and had experienced negative consequences as a result. For instance, 12% of participants had posted angry or aggressive comments on a social networking site in the last month. Eleven percent had posted something negative about someone online in the hopes that he or she would see it and 3% had actually threatened someone via a social networking site. Nine percent had gotten into an argument that they later regretted and three percent had lost a friend or damaged a relationship because of something they posted online. The types of angry behaviors were broader than you might think as well. Some participants reported "hacking" into someone's social networking account and saying things as if they were them (6%), intentionally posting an unflattering picture of someone (4%), or even creating an angry page or event online (4%).

Not surprisingly, there is no published research on the treatment of chronic online anger problems. Social networking is relatively new and there are enough challenges associated with online anger research so that we have not yet seen any sort of intervention research related to online anger. That said, it is reasonable to assume that the basic cognitive-behavioral treatments associated with anger would be useful and appropriate in treating those with online anger problems as well. Specifically, relaxation approaches and replacing maladaptive angry thoughts with more positive thoughts will likely be valuable in treating online anger problems.

9.6 Why Does Online Anger Happen?

To understand online anger, one needs to understand why people get angry in general. Deffenbacher (1996) argues that anger results from a combination of a precipitating event, the angered individual's preanger state, and the individual's appraisal of the precipitating event. The precipitating event is the event that served as the trigger (e.g., a long line at the grocery store, someone posting something you find offensive on Facebook). People often think of it as the cause of their anger but, ultimately, that is not entirely true. It is ultimately only one piece of the cause, contributing to the preanger state and the appraisal. Our preanger state is how we are feeling immediately before the precipitating event (e.g., stressed, tired, hungry, in a hurry). These feeling states can have the effect of exacerbating our angry response by affecting how we appraise the precipitant. For example, being tired is associated with poorer impulse control that may lead to a more intense angry response when faced with a provocation.

The final piece of Deffenbacher's model is appraisal, or how we interpret the precipitating event. Deffenbacher argues that we become angry because we appraise situations as blameworthy, unjustified, punishable, etc. So, if you are on Facebook one night and see a political post from a friend (the precipitating event) that you disagree with, you are likely to get angry if you interpret that post as blameworthy (e.g., "he should know better than that"), unjustified (e.g., "I should not have to read this sort of thing from him"), and/or punishable (e.g., "I am going to let him have it). If you interpret the situation a little differently, (e.g., "that is a foolish post, but people are allowed to believe whatever they want"), you are less likely to become angry.

It is important to note that when it comes to cognitive appraisal, anger-inducing interpretations or appraisals of a situation are not necessarily inaccurate. Sometimes people are absolutely correct in their interpretation of an event and anger is a perfectly reasonable emotion to feel. For instance, if an acquaintance posts something negative and hurtful about you, it would see totally reasonable to become angry in response. The next step, though, it figuring out how to handle your anger. Is it wise to respond with your own angry comment, call him or her to talk about it in person, decide the relationship is not worth it and block/unfriend the person? Each of those responses might be reasonable, depending on a host of contextual factors (e.g., the type of relationship you have with the person already, other mutual friends who might be involved in the discussion, the consequences of ending the relatationship).

Although anger online occurs just like anger anywhere else, there are a few elements of the online environment that make angry interactions more common or more problematic online. First, in those online settings that allow for truly anonymous posting (e.g., 4chan.org, Justrage.com), there is an increased likelihood of angry and aggressive posts. Ultimately, anonymity leads to what feels like consequence free emotional expressions and people become less afraid of expressing their anger. People may be more open to actively expressing their anger online when they know it cannot be tied back to them.

Although true anonymity is somewhat rare online, there is a related phenomenon that is relevant in most online environments. Online interactions through Facebook, Twitter, and even email, allow for greater social distance than in person interactions. What this means is that they feel somewhat anonymous to people even though they are not truly anonymous. The distance between you and the person you are interacting with may stop you from censoring yourself. As you type the post, you are not looking the person in the eye or seeing their facial expressions. In a face-to-face conversation, you might notice that he or she is really reflecting on or is hurt by what you are saying and you may back off before things get too heated. None of that happens in an online interaction so things can escalate quickly.

The online environment also has a tendency to exacerbate impulsivity problems. Posting on Facebook, Twitter, email, etc. are a little too quick and easy sometimes. You can respond to a provocation immediately, and when you are most angry, rather than giving yourself time to emotionally calm down you become less rational and less likely to think through the consequences of what you are writing. What you post might actually capture how you are feeling very well, but it is probably not expressing that frustration in the most effective way or, worse yet, may come off in a way that damages a relationship.

Finally, the online environment can also lead to misunderstandings. Because it is written, it can be somewhat difficult to understand the intent of other people's posts or emails. Similar to the difficulty in researching online anger that was addressed earlier, sarcasm, hyperboles, irony, etc. can often be hard to identify when written. For example, the day after President Obama won the Noble Peace Prize, I saw a friend post an article about it on Facebook with the following: "About time a Kenyan won!" Though I knew my friend well enough to know she was making a joke about the birther movement, another of her friends did not and responded with a lengthy, and somewhat cruel, angry response. The exchange, which escalated from there, was the result of a simple misunderstanding.

9.7 Avoiding the Anger Online Trap

Given the finding reported earlier, that almost one in ten report having an argument online in the last month that they later regretted, it seems clear that online anger is getting the best of many people. While it is completely reasonable that people want to voice their frustration in an online venue, it is also important to avoid becoming so angry that it leads to negative consequences. Here are some strategies people can use to avoid experiencing those consequences.

1. Don't respond electronically. Go talk to the person if you can. Email, Facebook, Twitter, etc. are sometimes the easy way out. They are what people do when they do not want to have an uncomfortable face-to-face conversation with someone. There are times when an online response is understandable, but if it is possible to avoid it, it might make sense to do so.
2. Wait. Emotions are usually short-lived. If you can wait it out until your anger starts to dissipate, your response might be better for it. If you really feel you need to do something in response to the provocation, go ahead and start writing but do not

post or send it until you have had a chance to cool off. Then, reread what you wrote, think it through, probably rewrite some parts, and post the new version.
3. Have it read. You may want to ask a friend you trust to read it before you post it. That person, who is ideally removed from the situation, might be able to offer some much needed perspective, tell you if it sounds rude, or if it is unclear.
4. Remember that being angry is not the same thing as being cruel. There are infinite ways to voice your anger and it is quite possible to do so respectfully. If you are angered by an article you just read and want to respond in the discussion forum, go for it. But avoid name-calling and other insults. Instead, focus on the ways you disagree with the article. Be responsible and respectful in your response and things are less likely to escalate.
5. Ask yourself why you are sending it. Make sure you are aware of the end result you are hoping for. Are you trying to change your friends' opinions or get an apology from someone? Regardless, make sure you think about why you are writing it and that you can obtain whatever the desired outcome is. If the point is just to vent, it's probably better not to send it at all and find some other way to deal with your anger.

9.8 In Conclusion

In summary, online anger is a very real and common problem that seems to be becoming even more common as more and more people take to social networking venues to vent about their concerns. Despite the frequent and severe consequences, there has been little research on online anger or online aggression. Likewise, there are few resources designed to provide guidance on how to manage or limit the expression of anger online. This chapter provided a framework for understanding online anger within the context of anger in general, provided solutions to some of the problems associated with researching online anger, and provided hands-on tips for managing online anger.

References

Badaly, D., Kelly, B. M., Schwartz, D., & Dabney-Lieras, K. (2013). Longitudinal associations of electronic aggression and victimization with social standing during adolescence. Journal of Youth and Adolescence, 42, 891-904. doi:10.1007/s10964-012-9787-2

Berger, J., & Milkman, K. L. (2012). What makes online content viral?. Journal of Marketing Research, 49, 192-205. doi:10.1509/jmr.10.0353

Bushman, B. J. (2002). Does venting anger feed or extinguish the flame? Catharsis, rumination, distraction, anger and aggressive responding. Personality and Social Psychology Bulletin, 28, 724-731. doi:10.1177/0146167202289002

Bushman, B. J., Baumeister, R. F., & Phillips, C. M. (2001). Do people aggress to improve their mood? Catharsis beliefs, affect regulation opportunity, and aggressive responding. Journal of Personality and Social Psychology, 81, 17-32. doi:10.1037/0022-3514.81.1.17

Derks, D., Bos, A. R., & von Grumbkow, J. (2008). Emoticons and online message interpretation. Social Science Computer Review, 26, 379-388.doi:10.1177/0894439307311611
Derks, D., Bos, A. R., & von Grumbkow, J. (2008). Emoticons in computer-mediated communication: Social motives and social context. Cyberpsychology & Behavior, 11, 99-101. doi:10.1089/cpb.2007.9926
Fan, R., Zhao, J., Chen, Y., & Xu, K. (2013). Anger is more influential than joy: sentiment correlation in Weibo. Reprint submitted to Elsevier, 10 September. Accessed January 2013. Avialable online at http://arxiv.org/abs/1309.2402.
Graham, K., Tremblay, P. F., Wells, S., Pernanen, K., Purcell, J., & Jelley, J. (2006). Harm, intent, and the nature of aggressive behavior: Measuring naturally occurring aggression in barroom settings. Assessment, 13, 280-296. doi:10.1177/1073191106288180
Lee, C. (2012). Exploring emotional expressions on YouTube through the lens of media system dependency theory. New Media & Society, 14, 457-475. doi:10.1177/1461444811419829
Lohr, J. M., Olatunji, B. O., Baumeister, R. F., & Bushman, B. J. (2007). The psychology of anger venting and empirically supported alternatives that do no harm. The Scientific Review of Mental Health Practice: Objective Investigations of Controversial and Unorthodox Claims in Clinical Psychology, Psychiatry, and Social Work, 5, 53-64.
Martin, R. C. (2013). [Online anger consequences]. Unpublished raw data.
Martin, R. C., Coyier, K., VanSistine, L. M., & Schroeder, K. L. (2013). Anger on the Internet: The perceived value of rant-sites. Cyberpsychology, Behavior, And Social Networking, 16, 119-122.
Nils, F., & Rimé, B. (2012). Beyond the myth of venting: Social sharing modes determine the benefits of emotional disclosure. European Journal of Social Psychology, 42, 672-681. doi:10.1002/ejsp.1880
Olatunji BO, Lohr JM, Bushman BJ. (2007) The pseudopsychology of venting in the treatment of anger: Implications and alternatives for mental health practice. In: Cavell TA, Malcolm KT, eds, Anger, aggression and interventions for interpersonal violence. Mahwah, NJ: Lawrence Erlbaum Associates Publishers, pp. 119-141.
Parlamis, J. D. (2012). Venting as emotion regulation: The influence of venting responses and respondent identity on anger and emotional tone. International Journal of Conflict Management, 23, 77-96. doi:10.1108/10444061211199322
Runions, K. (2013). Toward a Conceptual Model of Motive and Self-Control in Cyber-Aggression: Rage, Revenge, Reward, and Recreation. Journal Of Youth & Adolescence, 42, 751-771. doi:10.1007/s10964-013-9936-2
Spielberger, C. D. (1999). Professional manual for the State-Trait Anger Expression Inventory-2 (STAXI-2). Odessa, FL: Psychological Assessment Resources.
Teng, C., Tseng, F., Chen, Y., & Wu, S. (2012). Online gaming misbehaviours and their adverse impact on other gamers. Online Information Review, 36, 342-358. doi:10.1108/14684521211241387
Wolf, A. (2000). Emotional expression online: Gender differences in emoticon use. Cyberpsychology & Behavior, 3, 827-833. doi:10.1089/10949310050191809

Meagan A. Ramsey, Ann M. Oberhauser, Amy L. Gentzler

10 College Students' Use of Communication Technology with Parents: Influences of Distance, Gender, and Social Presence

Abstract: Information and communication technology (ICT) has significantly affected the way people maintain relationships despite spatial and other social and economic barriers. In the case of college students and their parents, ICT is a means of maintaining this parent-child relationship when students travel far from home to attend school. However, little research has examined college students' use of various types of technology for communicating with their parents and how it may affect their relationship with their parents. This chapter analyzes the socio-spatial aspects of how college students use a variety of communication channels (cell phones, text messaging, email, and social networking sites) to connect with their parents using both quantitative and qualitative methods. Specifically, the study addresses: 1) the impact of geographical distance between a college student and their parent on their use of communication technology and the qualities of their relationship, 2) how the gender of both the students and their parents influences the amount and type of communication technology students use with their parents, and 3) whether or not students' social presence mediates the association between using particular technologies to communicate with their parents and their relationship with their parents. Overall, this chapter contributes to our understanding of the social and spatial aspects of communication technologies within the parent-child relationship and has important implications for universities and families with students transitioning to college.

10.1 College Students' Use of Communication Technology with Parents: Influences of Distance, Gender, and Social Presence

The widespread use of information and communication technology (ICT) in society impacts how we maintain relationships and connections with others (Kim, Kim, Park, & Rice, 2007). This is important for college students and their parents, as college students may travel far from home to attend school. However, relatively little research has analyzed the use of ICT among college students and parents. Given the importance of these communication technologies for college students, this research aims to understand how particular factors influence students' use of these technologies to maintain relationships. This chapter examines the effect of geographical distance between college students and their parents on their use of

ICT and relationships, how ICT use may vary by gender of both the college students and their parents, and how students' social presence, or their perceived salience or presence of the other person, felt during ICT use influences their relationships with their parents.

10.2 Parent-Child Relationships and ICT Use

Studies on the impact of the internet and mobile communication on social relations tend to find that increased online social communities often complement offline social interaction (Crang, Crosbie, & Graham, 2007). It seems that this may especially be the case for parents and students who live long distances from each other, as they may rely on ICT more heavily to maintain their relationship if frequent face-to-face contact is not practical or possible. In support of this, research indicates that students communicate with their parents quite frequently, averaging 13 times a week when looking across multiple types of ICT (Hofer, 2008). Additionally, our research indicates that almost 100% of students use the phone to communicate with their parents, and that rates of student-parent communication by text and SNS are increasing (to 85% and 45% in 2011, respectively). However, e-mail communication with parents is declining (Ramsey, Gentzler, Morey, Oberhauser, & Westerman, 2013).

Our previous research has also revealed that the type of ICT that students use with their parents is related to unique relationship qualities. For instance, early research indicated that students who used a SNS with their parents were lonelier, more anxiously attached, and had more conflict with their parents (Gentzler, Oberhauser, Westerman, & Nadorff, 2011), but more recent research indicates that using an SNS with parents is no longer associated with poor outcomes (Ramsey et al., 2013). In addition, students' frequent telephone communication with parents is consistently associated with positive relationship qualities (Chen & Katz, 2009; Gentzler et al., 2011; Ramsey et al., 2013; Wei & Lo, 2006). Overall, communication between parents and college students (particularly using certain ICT channels) may enable students to maintain close, positive relationships with parents, which research suggests may help students more smoothly transition to college (Mattanah, Lopez, & Govern, 2011; Wintre & Yaffe, 2000). Although, an opposing concern noted by Hofer and Moore (2010) is that ICT could result in students' overreliance on parents. Thus it may be useful for colleges and universities to also be mindful that ICT could actually inhibit students' developing independence. The following sections outline how distance, gender, and social presence influence students' and parents' ICT use and relationship qualities.

10.3 Distance

The increased mobility of ICT allows students and parents to accomplish relational goals (e.g., keeping in contact) better than past technologies, as the increased mobility allows people to interact anywhere, and thus, reduces the time necessary for relational maintenance (e.g., engaging in activities that help preserve connections with close social partners) to take place (Castells, 2010). This mobility of today's ICT has clear significance for those trying to connect across large distances, including many college students and their parents. Recent research suggests that students who live very far from their parents choose different forms of ICT (e.g., Skype, email) to maintain the relationship (Yang, Brown, & Braun, 2013). Thus, we expected that distance will similarly influence the amount and type of ICT use that college students use with their parents. Additionally, we explored whether or not distance was related to students' relationships with their parents.

10.4 Gender

Many studies examine how socially constructed gender roles impact the use of communication technologies (e.g., Castells, Fernandez-Ardevol, Qiu, & Sey, 2007). Specifically, rates of ICT use differ by gender, as women tend to use online communication more than men (Hartsell, 2005), and tend to use the phone to contact their family more often as well (Chen & Katz, 2009; Wei & Lo, 2006). Thus students' ICT use is related to gender roles in society. Moreover, research suggests that it is important to consider the gender of the parent in addition to that of the student. For example, adolescents' SNS use with their family is related to their reported warmth and support with their fathers but not their mothers (Coyne, Padilla-Walker, Day, Harper, & Stockdale, 2013). In addition, college students are more likely to report wanting more communication with fathers than they currently have compared to their desired contact with mothers (Hofer, 2008). Therefore, it is necessary to take both student and parent gender into account when examining the influences of gender on ICT use.

10.5 Social Presence

Social presence, which refers to how salient or physically present the other person seems during the communication process (Biocca, Harms, & Burgoon, 2003; Short, Williams, & Christie, 1976), is another factor that may play a role in students' ICT use and relationships with their parents. Many factors may affect the amount of social presence a person feels during a particular interaction such as the features of the particular technology used, the relationship, the distance between the individuals, and type of communication used (Biocca et al., 2003; Gooch & Watts, 2013). We expect that social presence may be one reason that college students' use of ICT is related to their relationship quality with that parent. In other words, students who more frequently use ICT with their parent may report higher-quality relationships with them in part because they can feel connected and present during their communications. In our study we examine the role of social presence across multiple types of ICT, which is important because different types of communication may naturally elicit more presence (Biocca et al., 2003; Gooch & Watts, 2013).

10.6 Current Study

In the current study, we used mixed methods to examine how socio-spatial dimensions influence college students' use of phones, text messaging, email, and SNS to maintain relationships with their parents. The combination of quantitative and qualitative data from the surveys and focus groups gave us insight to the broad patterns and relationships, as well as the personal experiences that individual students shared with us about their use of ICT. The findings from both of these methods inform the results and the discussion of our research throughout this paper. We had three major research questions: 1) does the geographical distance between a college student and their parent influence their use of ICT or the qualities of their relationship?; 2) is the amount and type of ICT students use with their parents impacted by the gender of both the students and their parents?; and 3) does students' social presence mediate the association between using particular technologies to communicate with their parents and their relationship with their parents?

10.7 Method

10.7.1 Participants and Procedure

Focus group. Twenty-three students (5 females, 18 males) participated in the focus group portion of this study in 2009. An average of 7 students participated in each of the three focus group discussions. Nearly half of the participants were freshmen and were recruited from an introductory human geography class. The discussions were organized into the following three topics: 1) students' backgrounds such as year in college, major, and hometown; 2) the type, frequency of, and reason for their use of ICT, including family members with whom they communicate; and 3) students' opinions about and effectiveness of ICT in their relationships. Data from the focus groups were recorded, transcribed, and analyzed using QSR NVivo software. The analysis included the development of themes that corresponded with the research questions outlined above and provided a structure to identify the social relationships and impact of ICT.

Online survey. Two hundred and sixteen college students (171 females, 45 males) ages 18 to 22 ($M = 19.52$, $SD = 1.08$) participated in the online portion of this study in 2011. The racial-ethnic distribution of the final sample was 93% Caucasian, 3% African-American, 1% Native American, 1% Hispanic, 1% Asian, and 1% other. Participants were recruited from general psychology classes and received extra credit for participating. Participants first identified the family member they were closest to (180 mothers, 36 fathers) and then answered questions about their communication and relationship with this family member. These 216 students came from a larger sample of 302 participants. We excluded 22 participants ages 22 and older because we expected that they may have different patterns of ICT use with their parents, and 64 students for identifying a different family member (other than their parent) as closest.

10.7.2 Online Survey Measures

Use of ICT. Participants rated their frequency of using phone, e-mail, text messaging, and SNS to communicate with their parent on an 8-point scale ranging from 0 (never) to 7 (several hours a day).

Distance. Participants reported the location of their parent's home and this was then coded as miles to the town from where the university is located. Two extreme outliers that were more than three standard deviations away from the mean distance (1,203 and 4,231 miles) were recoded to the next highest amount (888 miles).

Social presence. Participants reported on two items that assessed social presence for each type of ICT. Participants rated each item on a 7-point Likert scale ranging from 1 (not at all) to 7 (very much). The items were, "When you interact with your closest family member using [ICT], to what extent do you feel like you are actually with your closest family member?" and "When you interact with your closest family member using [ICT], to what extent do you imagine being with your closest family member face-to-face?" The two items were highly correlated for each type of ICT (phone ($r = .78$, $p < .001$), text ($r = .85$, $p < .001$), e-mail ($r = .88$, $p < .001$), and SNS ($r = .88$, $p < .001$)) and were averaged to create one social presence subscale for each form of communication.

Relationship with parents. Participants completed five scales (3 items per scale) of the Network of Relationships Inventory (Furman & Buhrmester, 1985) which assessed participants' relationship satisfaction, intimacy, support, instrumental aid, and conflict with their parent. Participants rated all 15 items on a 5-point Likert scale ranging from 1 (little to none) to 5 (the most). Examples include: "How satisfied are you with your relationship with your closest family member?" (satisfaction, $\alpha = 0.93$); "How much do you share your secrets and private feelings with your closest family member?" (intimacy, $\alpha = 0.88$); "How much do you turn to your closest family member for support with personal problems?" (support, $\alpha = 0.87$); "How much does your closest family member help you when you need to get something done?" (instrumental aid, $\alpha = 0.84$); and "How much do you and your closest family member disagree and quarrel?" (conflict, $\alpha = 0.88$).

10.8 Results

10.8.1 Focus Group Themes

Several themes emerged from the focus groups that relate to our questions about types of ICT communication, distance, and social presence in their interactions with their parents. First, several students commented on the use of various forms of ICT in communicating with their parents. Specifically, they are more apt to text about logistics or appointments, but use phone calls for more in-depth or personal conversations. For example, one student reported:

> I won't sit there and text them all day in class, but they know how, and if they want to send me something that's imperative, ya know, every once in awhile I'll get a text message from my mom that says "You have a doctor's appointment this day" or "You need to get to the dentist" or "you need to call me about something important later."

In this case, the student's mother communicates with her son to remind him about various things. However, several students also mentioned the lower level of access to and use of particular forms of ICT among their parent's generation. "It's like my parents and technology, they have no idea how to text, so I've lucked out so far." "Like, I don't text my parents, I just call them at home. They don't really like if I text them at all." "My mom doesn't know how to text, so I always have to call her."

Geographical issues were also mentioned among students in the focus groups in that some of their parents lived in areas that made communication with them difficult. Specifically, one student said, "Where I come from, my hometown, I don't have cell phone service." This geographical barrier may affect students' communication with their parents and indicates that distance may not be the only geographical factor in college students' use of ICT with their parents.

Although students did not use the term social presence, they also highlighted key issues pertaining to this construct. Some students lamented the lack of "personal immediacy between people" through texting and other forms of social media. As one student stated:

> There's nothing that compares with sitting down and talking to her (student's mother) face to face or getting a hug from her. Ya know, there's nothing that can replace that. ... But, I do feel that Facebooking and texting ... and all that; I think it's almost kind of desensitizing us a little bit to like human emotion.

10.8.2 Influence of Distance

Using the online survey data, we first examined if the geographical distance between a college student and their parent influences their use of ICT. Bivariate correlations revealed that distance was associated with phone use between parents and students, but not with use of text, SNS, or email (see Table 1). Specifically, students living farther from their parents reported less phone use with them. We also examined if the geographical distance between a college student and their parent was related to the qualities of their relationship. However, bivariate correlations revealed that distance was not associated with parent-child relationship qualities.

Table 10.1. Correlations among key variables

	1	2	3	4	5	6	7	8	9	10	11	12	13
1. Distance	-												
2. Phone Use	-.18**	-											
3. Text Use	.02	.21**	-										
4. SNS Use	.13	-.01	.18**	-									
5. Email Use	.08	-.01	-.07	.08	-								
6. Phone SP	-.03	.16*	-.03	.04	.12	-							
7. Text SP	-.03	.14	.26***	.22**	.18*	.71***	-						
8. SNS SP	.04	.01	.01	.58***	.19*	.47***	.70***	-					
9. Email SP	.02	-.10	-.04	.37***	.55***	.38***	.57***	.70***	-				
10. Satisfaction	-.02	.35***	.19**	-.02	-.05	.15*	.13	.00	-.05	-			
11. Intimacy	-.02	.45***	.13	.06	.03	.21**	.17*	.06	.03	.55***	-		
12. Support	-.08	.50***	.13	.02	.04	.14*	.14	.02	-.02	.70***	.78***	-	
13. Aid	-.01	.44***	.11	-.07	.13	.18*	.17*	.01	.03	.61***	.64***	.80***	-
14. Conflict	-.03	-.07	-.05	.04	.05	-.07	-.03	.08	.15	-.30***	-.01	-.16*	-.10

Note. SP = Social presence. *$p < .05$, **$p < .01$, ***$p < .001$.

10.8.3 Influence of Student and Parent Gender

To examine effects of parent and student gender on the use of the various types of communication technology, a 2 (parent gender) by 2 (student gender) MANOVA was conducted. There was a significant main effect of parent gender (Wilks' Lambda (4, 203) = .95, F = 2.60, p = .038, $\eta_p^2 = .049$). This effect was qualified by a significant interaction between parent and student gender (Wilks' Lambda (4, 203) = .94, F = 3.21, p = .014, η_p^2 = .060). Follow up ANOVAs using Bonferroni corrected alphas revealed that females were more likely to text their fathers than males (F(1, 206) = 5.71, p = .018, η_p^2 = .027). Additionally, males were more likely to use text messaging (F(1, 206) = 5.62, p = .019, η_p^2 = ..027) and SNS (F(1, 206) = 9.10, p = .003, η_p^2 = .042) to communicate with their mothers than with their fathers (see Figure 10.1).

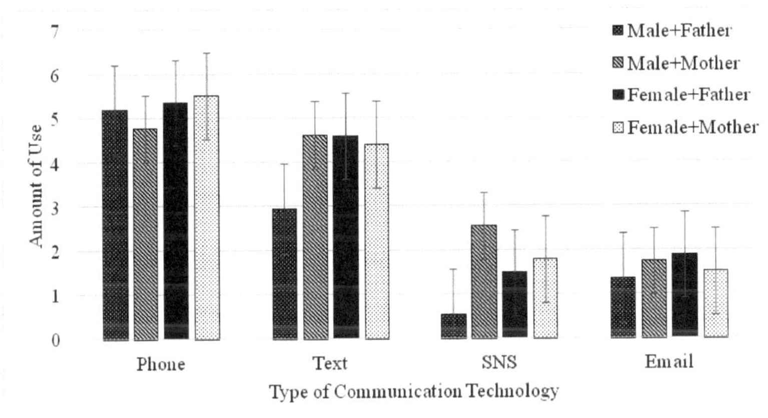

Figure 10.1. Amount of using each type of communication technology by student and parent gender.
**p* < .05

10.8.4 Influence of Social Presence

To examine if students' social presence mediated the association between using particular technologies to communicate with their parents and their relationship with their parents, we used PROCESS with SPSS (Hayes, 2013) to assess indirect effects. Separate regressions were conducted for each type of ICT (phone, text, SNS, email) and for each type of relationship outcome (satisfaction, intimacy, support, aid, conflict). For each regression, the amount of a particular type of ICT was the predictor, the social presence students felt for that particular ICT was the mediator, and a quality of the parent-child relationship was the outcome. Although increased phone use with parents was directly associated with greater satisfaction, intimacy, support, and, aid, and more frequent text communication was directly associated with satisfaction and support, only two significant indirect effects of social presence emerged (as evidenced by the 95% confidence intervals associated with the bootstrapped estimates (5,000 samples) that did not contain zero). First, there was an indirect effect of phone-related social presence on the association between amount of phone use and intimacy with parents (b = .025, SE = .018, 95% CI: .001-.074). There was also an indirect effect of text-related social presence on the association between students' amount of text communication with their parents and instrumental aid from parents (b = .022, SE = .014, 95% CI: .000-.058).

10.9 Discussion

This analysis of the social and spatial dynamics of ICT provides a more thorough understanding of the factors that influence ICT use among college students and their parents in contemporary society. This study advances the literature on the effects of geographical distance, parents' and students' gender, and feelings of social presence on students' use of ICT to connect with their parents and students' relationships with parents. Studies such as these are an important step toward understanding the role of parental communication in students' transition to and satisfaction in college. College students' adjustment is predicted by having supportive relationships with parents but also developing healthy levels of individuation from them (Mattanah, Hancock, & Brand, 2004; Mattanah et al. 2011). Moreover, students' social and emotional adjustment predicts college retention (Gerdes & Mallinckrodt, 1994). Thus, gaining a better understanding of how students use ICT to maintain healthy levels of communication and closeness with parents may allow us to better predict their success and retention in college.

10.9.1 Distance and Students' and Parents' ICT Use and Relationships

The spatial dimensions of ICT are important in young adults' use of this form of communication in order to maintain relationships with their parents. Specifically, we found that students whose parents lived closer to the university reported talking with their parent more on the phone. This finding is in line with other research indicating that students tend to communicate more with local relatives than with distant relatives using the phone and other forms of ICT (Baym, Zhang, & Lin, 2004; Quan-Haase, 2007). There may be several explanations for this finding. First, it is possible that young adults who move far from home to attend college are different than students who choose to stay closer to their family (Mattern & Wyatt, 2009). However, in opposition to past research (Flanagan, Schulenberg, & Fuligni, 1993), we found that distance was not associated with better or worse parent-student relationship qualities. It is also plausible that students who live closer to their parents call them more often for practical reasons (e.g., to ask when dinner is ready, to let them know they are coming home) than students living far from their parents. The issue raised in the focus groups regarding lack of cell phone service highlights a plausible reason for this finding. It is possible that some students' parents live in an area where cell phone service is lacking, and that cell phone accessibility is impeding students' communication with family members. The lack of reliable cell phone and Internet service is not uncommon in rural parts of West Virginia where a significant portion of the student who participated in this research live.

It is also surprising that distance did not influence usage rates of other types of ICT (email, text, SNS). Perhaps these online forms of communication technology have widespread use regardless of distance, or perhaps other factors are more critical determinants of students' use of particular types of ICT with parents (Agosto, Abbas, & Naughton, 2012). For instance, in our focus groups, several students mentioned the lower level of access to and use of particular forms of ICT among their parent's generation. These comments illustrate the generational differences in use of ICT, as well as some of the distance factors that relate to use of ICT discussed above (Castells et al., 2007).

10.9.2 Gender and Students' and Parents' ICT Use

This research also examined parent-student relationships as being related to gender identities and norms, and indicated that it is important to take this system into consideration when assessing how students and parents use ICT. Specifically, female students were more likely to use text messaging to communicate with their fathers than male students. This finding is similar to other relevant literature that girls use more SNS to communicate with family in general (Coyne et al., 2013), although it is unclear why this result only emerged for text messaging and not for other types of ICT. Male students were also much less likely to use text messaging or a SNS to communicate with their fathers than with their mothers. This finding is consistent with research indicating that college students communicate with their mothers more than their fathers (Noller & Bagi, 1985). However, it is not clear why this finding only holds for males and why it is specific to text and SNS communication. Although our findings do not replicate past literature on gender differences in phone use with family (Chen & Katz, 2009; Wei & Lo, 2006), several new interesting trends emerged.

10.9.3 Indirect Effects of Social Presence on ICT Use and Relationship Qualities

Social presence has also been identified as an important influence on ICT use (e.g., Biacco et al., 2003), and we expected that it would also affect qualities of the parent-student relationship. In line with our expectations, there was a significant indirect effect of social presence on the association between phone use and intimacy. Thus, one reason that more frequent phone use is linked to greater intimacy is due to feeling more connected and present with the parent during the conversation. Social presence may directly promote intimacy if people feel more willing to be open and self-disclose. Researchers have even indexed social presence using scales of intimacy (e.g., Burgoon & Hale, 1987). However, given our cross-sectional data, the direction could be reversed where intimacy drives feelings of presence and the resulting choice to talk by phone more frequently. Surprisingly, social presence did not mediate the association between phone use and other positive relationship outcomes (satisfaction, support, aid) that has been linked to greater phone frequency (e.g., Gentzler et al., 2011; Ramsey et al.,

2013). Other factors may be more relevant to these outcomes such as feeling positively validated during the conversations rather than just feeling social presence.

Social presence also mediated the association between text use and aid. Again, it is unclear why presence only mediated this outcome, but parents may take advantage of the convenience of text communication and only use texting with their college student for practical reasons or reminders (Smith, Nguyen, Lai, Leshed, & Baumer, 2012). Data from the focus group discussions expanded these findings by revealing that many students' parents prefer phone communication, some parents are unable to text or use SNS, and email is seen as too formal for casual conversations. Thus, texting between today's college students and parents may be reserved for particular types of communication and messages. Due to the specificity with which text messaging may be used between parents and students, perhaps students feel like their parents are physically there with them during those messages.

10.10 Limitations and Future Directions

Despite the many strengths of this study, there are also several limitations that should be considered. First, although we propose directional models, we cannot be certain of the direction given the correlational and cross-sectional nature of the data. For example, we propose that use of certain communication technologies and the social presence felt for the various forms of ICT influence relationship qualities such as intimacy, but it is also possible that qualities such as intimacy actually dictates ICT use as outlined above, or that the associations are bidirectional.

There are also important variables and factors that were not measured. For instance, video conferencing is another form of ICT that plays an important role in connecting student and parents across long distances (Furukawa & Driessnack, 2013). Also, location may be particularly important for studies on communication technology, as one student in our focus group pointed out that some areas may not have easy access to certain forms of ICT. In relation to this, our research does not allow us to make inferences about how ICT use may change as students transition from living with parents during high school to living away from home during college. Longitudinal research is needed to examine how students' and parents' ICT use changes during this transitional phase.

This research is highly relevant to both the changing use of ICT in society, as well as the role of mobile communication in maintaining relationships among family across long distances. Our study focuses on the use of ICT among college students and their parents, particularly in the early years of transitioning from dependence on family support and guidance to independence and autonomous decision-making. This research has important implications for universities and families that can help smooth their students' transitions from home to college by modulating their use of ICT. For example, it may be important for many families to shift their use of ICT by relying on new forms that fit with both party's preferences. Additionally, some parents and students may even be encouraged to rely on ICT less frequently if the ease and availability of ICT promotes students' dependency on parents (e.g., for advice on managing interpersonal conflicts, professional advice, and help with classwork) and inhibits autonomous behaviors in the students (Hofer & Moore, 2010). If universities understand what factors influence parent-student ICT use (e.g., distance, gender) and how parents and students can use ICT to promote social presence and aid in the maintenance of a positive and healthy relationship, then schools can begin using this information to educate parents and students during events such as freshman orientation. The successful use of ICT in promoting and maintaining quality parent-child relationships may then enhance students' adjustment to and success in college and aid in their retention.

References

Agosto, D. E., Abbas, J., & Naughton, R. (2012). Relationships and social rules: Teens' social network and other ICT selection practices. Journal of the American Society for Information Science and Technology, 63(6), 1106-1124.

Baym, N. K., Zhang, Y. B., & Lin, M. C. (2004). Social interactions across media: Interpersonal communication on the internet, telephone and face-to-face. New Media and Society, 6(3), 299-318.

Biocca, F., Harms, C., & Burgoon, J. K. (2003). Toward a more robust theory and measure of social presence: Review and suggested criteria. Presence, 12(5), 456-480.

Burgoon, J. & Hale, J. L. (1987). Validation and measurement of the fundamental themes of relational communication. Communication Monographs, 54, 19-41.

Castells, M. (2010). The rise of the network society. New York: Blackwell.

Castells, M., Fernandez-Ardevol, M., Qiu, J. L., & Sey, A. (2007). Mobile communication and society: A global perspective. Cambridge, MA: MIT Press.

Chen, Y. F., & Katz, J. E. (2009). Extending family to school life: College students' use of the mobile phone. International Journal of Human-Computer Studies, 67(2), 179-191.

Coyne, S. M., Padilla-Walker, L. M., Day, R. D., Harper, J., & Stockdale, L. (2013). A friend request from dear old dad: Associations between parent–child social networking and adolescent outcomes. Cyberpsychology, Behavior, and Social Networking. Advance online publication.

Crang, M., Crosbie, T., & Graham, S. (2007). Technology, time-space, and the remediation of neighbourhood life. Environment and Planning A, 39, 2405-2422.

Flanagan, C., & Schulenberg, J. (1993). Residential setting and parent-adolescent relationships during the college years. Journal of Youth and Adolescence, 22(2), 171-189.

Furman, W., & Buhrmester, D. (1985). Children's perceptions of the personal relationships in their social networks. Developmental Psychology, 21(6), 1016-1024.

Furukawa, R., & Driessnack, M. (2013). Video-mediated communication to support distant family connectedness. Clinical Nursing Research, 22(1), 82-94.

Gentzler, A. L., Oberhauser, A. M., Westerman, D., & Nadorff, D. K. (2011). College students' use of electronic communication with parents: Links to loneliness, attachment, and relationship quality. Cyberpsychology, Behavior, and Social Networking, 14(1-2), 71-74.

Gerdes, H., & Mallinckrodt, B. (1994). Emotional, social, and academic adjustment of college students: A longitudinal study of retention. Journal of Counseling and Development, 72(3), 281-288.

Gooch, D. & Watts, L. (2013). Social presence and the void in distant relationships: How do people use communication technologies to turn absence into fondness of the heart rather than drifting of the mind? AI & Society. Advance online publication.
Hartsell, T. (2005). Who's talking online? A descriptive analysis of gender and online communication. International Journal of Information and Communication Technology Education, 1(1), 42-54.
Hayes, A. F. (2013). Introduction to mediation, moderation, and conditional process analysis: A regression-based approach. New York: Guilford Press.
Hofer, B. K. (2008). The electronic tether: Parental regulation, self-regulation, and the role of technology in college transitions. Journal of the First-year Experience and Students in Transition, 20(2), 9-24.
Hofer, B. K., & Moore, A. S. (2010). The iConnected parent: Staying close to your kids in college (and beyond) while letting them grow up. New York: Simon and Schuster.
Kim, H., Kim, G. J., Park, H. W., & Rice, R. E. (2007). Configurations of relationships in different media: FtF, email, instant messenger, mobile phone, and SMS. Journal of Computer-Mediated Communication, 12(4), 1183-1207.
Mattanah, J. F., Hancock, G. R., & Brand, B. L. (2004). Parental attachment, separation-individuation, and college student adjustment: A structural equation analysis of mediational effects. Journal of Counseling Psychology, 51(2), 213-225.
Mattanah, J. F., Lopez, F. G., & Govern, J. M. (2011). The contributions of parental attachment bonds to college student development and adjustment: A meta-analytic review. Journal of Counseling Psychology, 58(4), 565-596.
Mattern, K. & Wyatt, J. N. (2009). Student choice of college: How far do students go for an education? Journal of College Admission, 203, 18-29.
Noller, P., & Bagi, S. (1985). Parent—adolescent communication. Journal of Adolescence, 8(2), 125-144.
Quan-Haase, A. (2007). University students' local and distant social ties: Using and integrating modes of communication on campus. Information, Communication & Society, 10(5), 671-693.
Ramsey, M. A., Gentzler, A. L., Morey, J. N., Oberhauser, A. M., & Westerman, D. (2013). College students' use of communication technology with parents: Comparisons between two cohorts in 2009 and 2011. Cyberpsychology, Behavior, and Social Networking, 16(10), 747-752.
Short, J., Williams, E., & Christie, B. (1976). The social psychology of telecommunications. London: John Wiley.
Smith, M. E., Nguyen, D. T., Lai, C., Leshed, G., & Baumer, E. P. S. (2012). Going to college and staying connected: Communication between college freshmen and their parents. CSCW'12: Proceedings of the ACM 2012 conference on computer supported cooperative work (pp. 789-798). New York: ACM.
Wei, R., & Lo, V. H. (2006). Staying connected while on the move: Cell phone use and social connectedness. New Media and Society, 8(1), 53-72.
Wintre, M. G., & Yaffe, M. (2000). First-year students' adjustment to university life as a function of relationships with parents. Journal of Adolescent Research, 15(1), 9-37.
Yang, C. C., Brown, B. B., & Braun, M. T. (2013). From Facebook to cell calls: Layers of electronic intimacy in college students' interpersonal relationships. New Media and Society. Advance online publication.

Deborah Ko, Mike Yao

11 Internet addiction: an cross-cultural perspective

11.1 Introduction

Excessive and compulsive use of the Internet, or Internet addiction, has received much attention from the public. Until recently, social and behavioral scientists have primarily focused their attention on the ontological and epidemiological issues surrounding this problem, and its relationship to a number of psychiatric conditions such as depression and loneliness. While empirical studies in this area generally show that Internet addiction is a phenomenon widely observed in different countries around the world, the reported pervasiveness of this problem varies quite significantly from one sample to another. Moreover, although previous studies have identified a number of socio-economic and psychological correlates of Internet addiction, the existing research has largely ignored cross-cultural differences. We hold the view that excessive and unhealthy Internet use is more than a psychiatric condition; it is a social phenomenon that is affected by environmental, cultural, and technological factors. Research on Internet addiction urgently needs a new direction that looks beyond epidemiological characteristics of the problem and their individual level correlates. In this chapter, we will review empirical studies on Internet addiction, identify a number of lingering theoretical and methodological issues, and offer some new thoughts on this line of research from a cross-cultural perspective.

11.2 (Re)conceptualizing Internet Addiction

It has been nearly twenty years since Dr. Ivan Goldberg, a clinical psychiatrist, first proposed Internet Addiction Disorder (IAD) as a satirical hoax (Young, 1998). Today, Internet addiction has been widely recognized as a serious mental health issue worldwide. For example, in Korea, Internet addiction has been estimated to affect up to 30% of Internet users under 18 and deemed a national health concern (Fackler, 2007; Ha, et al., 2007). In China, more than 10% of adolescent Internet users were identified as Internet addicts (Wu & Zhu, 2004); government sponsored treatment clinics and military style "detox" camps were established all over the country to treat this new "addiction".

Perhaps it was because the empirical research on Internet addiction first emerged in a clinical context (Young, 1998). Perhaps it was because the conditions experienced by those affected indeed share similar symptoms and consequences as found in other classified substance and behavioral addictions, or perhaps it was simply because the word "addiction" deeply resonated with the public; much of the existing research on

Internet addiction has focused on establishing the condition as a classified psychiatric disorder. From such an epidemiological perspective, researchers of Internet addiction primarily focused their attention on the following questions: 1) what is Internet addiction; 2) what are its symptoms; 3) how pervasive is the problem; 4) what are the causes and consequences of having this disorder; and 5) how to treat it. They used various labels—compulsive Internet use, pathological Internet use, Internet dependency, Internet addiction disorder, Internet usage disorder, and problematic Internet use—to describe the phenomenon. Different diagnostic criteria have been proposed, ranging from clinical interviews to structured questionnaires. In a recent comprehensive literature review of 69 large-scale empirical studies published since 2000, Kuss et al (2014) identified 21 different diagnostic instruments in six different languages. They also found that the reported prevalence rate of Internet addiction in these studies differ significantly as a consequence of different assessment tools and cut-offs.

Although researchers might disagree on the labeling, causes, and pervasiveness of the problem, most seem to agree that excessive use of the Internet can adversely affect users' physical, psychological, as well as social wellbeing (Beard, 2005; Ko et al, 2009; Leung & Lee, 2012; Yao, Ho, Ko, & Pang, 2013; Young, 2010). Heavy Internet users may develop a preoccupation with various online activities, increasingly feel the need to escape into cyberspace, and become irritable when trying to cut back their Internet use (Dell'Osso et al., 2006). These individuals may also experience a number of functional impairments as a result of Internet use, such as marital or family strife, job loss or decreased job productivity, and legal difficulties or school failure (Chou & Hsiao, 2000). Tokunaga and Rains (2010) conducted a meta-analysis of 94 studies from 22 different countries and found moderate and consistent links between loneliness, depression, and problematic Internet use. Kuss et al. (2013) also found that Internet addiction has been consistently associated with a number of sociodemographic and psychosocial factors, as well as being comorbid with other disorders in adolescents and adults.

Notwithstanding the value of the growing body of existing literature on Internet addiction, there are a number of lingering issues. First, previous research on Internet addiction seems to overlook the impact of technological changes on conceptual issues related to Internet addiction. In the past two decades, the "Internet" has gone from being a novel communication medium used by a tiny fraction of people in a handful of developed countries to being an omnipresent technological web connecting more than 40% of the world's population. Instead of merely allowing its users to exchange text messages with each other and retrieve static information from crudely designed webpages, the Internet today is deeply integrated into all aspects of human lives. It connects billions of people around the globe and provides them with useful information, facts, and entertainment almost anywhere at any time. As such, does it still make sense for researchers to treat "Internet use" as a generalized concept when discussing "internet addiction"? To this extent, some researchers proposed to study the potentially addictive online activities, such as gambling, gaming, and shopping, as separate conditions. However, as Internet users are spending more time and engage in more diverse social activities online, every online activity can potentially be abused.

Second, while previous research found various psychosocial and personality factors to be predictive of Internet addiction, the causal directions of the relationships between these variables and Internet addiction have not been clearly established (Chou et al., 2005; Kardefelt-Winther, 2014). For instance, does Internet addiction lead to depression and loneliness? Or, are depressed and lonely people more likely to be addicted to the Internet? Two competing views emerged in previous literature. On the one hand, Davis (2001) posited that existing psychopathological disorders, such as depression, loneliness, social anxiety, and substance dependence were necessary elements in the etiology of pathological Internet use. Specifically, people with these psychosocial dispositions would be more likely to use the Internet to escape from reality and thus are particularly prone to Internet addiction. On the other hand, Young and Roger (1998) suggested that excessive Internet use would damage users' real life social relationships and lead to social isolation, and in turn lead to more serious psychological problems such as depression. Although the results from two recent studies that utilized multiple-wave panel design show that Internet addiction might be the cause of depression and loneliness (Lam et al, 2012; Yao & Zhong, 2014), this finding is far from being conclusive.

A third concern, which is also the focus of this chapter, is the cross-cultural issue. For example, the prevalence rate of Internet addiction reported in Asian countries (e.g., Korea, Taiwan, & China) are consistently greater than in samples collected from European and North American countries. Although this pattern might be the result of measurement issues and sampling errors, there may be real cultural differences at work. Indeed, in much of the existing research on Internet addiction, mostly from an epidemiological perspective, researchers focus primarily on internal and individual variables; the cultural and societal level factors have been largely ignored. The cross-cultural validity of various diagnostic instruments is also seldom discussed. Furthermore, although Internet addiction was first proposed and studied by American researchers based on the diagnostic instruments developed in the American clinical context (Young, 1998), the bulk of recent studies seem to have been conducted in other countries. To illustrate this point, we searched PsycINFO, Proquest Health, and Medical Complete for articles concerning Internet addiction from 2003 to 2013 and identified a total of 179 empirical studies on Internet addiction with primary data. As can be seen from the summary table below (see Table 1), Taiwan, China, and South Korea accounted for nearly 42% of the studies on Internet addiction whereas only about 6% of the studies from the U.S. There is also a clear increase of studies conducted in Mediterranean and Eastern European countries in the recent years. The pattern clearly illustrates the urgency in adopting a cross-cultural approach to studying Internet addiction. In the following sections of this chapter we will review the existing literature on Internet addiction from a cross-cultural perspective. We will also propose several key methodological and theoretical issues to be considered in future research.

11.3 Cross cultural issues in IAD research

11.3.1 A cross-cultural consideration of IAD measurement

Prevalence of IAD worldwide differs based on region as well as age. For instance, some estimates in the US claim that 6% are considered addicted to the Internet (Greenfield, 1999), whereas one US university reported 15% of its student body could be considered addicted (Fortson, Scotti, Chen, Malone, & Del Ben, 2007), while another study suggested 18% of British students were (Niemz, Griffiths, & Banyard, 2005). In China, around 6% met the criteria for addiction (Deng, Hu, Hu, Wang, & Sun, 2007; Cao, Su, Liu, & Gao, 2007; Ni, Yan, Chen, & Liu, 2009). In a Taiwanese University, 17.9% were reportedly addicted to the Internet (Tsai et al., 2009). In South Korea, an estimated 18.1% of middle school students meet the criteria for Internet addiction (Seo, Kang, & Yom, 2009). However, there are many methodological issues in measurement that can cause fluctuations in the data. For example, depending on what measures are used, these reports vary widely, for instance, in South Korea alone, some reports show as low as 1.6% (Kim et al., 2006) or as high as 20.3% (Ha et al., 2007).

In a recent literature review, Kuss et al. (2013) identified and analyzed 21 different assessment instruments of IAD used in 68 epidemiological studies of Internet addiction published after 2000 with sample size larger than one thousand participants (see Kuss et al., 2013 for a full review of the principle characteristics of these measures). They attributed the inconsistencies in the prevalence rate of IAD to validity and reliability issues with the instruments. However, given the fact that out of the 68 studies reviewed in this research, 11 were conducted in China, 17 were from Taiwan, and 5 were from South Korea, and only 3 used samples from the U.S., a cultural difference explanation seems to be a strong alternative explanation that should be considered. In fact, Frangos and colleagues (2012) conducted a meta-analysis of problematic Internet usage to examine the reliability of using Young's Internet addiction test. They found that there are indeed cultural differences in the reliability of the measure in 20 studies. Specifically, the measure was more reliable when used in Asian populations than it was in Western populations like Europe. Although China and South Korea have deemed Internet Addiction a mental disorder and are creating programs to combat this, one must take pause on our reliance on self-reported IAD measures and its reliability in cross-cultural comparison.

Cross-cultural studies have shown that cultures may psychologically differ on a host of different areas, such as cognition (Bloom, 1984), sense of self (Markus & Kitayama, 1991), self-esteem (Heine, Lehman, Markus, & Kitayama, 1999; Kitayama, Markus, Matsumoto, & Norasakkunkit, 1997), emotions (Aaker & Williams, 1998), coping strategies (Kim, Sherman, Ko, & Taylor, 2006; Tweed, White, & Lehman, 2004), and causal attributions (Choi, Nisbett, & Norenzayan, 1999; Morris & Peng, 1994). Two cultural groups that have often been compared are Asian and Western samples because of the vast range in which they differ on some of these dimensions.

Table 11.1. A summary of Internet addiction prevalence studies 2003-2013 by origin of sample

	2003	2004	2005	2006	2007	2008	2009	2010	2011	2012	2013	Total	Percent
China		1		4	1	1	6	5	5	6	4	33	18.44%
Turkey						2	2	2	6	5	8	25	13.97%
Korea	1	1	2	1		2			3	3	8	21	11.73%
Taiwan	1	1		1	2	3	7	1	2		2	20	11.17%
U.S.	1	1		1	1		3		2	2		11	6.15%
Italy					1		4			3	1	9	5.03%
Greece						1		1		4	2	8	4.47%
Online general			1	1		1			1		3	7	3.91%
Iran						1		1	2	2		6	3.35%
Germany								2	1	1		4	2.23%
India	1								1		2	4	2.23%
Spain										1	2	3	1.68%
Unspecified						1		1			1	3	1.68%
Australia							1			1		2	1.12%
Czech Republic		1								1		2	1.12%
German								1	1			2	1.12%
Netherlands				1							1	2	1.12%
Northern Cyprus									1		1	2	1.12%
Norway		1					1					2	1.12%
U.K.						1					1	2	1.12%
Asian (general)										1		1	0.56%

continued **Table 11.1.** A summary of Internet addiction prevalence studies 2003-2013 by origin of sample

	2003	2004	2005	2006	2007	2008	2009	2010	2011	2012	2013	Total	Percent
Cremona										1		1	0.56%
Finland		1										1	0.56%
Hong Kong		1										1	0.56%
Hungary											1	1	0.56%
Israel										1		1	0.56%
Lebanon										1		1	0.56%
MMORPG players						1						1	0.56%
Serbia								1				1	0.56%
South Africa						1						1	0.56%
Sweden									1			1	0.56%
Grand Total	4	8	3	9	5	15	24	15	26	33	37	179	100.00%

Because psychological theory and diagnosis has arisen in the West, it is important to recognize the boundaries and cultural biases that may be inherent in the measures and assumptions it produces.

For instance, two important dimensions implicated in the study of IAD are individualism/collectivism (Triandis, 1989) and independent/interdependent self-construals (Markus & Kitayama, 1991). Cultures may differ on a societal level. For instance, Individualistic cultures such as those found in the West, like North America and Europe, may focus more on the individual and his/her own autonomy and personal feelings and reactions to his/her own environment (Triandis, 1989). Collectivist cultures such as those found in Asia, like China, Japan, and, Korea may focus more on the group or on maintaining strong relationships among individuals (Triandis, 1989). This is important in understanding the societal artifacts and values that influence individuals of that culture.

Likewise, cultures may differ on an individual level. For instance, culture may shape how an individual perceives the self. An independent self-construal is associated more with individualist cultures (Markus & Kitayama, 1991), focusing on the self as an autonomous being whose actions, thoughts, and beliefs are managed by and relate solely to the individual. On the other hand, an interdependent self-construal (Markus & Kitayama, 1991), associated more with collectivist cultures, focuses on the self as connected and interrelated to close others such that thoughts may be evaluated on how they are shared with close others and actions are evaluated on how they may affect social relationships and their societal roles. Culture influences how individuals see themselves and it provides guidance on what components of the self are important to protect and nurture.

Cultural motivations in terms of how and why individuals use the Internet are often neglected but may be driving forces in explaining the prevalence and also the difference of Internet addiction between cultures.

One of the problems in bridging the cultural gap may be in how IAD measurement has arisen. As a clinical disorder based off of gambling addiction from the DSM-IV (Young, 1998), most IAD measurements have been founded on a Western model of mental illness and have subsequently been translated but perhaps not adjusted to culturally express mental illness. Although IAD has been addressed from a clinical perspective, it has neglected to abide by common clinical practices in confronting the universality and cultural diversity of the "disorder." Westermeyer and Janca (1997) outlined cultural factors that needed to be addressed for accurate psychiatric diagnosis. For instance, patient perceptions regarding illness and the way in which an individual describes problems may differ by culture. Similarly, individuals may vary by culture on how often they report symptoms depending on how taboo or how acceptable it is to disclose.

This poses a few problems in determining external validity of IAD measures. First, problems or consequences from heavy Internet usage may be different from one culture to another. Lortie and Guitton (2013) examined 14 questionnaires measuring

Internet addiction among 360 studies from 1993-2011. For most studies that they examined, authors did not publish evidence of criterion validity, suggesting that these measures do not differentiate between normal and "pathological" users. Behaviors or mental states are considered problematic or pathological when they disrupt daily life and cause the individual distress. For instance, individuals from a collectivist culture may not consider constantly connecting to the Internet a problem until it damaged personal relationships and harmed one's capacity to fulfill societal roles (Suh et al., 1998). Likewise, for those from individualistic cultures, Internet addiction may only become problematic when it leads to negative personal thoughts like depression or diminished self-worth (Heine et al., 2001; Lee, Aaker, & Gardner, 2000).

Secondly, individuals may look to their environment to gain information about what is considered "abnormal" and also what may be considered shameful. Because IAD measures are largely self-reported, individual responses can be colored by their own reference group or cultural standards (Heine, Lehman, Peng & Greenholtz, 2002; Peng, Nisbett, & Wong, 1997). For instance, individuals from collectivist cultures, specifically Asian cultures, have been shown to emphasize self-criticism and self-improvement over self-promotion or self-enhancement as it is more beneficial in harmonizing with groups (Heine et al., 1999; Kitayama, Markus, Matsumoto & Norasakkunkit, 1997). Those from collectivist cultures may be more attuned to negative consequences from Internet usage, especially if it damages their ability to perform social responsibilities. For instance, Asians may respond to items from Young's IAT (1998) such as "how often do others in your life complain to you about the amount of time you spend on-line?" "how often do you choose to spend more time on-line over going out with others?" more negatively because they attend to these issues more or these issues are more disruptive to their everyday lives than for those from the West.

Similarly, Heine and colleagues (2002) found that manipulating one's reference group influenced responses to common likert-type scales, such as those used in all IAD measures. Participants filled out questionnaires either with no prompt or with a prompt saying "in comparison to" either their ingroup or an outgroup. Consistent with their hypotheses, Japanese responses were largely influenced by reference groups whereas European Canadian responses were not, suggesting that those from collectivist cultures such as Japan may look towards important reference groups to evaluate their own behaviors and values, whereas those from individualistic cultures such as Canada use internal standards rather than reference groups. Similarly, for a highly technologically integrated society, depictive of much of Asia, an individual may judge the frequency of their actions as normal, whereas in another culture the frequency would be considered abnormal. Currently, most IAD measures have standardized scoring systems marking normal to dysfunctional Internet usage based mostly on Western data (CITE). By defining culturally meaningful baselines of Internet usage, researchers may more accurately assess individuals who are at more psychological risk from overusage of the Internet.

Not only do most IAD measures disregard reference groups and cultural norms in their self-report measures, the anchors for the Likert-type scales are highly subjective. For instance, Young's IAT (1998) uses anchors such as "rarely", "occasionally", "frequently", "often", and "always". These items can mean different things to different people in a single culture, and even more when looking at more than one culture. For instance, individuals from a mature Internet-integrated culture may believe "frequently" means over 10 hours a day, whereas for an individual from emerging Internet-integrated cultures, "frequently" may mean 3 hours a day. Indeed, Internet penetration differs widely, and the numbers for Asian countries speaks to the differences in IAD. Although North America has an Internet penetration level of 78.6% and Europe at 63.2%, top Asian countries' Internet penetration levels such as Taiwan (75.4%), South Korea (82.5%), and Hong Kong (74.5%) show massive growth, with China, accountable for 50% of Internet users in Asia, has an Internet penetration of 40% (Internet World Stats, 2012). Using subjective or abstract anchors can reduce cultural comparability because the definitions may vary from culture to culture.

In sum, although there are marked differences between Asia and the West in their responses to IAD measures, methodological issues should be taken into consideration before jumping to conclusions or creating government task forces to tackle this new social problem. For instance, the definition of problematic use and the consequences of Internet usage may differ between cultures. Using ambiguous anchors and neglecting possible referential group factors can create cultural artifacts that adversely affect an accurate diagnosis. These aspects challenge the assumptions of current IAD measures and should impel us to reconsider the ways in which we construct Internet diagnostic material.

Although more cross-cultural research should be done on definitions, behaviors, and consequences of Internet usage, simple adjustments to current measures can help to address some of the methodological problems posed in this chapter. For instance, Lortie and Guitton (2013) recommend verifying questionnaires with reports from close family and friends. Further, they offer improvements to existing internet addiction questionnaires, suggesting that they rely on the negative and maladaptive consequences of overuse in personal, familial, and professional settings as well as personal distress caused. Heine and colleagues (2002) suggest creating questionnaires that specify contexts and concretize anchors. For instance, "frequently" is more subjective than "twice a day" and more prone to reference group effects. Psychological symptoms such as control over emotions or thoughts, definition of harm, and awareness of the environment may differ between cultures (Westermeyer & Janca 1997), whereas concrete behaviors, scenarios, and biometric data may be more useful to compare cross-culturally (Peng, Nisbett, & Wong, 1997). Lastly, we propose adapting IAD measures to have more culturally relevant scoring systems by taking into account baseline measures of normal and abnormal Internet usage and behavior. If there truly is an Internet addiction "epidemic" in Asia then the materials should take the cultural context into consideration in how the data is obtained.

11.3.2 A cross-cultural consideration in Internet adoption and user behavior

Another aspect that one must consider in cross-cultural research is what understanding of cultural differences actually means. For instance, Van de Vijver and Leung (2000) argue that observed differences do not always constitute real cross-cultural differences. As an example, heightened Internet usage may look detrimental in the West but is considered normal in Asia because of structural constraints in Internet connectivity of a given country or region. They suggest that one problem in conducting psychological research cross-culturally is that researchers neglect the environmental and social context in which they take their samples.

Although much research has been conducted on IAD, few measures look at the important social drives nurtured in online interaction. For instance, taking other important contextual variables such as need to belong and Internet penetration into consideration may explain some of the cultural differences observed. Lortie and Guitton (2013) reported that current assessment tools and the DSM-IV-TR and ICD-10 base measurement on criteria focus on compulsion, consequences, and salience towards excessive Internet usage. Because social rewards may be a large motivating factor for individuals to use the Internet (Caplan, 2007; Chak & Leung, 2004; Douglas et al., 2008; Erwin, Heimberg, Fresco, & Hantula, 2003), its absence in measurement is startling. Kuss and colleagues (2013) confirmed that social applications (such as Twitter and social networking sites) strongly predicted Internet addiction. Similarly, Kardefelt-Winther (2014) proposes that it is not the compulsiveness or mental illness that causes excessive Internet use, but the Internet's ability to fill social needs or act as a coping strategy for negative feelings.

Not only are rates of adoption different between the East and the West, the way in which Internet is used may also differ. Qiu, Lin, and Leung (2013) suggest that online environments may act similarly to offline environments in how they enforce and promote cultural norms. Looking at different social networking sites between the East and West also sheds light on how cultures influence the way that social networking is established and structured. For instance, those from collectivist cultures and individualist cultures differ in how they structure relationships and how they communicate ideas and feelings. de Mooji (2014) suggests that individuals from the West use the Internet more for information searching and sharing, whereas those in the East use the Internet more for maintaining and strengthening social ties. If individuals from different cultures derive a different sense of utility from the Internet, it also implies that the motivations towards Internet use and perhaps problematic use differ as well.

Even the same platform can expose cultural differences as individuals may utilise them for culturally specific social goals. Chapman and Lahav (2008) showed that even within social media, user behavior differed by country. For those from the West, individuals were more user-centric and less intimate; Americans used SNS to self promote and share pictures of themselves and the French have nonpersonal conversations or discussions. For those from the East, individuals were more ingroup-oriented; Koreans shared pictures only with close others in a tight ingroup and Chinese users played multi-user games and shared resources together (Chapman & Lahav, 2008). Thus the Internet may serve different purposes, highlighting different types of needs for belonging and cultural expression.

Although the same Internet structures can provide a glimpse into how different cultures' values and beliefs influence their online behavior, so too can one look towards how cultures create Internet structures that promote cultural norms and values. Social networks that develop in different countries also may inherently structure their sites to reflect the norms of relationships within that society. For instance, in Cyworld, the largest social networking site in Korea, Cho (2010) found that individuals had a stronger division between ingroups and outgroups through their use of privacy settings. Americans were also shown to use more direct speech, whereas Koreans used more nonverbal expressions (e.g., emoticons), in line with predictions based on cultural differences in communication expression.

Individuals may also be sensitive to cultural influences on different Internet platforms. Japanese users on both Japanese social networking sites (SNS) Mixi and American SNS Facebook develop and maintain relationships in different ways (Thomson & Ito, 2012). Japanese users on Mixi have fewer friends but stronger commitment and connection to those friends with fewer direct self-disclosures. However, on Facebook, the same Japanese participants used more self-disclosure and had a broader friend network with less commitment, indicative of a Western framework of relationship formation. They suggest that these differences are due to the Japanese participants' perception of differences in relational mobility (Thomson & Ito, 2012), similar to the concept of independent and interdependent self-construals in which an individual can fluidly make and break social relationships (independent self-construal) because they are not interconnected and extrinsically linked to one another (interdependent self-construal), diminishing mobility in and out of social groups.

These studies suggest that Internet structures such as SNS are artifacts of their culture and promote specific types of behaviors and beliefs. The way in which individuals use the Internet may be guided by the various platforms that sustain these distinct cultural norms.

This poses a problem in how psychologists have approached Internet addiction in a number of ways. First, the social motivations to connect to the Internet are not measured in the majority of IAD measures (Lortie & Guitton, 2013; Van de Vijver & Leung, 2000). Young people are often the largest focus of IAD and they also are most motivated towards social interaction. Secondly, IAD measures do not distinguish between cultures on the social implications that the Internet presents. For those from highly collectivist cultures, high Internet usage may indicate strong relational cohesion and maintenance of group norms if they use the Internet for social purposes. On the other hand, for those from highly individualistic cultures, high internet usage may indicate a stronger need for self-expression and individual acceptance. Although both may require an audience, the needs of the individual and subsequent social consequences differ. For instance, excessive Internet usage in the West may be linked to depression and low self-esteem, whereas in the East it may be linked with social anxiety and loneliness. Kardefelt-Winther (2014) criticized IAD research because of its inability to identify clear causal links to IAD. Predictive validity may be confounded not only by the lack of social motivation measures, but also because of the cultural consequences an individual anticipates.

A cross-cultural consideration in mental health problem diagnosis and treatment

In comparison to other groups in America, Asians are consistently low in utilizing mental health services (Atkinson, Lowe, & Matthews, 1995; Chang, Yeh, & Krumboltz, 2001; Matsuoka, Breaux, & Ryujin, 1997; Sue, Fujino, Hu, Takeuchi, & Zane, 1991). Broadly speaking across Asia, mental health care varies from country to country (Deva, 2002) with most psychiatric care residing in urban areas (Lauber & Rössler, 2006). Further, depending on the Asian country treatment varies, sometimes using local alternative medicines, healers, mental health professionals, or combinations of these treatments (Ng, 1997). Similarly, the dialogue around mental illness is different from the West because of the focus on physical problems, as well as the holistic belief that mental and physical ailments are intertwined (Fabrega, Jr., 2001). For instance, the symptoms that Asians may notice in IAD may focus on or add entirely different symptoms to IAD compared to how it is described in the West because of how one experiences mental illness in different cultures. Thus how cultures talk about and treat mental illnesses such as IAD should be researched further and accounted for in culturally appropriate IAD measurements.

Further barriers which may partly explain why Asians (in both America and Asia) are less likely to seek help is the stigma attached to mental illness (Tseng et al., 2001). A study in Hong Kong showed that individuals found symptoms of mental illness to be merely reactions to stress, not recognizing them as symptoms of mental disorders, and are more likely to focus on somatic versus psychological symptoms (Chung, Chen, Lam, Chen & Chan, 1997). This may be dangerous because it suggests that mental illnesses should be within an individual's control to handle and reduces the need to seek help for such illnesses.

Mental illness may be stigmatic not only because of how individuals perceive mental illness in general, but also because of the implications it presents to relationships and social perception (Kim, Sherman, & Taylor, 2008; Ng, 1997; Taylor et al., 2004). Ng (1997) found that most Asian societies, mental illnesses are first handled within the family, with family members providing support financially or instrumentally through known channels before seeking outside help. Further, the individual shame associated with mental disorders in the West are expanded within collectivist cultures such that mental disorders may be associated with shame towards individuals and their families and close friends. Therefore seeking help for mental illness in Asian cultures means not only shaming the family, but also tasking them with the responsibility of providing help. Indeed, Kim, Sherman, Ko, and Taylor (2006) found that in social support seeking among Asians as compared to European Americans, Asians seek support less from close family and friends and their stress is aggravated by seeking help from close others. This finding suggests that seeking help may have relational consequences.

Kim and colleagues (2006) found that implicit forms of social support seeking, such as being reminded of one's social network and interacting with close others without disclosing stressful information, was more effective in reducing stress for Asian Americans than explicit forms of social support seeking, such as talking to someone about one's problems or stress. Thus how individuals may seek help for IAD may differ by culture. This may also point to an alternative explanation for how excessive Internet usage may be confounded with help-seeking behaviors.

As we have suggested earlier on, the importance of certain functions online may differ from culture to culture. We've looked at cultural differences in social networking sites, with Asians showing more personal and smaller friendship groups and exhibiting more intimate interactions online than those from the West. Heavy usage of the Internet may be problematic in and of itself, however it may serve as a culturally acceptable coping strategy in Asian culture.For instance, Chang, Yeh, and Krumbholtz (2001) created an online support group for Asian American males, as they are demographic that is most likely to not use mental health services and are more likely to prematurely terminate care (O'Sullivan, Peterson, Cox, & Kirkeby, 1989; Sue, 1977). As online networks may help to reduce shame (since interactions are not face-to-face and may be anonymous), allow individuals to think and edit before providing responses, and are more easily accessible, not only did individuals feel supported by the group, all participants stayed in the online support group for the 4 week intervention (Chang et al., 2001). Thus Asian males may receive psychological benefits from interacting online because it reduces social anxiety and the shame associated with turning to their family or friends for explicit help or social support. One of the problems with IAD measures is only focusing on the possible consequences of Internet overuse, but not taking into account the benefits of Internet use which reward and encourage this overuse. Merely focusing on the negative consequences of and solutions to minimize problematic Internet use is short-sighted if reducing Internet use may cut off avenues of social support and cause more problems.

11.4 Conclusion

Internet addiction, although very real, suffers from many methodological and social oversights since its inception in the late 90s. Much has changed in our relationship with the Internet and what purpose itis used for, although we still use the same few IAD measures as when the Internet was in its infancy. Addressing cultural nuances is an exercise not only in conceptualizing Internet addiction but also creating meaningful tools to measure it.

Methodological issues often become more apparent when trying to compare cross-culturally. For instance, the lack of concrete anchors or behaviors leaves many of the statements too open ended. These generalized items are subject to the biased interpretations inherent within one's culture. Individuals also often turn to meaningful referent groups to assess what is considered acceptable and what is considered excessive. Cultural differences in value systems may also cause individuals to emphasize some consequences over others. Is hypersocialization over the internet considered dysfunctional or is it an acceptable means of maintaining one's social capital? Rethinking the structure of IAD measures to describe more of the context in which individuals use the Internet, what specific consequences arise, and quantify responses may be a first step in giving researchers a more "apples to apples" comparison between cultures. Further, establishing baselines as to what is considered abnormal or acceptable within each culture and what thresholds cause psychological harm will make results more meaningful, rather than having Western standardized cut-off points in scoring.

More importantly, in order to treat problematic Internet usage and addiction the cultural context needs to be examined because of its relevance tounderstanding underlying motivations and rewards for Internet usage. As previously discussed, the East and the West have been shown to differ on motivations towards information sharing and maintaining social relationships online. Even within social behavior online, motivations between the two can still be seen in how individuals nurture either individualistic concerns for self-presentation versus collectivistic concerns for relational cohesion. Because cultures carry many of their offline values into their online presence, researchers must acknowledge these values and drives in interpreting certain online behaviors. Further, practitioners need to understand what benefits are derived from using the Internet in order to help clients reduce their usage in a healthy and sustainable way. Knowing how culture promotes these benefits can help drive more effective therapies. Similarly, one issue practitioners and researchers must consider is whether or not problematic Internet usage is actually a beneficial coping strategy, especially in Asian cultures, where reducing Internet usage would actually take away important psychological, social, and instrumental resources.

Although this is not a comprehensive list of cross-cultural considerations, this chapter serves to open a dialogue among researchers internationally to more accurately examine and help individuals suffering from IAD, as well as to lay a conceptual foundation that takes into account the dynamic ways in which cultures use and are affected by the Internet.

References

Aaker, J. L., & Williams, P. (1998). Empathy versus pride: The influence of emotional appeals across cultures. Journal of Consumer Research, 25(3), 241-261.

Atkinson, D. R., Lowe, S., & Matthews, L. (1995). Asian-American Acculturation, Gender, and Willingness to Seek Counseling. Journal of Multicultural Counseling & Development, 23(3), 130-138. doi: 10.1002/j.2161-1912.1995.tb00268.x

Beard, K. W. (2005). Internet addiction: A review of current assessment techniques and potential assessment questions. Cyberpsychology & Behavior, 8(1), 7-14. doi: 10.1089/cpb.2005.8.7.

Cao, F., Su, L., Liu, T., & Gao, X. (2007). The relationship between impulsivity and Internet addiction in a sample of Chinese adolescents. European Psychiatry, 22(7), 466-471.

Caplan, S. E. (2007). Relations Among Loneliness, Social Anxiety, and Problematic Internet Use. Cyberpsychology & Behavior, 10(2), 234-242. doi: 10.1089/cpb.2006.9963

Chak, K., & Leung, L. (2004). Shyness and locus of control as predictors of Internet addiction and Internet use. Cyberpsychology & Behavior, 7(5), 559-570.

Chang, T., Yeh, C. J., & Krumboltz, J. D. (2001). Process and Outcome Evaluation of an Online-Support Group for Asian American Male College Students. Journal of Counseling Psychology, 48(3), 319-329.

Cho, S. E. . (2010). Cross-cultural comparison of Korean and American social network sites: exploring cultural differences in social relationships and self-presentation. (Doctoral dissertation), Rutgers University, New Brunswick. Retrieved from http://mss3.libraries.rutgers.edu/dlr/showfed.php?pid=rutgers-lib:26520

Choi, I., Nisbett, R. E., & Norenzayan, A. (1999). Causal attribution across cultures: Variation and universality. Psychological Bulletin, 125(1), 47-63.

Chou, C., Condron, L., & Belland, J. C. (2005). A review of the research on Internet addiction. Educational Psychology Review, 17(4), 363-388. doi: 10.1007/s10648-005-8138-1

Chou, C., & Hsiao, M. C. (2000). Internet addiction, usage, gratification, and pleasure experience: the Taiwan college students' case. Computers & Education, 35(1), 65-80. doi: 10.1016/S0360-1315(00)00019-1

Chung, K. F., Chen, E. Y. H., Lam, L. C. W., Chen, R. Y. L., & Chan, C. K. Y. (1997). How are psychotic symptoms perceived? A comparison between patients, relatives and the general public. Australian and New Zealand Journal of Psychiatry, 31(5), 756-761. doi: 10.3109/00048679709062691

Davis, R. A. (2001). A cognitive-behavioral model of pathological Internet use. Computers in Human Behavior, 17(2), 187-195. doi: 10.1016/S0747-5632(00)00041-8

Dell'Osso, B., Altamura, A. C., Allen, A., Marazziti, D., & Hollander, E. (2006). Epidemiologic and clinical updates on impulse control disorders - A critical review. European Archives of Psychiatry and Clinical Neuroscience, 256(8), 464-475. doi: 10.1007/s00406-006-0668-0

Deng, Y.X., Hu, M., Hu, G.Q., Wang, L.S., & Sun, Z.Q. (2007). An investigation on the prevalence of Internet addiction disorder in middle school students of Hunan province. Zhonghua Liu Xing Bing Xue Za Zhi, 28(5), 445-448.

Deva, M. (2002). Mental health and mental care in Asia. World Psychiatry, 1, 118-120.

Douglas, A. C., Mills, J. E., Niang, M., Stepchenkova, S., Byun, S., Ruffini, C., . . . Blanton, M. (2008). Internet addiction: Meta-synthesis of qualitative research for the decade 1996-2006. Computers in Human Behavior, 24(6), 3027-3044. doi: 10.1016/J.Chb.2008.05.009

Erwin, B. A., Turk, C. L., Heimberg, R. G., Fresco, D. M., & Hantula, D. A. (2004). The Internet: home to a severe population of individuals with social anxiety disorder? Journal of Anxiety Disorders, 18(5), 629-646. doi: 10.1016/j.janxdis.2003.08.002

Fabrega, H., Jr. (2001). Culture and history in psychiatric diagnosis and practice. Psychiatric Clinics of North America, 24(3), 391-405. doi: 10.1016/S0193-953X(05)70236-7
Fackler, M. (2007). In Korea, a Boot Camp Cure for Web Obsession, New York Times. Retrieved from http://www.nytimes.com/2007/11/18/technology/18rehab.html?pagewanted=all&_r=0
Fortson, B. L., Scotti, J. R., Chen, Y-C., Malone, J., & Del Ben, K. S. (2007). Internet Use, Abuse, and Dependence Among Students at a Southeastern Regional University. Journal of American College Health, 56(2), 137-144. doi: 10.3200/JACH.56.2.137-146
Greenfield, D. (1999). Virtual addiction: Help for netheads, cyberfreaks, and those who love them. Oakland, CA: New Harbinger.
Griffiths, D. (2005, October 10). Treating China's online addicts. BBC News. Retrieved March 20, 2014, from http://news.bbc.co.uk/2/hi/4327258.stm
Ha, J. H., Kim, S. Y., Bae, S., C., Bae, S., Kim, H., Sim, M., . . . Cho, S. C. (2007). Depression and Internet Addiction in Adolescents. Psychopathology, 40(6), 424-430. doi: 10.1159/000107426
Heine, S. J., Lehman, D. R., Markus, H. R., & Kitayama, S. (1999). Is there a universal need for positive self-regard? Psychological Review, 106(4), 766-794.
Heine, S. J., Lehman, D. R., Peng, K. P., & Greenholtz, J. (2002). What's wrong with cross-cultural comparisons of subjective likert scales?: The reference-group effect. Journal of Personality and Social Psychology, 82(6), 903-918. doi: Doi 10.1037//0022-3514.82.6.903
Kardefelt-Winther, Daniel. (2014). A conceptual and methodological critique of internet addiction research: Towards a model of compensatory internet use. Computers in Human Behavior, 31, 351-354. doi: 10.1016/j.chb.2013.10.059
Kim, H. S., Sherman, D. K., Ko, D., & Taylor, S. E. (2006). Pursuit of comfort and pursuit of harmony: Culture, relationships, and social support seeking. Personality and Social Psychology Bulletin, 32(12), 1595-1607. doi: 10.1177/0146167206291991
Kim, H. S., Sherman, D. K., & Taylor, S. E. (2008). Culture and social support. American Psychologist, 63(6), 518-526. doi: 10.1037/0003-066x
Kim, K., Ryu, E., Chon, M. Y., Yeun, E. J., Choi, S. Y., Seo, J. S., & Nam, B. W. (2006). Internet addiction in Korean adolescents and its relation to depression and suicidal ideation: A questionnaire survey. International Journal of Nursing Studies, 43(2), 185-192. doi: 10.1016/j.ijnurstu.2005.02.005
Kitayama, S., Markus, H. R., Matsumoto, H., & Norasakkunkit, V. (1997). Individual and collective processes in the construction of the self: Self-enhancement in the United States and self-criticism in Japan. Journal of Personality and Social Psychology, 72(6), 1245-1267.
Ko, C. H., Yen, J. Y., Chen, C. S., Yeh, Y. C., & Yen, C. F. (2009). Predictive Values of Psychiatric Symptoms for Internet Addiction in Adolescents A 2-Year Prospective Study. Archives of Pediatrics & Adolescent Medicine, 163(10), 937-943. doi: 10.1001/archpediatrics.2009.159
Ko, C. H., Yen, J. Y., Liu, S. C., Huang, C. F., & Yen, C. F. (2009). The Associations Between Aggressive Behaviors and Internet Addiction and Online Activities in Adolescents. Journal of Adolescent Health, 44(6), 598-605. doi: 10.1016/j.jadohealth.2008.11.011
Kuss, D. J., Griffiths, M. D., Karila, L., & Billieux, J. (2013). Internet Addiction: A Systematic Review of Epidemiological Research for the Last Decade. Current Pharmaceutical Design, 19, 1-26. doi: 10.2174/13816128113199990617
Lee, A. Y., Aaker, J. L., & Gardner, W. L. (2000). The pleasures and pains of distinct self-construals: The role of interdependence in regulatory focus. Journal of Personality and Social Psychology, 78(6), 1122-1134. doi: 10.1037//0022-3514.78.6.1122
Leung, L., & Lee, P. S. N. (2012). Impact of Internet Literacy, Internet Addiction Symptoms, and Internet Activities on Academic Performance. Social Science Computer Review, 30(4), 403-418. doi: 10.1177/0894439311435217

Leung, L., & Lee, P. S. N. (2012). The influences of information literacy, internet addiction and parenting styles on internet risks. New Media & Society, 14(1), 117-136. doi: 10.1177/1461444811410406

Lortie, C. L., & Guitton, M. J. (2013). Internet addiction assessment tools: dimensional structure and methodological status. Addiction, 108(7), 1207-1216. doi: 10.1111/Add.12202

Markus, H. R., & Kitayama, S. (1991). Culture and the Self: Implications for Cognition, Emotion, and Motivation. Psychological Review, 98(2), 224-253. doi: 10.1037/0033-295X.98.2.224

Matsuoka, J. K., Breaux, C., & Ryujin, D. H. (1997). National utilization of mental health services by Asian Americans Pacific Islanders. Journal of Community Psychology, 25(2), 141-145. doi: Doi 10.1002/(Sici)1520-6629(199703)25:2<141::Aid-Jcop3>3.0.Co;2-0

Morris, M. W., & Peng, K. (1994). Culture and Cause: American and Chinese Attributions for Social and Physical Events. Journal of Personality and Social Psychology, 67(6), 949-971.

Ng, C. H. (1997). The stigma of mental illness in Asian cultures. Australian and New Zealand Journal of Psychiatry, 31(3), 382-390. doi: 10.3109/00048679709073848

Ni, X., Yan, H., Chen, S., & Liu, Z. (2009). Factors Influencing Internet Addiction in a Sample of Freshmen University Students in China. Cyberpsychology & Behavior, 12(3), 327-330. doi: 10.1089/cpb.2008.0321

Niemz, K., Griffiths, M., & Banyard, P. (2005). Prevalence of pathological Internet use among university students and correlations with self-esteem, the general health questionnaire (GHQ), and disinhibition. Cyberpsychology & Behavior, 8(6), 562-570. doi: 10.1089/cpb.2005.8.562

O'sullivan, M. J., Peterson, P. D., Cox, G. B., & Kirkeby, J. (1989). Ethnic Populations - Community Mental-Health Services 10 Years Later. American Journal of Community Psychology, 17(1), 17-30. doi: 10.1007/Bf00931200

Peng, K. P., Nisbett, R. E., & Wong, N. Y. C. (1997). Validity problems comparing values across cultures and possible solutions. Psychological Methods, 2(4), 329-344. doi: 10.1037/1082-989x.2.4.329

Qiu, L., Lin, H., & Leung, A. K. Y. (2013). Cultural Differences and Switching of In-Group Sharing Behavior Between an American (Facebook) and a Chinese (Renren) Social Networking Site. Journal of Cross-Cultural Psychology, 44(1), 106-121. doi: 10.1177/0022022111434597

Seo, M., Kang, H. S., & Yom, Y. H. (2009). Internet Addiction and Interpersonal Problems in Korean Adolescents. Computers Informatics Nursing, 27(4), 226-233. doi: 10.1097/NCN.0b013e3181a91b3f

Sue, S. (1977). Community mental health services to minority groups: Some optimism, some pessimism. American Psychologist, 32(8), 616-624. doi: 10.1037/0003-066X.32.8.616

Sue, S., Fujino, D. C., Hu, L. T., Takeuchi, D. T., & Zane, N. W. S. (1991). Community mental health services for ethnic minority groups: A test of the cultural responsiveness hypothesis. Journal of Consulting and Clinical Psychology, 59(4), 533-540. doi: 10.1037//0022-006x.59.4.533

Suh, E., Diener, E., Oishi, S., & Triandis, H. C. (1998). The Shifting Basis of Life Satisfaction Judgments across Cultures: Emotions versus Norms. Journal of Personality and Social Psychology, 74(2), 482-493.

Thomson, R., & Ito, N. (2012). The effect of relational mobility on SNS user behavior : A study of Japanese dual-users of Mixi and Facebook. The Journal of International Media, Communication, and Tourism Studies, 14, 3-22.

Tokunaga, R. S., & Rains, S. A. (2010). An Evaluation of Two Characterizations of the Relationships Between Problematic Internet Use, Time Spent Using the Internet, and Psychosocial Problems. Human Communication Research, 36(4), 512-545. doi: 10.1111/j.1468-2958.2010.01386.x

Triandis, H. C. (1989). The self and social behavior in differing cultural contexts. Psychological Review, 96(3), 506-520. doi: 10.1037//0033-295x.96.3.506

Tsai, H. F., Cheng, S. H., Yeh, T. L., Shih, C-C., Chen, K. C., Yang, Y. C., & Yang, Y. K. (2009). The risk factors of Internet addiction-A survey of university freshmen. Psychiatry Research, 167(3), 294-299. doi: 10.1016/j.psychres.2008.01.015

Tseng, W-S., Ebata, K., Kim, K-I., Krahl, W., Kua, E. H., Tan, E-S., & Yang, M-J. (2001). Mental health in Asia: social improvements and challenges. International Journal of Social Psychiatry, 47(1), 8-23. doi: 10.1177/002076400104700102

Tweed, R. G., White, K., & Lehman, D. R. (2004). Culture, stress, and coping

Internally- and externally-targeted control strategies of European Canadians, East Asian Canadians, and Japanese. Journal of Cross-Cultural Psychology, 35(6), 652-668. doi: 10.1177/0022022104270109

Van de Vijver, F. J. R., & Leung, K. (2001). Personality in cultural context: Methodological issues. Journal of Personality, 69(6), 1007-1031.

Wu, H. R., & Zhu, K. J. (2004). Path analysis on related factors causing internet addiction disorder in college students. Chinese Journal of Public Health, 20, 1363-1364.

Yao, M. Z., He, J., Ko, D. M., & Pang, K. (2014). The influence of personality, parental behaviors, and self-esteem on Internet addiction: A study of Chinese college students. CyberPsychology, Behavior & Social Networking, 17(2), 104-110. doi: 10.1089/cyber.2012.0710

Yao, M. Z., & Zhong, Z-j. (2014). Loneliness, social contacts and Internet addiction: A cross-lagged panel study. Computers in Human Behavior, 30, 164-170. doi: 10.1016/j.chb.2013.08.007

Young, K. (2010). Killer surf issues: Crafting an organizational model to combat employee Internet abuse. Information Management Journal, 44(1), 34-38.

Young, K. (2010). Policies and procedures to manage employee Internet abuse. Computers in Human Behavior, 26(6), 1467-1471. doi: 10.1016/j.chb.2010.04.025

Young, K. S. (1998). Caught in the net: How to recognize the signs of Internet addiction and a winning strategy for recovery. New York, NY: J. Wiley.

Young, K. S., & Rogers, R. C. (1998). The Relationship Between Depression and Internet Addiction. Cyberpsychology & Behavior, 1(1), 25-28. doi: 10.1089/cpb.1998.1.25

Nicholas David Bowman, Jaime Banks, Edward Downs

12 My pixels or my friends? Game characters as a lens for understanding user avatars in social networks

Abstract: In various interactive digital media, users create representations for themselves – be they images, texts, or interactive characters – that are used mark the user's identity, function, role, or position in the social landscape. These representations, or avatars, can exist separate from the user who created them. As such, they can be crafted, performed, experimented with, and reflected upon. In this separation, users may experience their own avatars, engaging them more or less as 'me' or 'not-me' as a function of user and avatar agencies. To better understand these dynamics, in this chapter we draw from current perspectives on a particular type of user-avatar pair – video game players and their graphic in-game characters – to theoretically and empirically contextualize the range of relationships users may have with their digital representations in a variety of social networking platforms, and how those relationships may differently influence social interactions online. Tracing the trajectory of the earliest audience-character scholarship from 1920s scholarship (the parasocial perspective) to emerging findings that gamers sometimes engage their avatars as autonomous social agents, we argue for a relational continuum that demonstrates the full range of non-social, parasocial and fully social relationships that communication technology users can have with their digital avatars.

12.1 Introduction

> Snot: "Steve, you are the king of Dragonscuffle"
> Steve: "Peasant! I am not Steve."
> Snot: "Forgive me, oh, great and powerful Agathor!"
> Steve: "As punishment for your insolence, you must now carry my Backpack of Holding"
> [later]
> Jeff: "Don't you feel like you're kind of missing out on your actual life?"
> Steve: "See, the problem is that in the "real world," things often suck. But when I'm Agathor ... there is no pain, no wedges, no heartache, only ... victory.

In the above dialogue – from the US animated comedy "American Dad" – best friends Steve and Snot debate the influence of Steve's video game supremacy (as the user behind Agathor, the most powerful warrior in the fictitious Kingdom of Krathnor) on his relative supremacy in their hometown of Langley Falls, Virginia. When questioned later by a mutual friend, Steven explains that Agathor is a far more powerful and successful person that he could ever hope to be (several scenes in the episode "Dungeons and Wagons" show flocks of in-game characters gathering around Agathor to celebrate his many battle victories), and spends the balance of the episode attempting to exert his in-game popularity into the "real world", with predictably hilarious results.

In the same way that Steve crafted and performed a warrior persona in his digital world as a way of experimenting with social desirability (and reflecting upon the effectiveness of this in his out-of-game interactions with Snot), social networking users often create idealized representations of themselves as a part of their daily social interactions (cf. Walther, 1996). As these interactions reach seeming ubiquity and deeper intimacy, the nature and function of users' digital presences plays an increasingly important role in social networking. From profile images and screen names to more complex digital bodies, these representations – or avatars – mediate these interactions and by design permit users to craft purposeful identities in digital spaces.

'Avatar' is a derivative of the Sanskrit avatara, which translates into the word 'descent' (Sheth, 2002). In Hindu culture, descent was a reference to the incarnation of a deity coming down to Earth to fulfill some purpose (Holzwarth, Janiszewski, & Neumann, 2006), just as users engage digital in social networks to fulfill particular purposes. Most closely associated with the innumerable embodiments of the Hindu god Vishnu (Sheth, 2002), each taken to accomplish specific tasks, users may shift from representation to representation as the digital environment, social network, and task-at-hand require. Indeed, as these representations are crafted, used, and reflected upon, users connect with their avatars in many different ways. In this chapter, we explore the relationship between a particular user-avatar pair – gamers and their graphic in-game characters – and how these relationships differently influence social interactions in play. The technological notion of avatars can be traced to the mid-1980s when F. Randall Farmer and Chip Morningstar (both software developers at Lucasfilms) needed a term to refer to controllable, humanoid, animated figures in the multiplayer online game Habitat (Britt, 2008). In the social science literature, an avatar may be a static picture or image that a person uses to represent the self in a social networking setting (Kang & Yang, 2006). Sometimes, an avatar is a primary character in a video game that is controlled by a video game player (Downs & Oliver, 2009; Jin & Park, 2009). In other cases, an avatar is the embodiment of an individual into a virtual space through the use of virtual technologies (Biocca, 1997; Fox & Bailenson, 2009), or an avatar could be a reference to an animated, artificially-intelligent bot that assists a person through some process in an online environment (Holzwarth, Janiszewski, & Neumann, 2006). Lessig (2000) broadly explains that avatars are the graphical representations and embodiments of our virtual characters, existing on screen in a variety of different modalities but serving as our primary conduit for experiencing a given virtual world. Avatars can be more than the pixels on-screen, however, sometimes construed to represent the personality that one associates with their avatar's form and function (Jordan, 1999).

Because avatars (broadly defined) are the primary vehicle by which users experience digital environments and their constitutive social networks, they tend to be considered as tools – devices that human users engage to mediate online activities. Yet, such a singular focus might obfuscate deeper questions about the player-avatar relationship. How do humans experience avatars? How do avatars 'experience' humans? Is there a meaningful relationship between both? How might these phenomenal experiences impact how we study media psychology? In approaching these questions, we draw from current perspectives on how video gamers relate with their avatars to theoretically and empirically demonstrate the range of relationships users may have with their digital representations in other mediated contexts.

12.2 A (Brief) History of On-Screen Relationships

Since the earliest days of media studies, researchers have sought to understand how media audiences connect with on-screen characters. In the late 1920s, Frances Payne Bolton funded some of the earliest studies on children's identification with movie characters (Lowery & DeFleur, 1995), finding children to learn from and imitate many of their favorite actors and their on-screen personae. The infamous Seduction of the Innocent studies of Wertram (1955) examined similar associations between juvenile delinquents and behaviors learned by imitating salacious comic book characters. Forward some 20 years, and a primary reason given for the critical and economic success of the racially charged 1970s sitcom All in the Family was the portrayal of "America's Favorite Bigot" Archie Bunker -- Norman Lear's approach at demonstrating the absurdity of bigotry. The caricature was loved by progressives for representing the ignorance of racism while at the same time loved by conservatives who heavily identified with the character's critiques of modern-day society (Vidmar & Rokeach, 1974), highlighting individual differences in responses to on-screen personalities. Indeed in each of these scenarios, we see the gestation of Horton and Wohl's parasocial relationship (PRS) hypothesis (Horton & Wohl, 1956): media audiences enjoy and seek out faux relationships with media characters -- even if these relationships are one-way, non-dialectical, and often of far greater importance to the audience member than the on-screen character.

PSRs are known to be key in understanding the uses and effects of entertainment media. For example, in affective disposition theory (ADT, Zillmann & Cantor, 1977; Raney, 2004) the key factor in the appeal and enjoyment of an entertainment product is the dispositions held towards main characters, such as a liked protagonist and disliked antagonist. However, these PSRs have always existed behind a fourth wall (Stevenson, 1995) -- an invisible barrier between the audience and the mediated world that allows each to exist without cognitive, affective, or behavioral interference from the other. That is, media audiences are able to safely engage in PSRs with their favorite (and hated) media characters by passively witnessing their actions, suspending their disbelief about the narrative (Coleridge, 1960; Boecking & Wirth, 2005), and suspending moral judgments made in those narratives (Shafer, 2009; Raney, 2011) in order to ensure an enjoyable experience.

However, the introduction of interactivity -- the ability of an audience member to alter the form and content of the on-screen product (Steuer, 1992) -- has forced us to reconsider the very foundation of the PSR. Entering a mediated environment via an avatar and interacting with that avatar and other avatars effectively breaks down the fourth wall, removing the separation of the off-screen and on-screen persona and shifting the role of passive audience member to one of an active user. Moreover, the great majority of interactive media – such as video games and more popular social media platforms (e.g., Facebook and Twitter) – require the user to create the very "characters" (or avatars) that occupy the digital environment, potentially allowing for a much greater range of relational possibilities between the user (the active audience member) and the avatars on-screen.

12.3 Interactivity and the Active Audience

Because the key marker of interactivity is the extent to which one can influence form and content of on-screen media content (Steuer, 1992), one can challenge the extent to which the assumption of the one-way, non-dialectical nature of audience-character relationships might hold true with newer media. For example, Bowman (2013) argues that the widespread use of social media by professional athletes has given sports fans unparalleled access to sports celebrities, continuing the tradition of using media to bring fans closer to the on-field (and off-field) action and providing spaces of discourse to engage fans on a one-to-one level. In this way, sports fans have evolved from being passive audiences members to full-fledged agents in the production of sports as a media product. Similarly, pop star Lady Gaga interacts intimately with her fans as a "Mother Monster" persona in digital spaces like Twitter, interactions that facilitate the active co-construction of fan and celebrity identities (Banks, 2010). Such effects have been found with interactive social television technologies (Ducheneaut, Moore, Oehlberg, Thornton, & Nickell, 2008; Cesar & Geerts, 2011) – in which traditional television sets are augmented with social media and other networked technologies to allow users to connect with each other and, ostensibly, with the on-screen content.

In no other environment is this passive-to-active shift clearer than in digital worlds. In such environments, media users are co-creators of the on-screen content - be it the numerous personal profiles and accounts that populate social media platforms (each representing a unique social agent) to the user-created avatars that comprise the populations of virtual worlds such as Second Life and Azeroth (the universe of World of Warcraft lore). As "members of the cast," users are expected - and sometimes even required - to play a role in the on-screen narrative. In fact, the worlds as they are known would not exist without users' active participation. One way this participation is accomplished is through interactions with the characters of these worlds, including interactions between users and their own avatars.

12.3.1 Interactivity and Player Experiences

Players' active participation in virtual worlds unfolds through information exchanges between the player and the avatar as they jointly engage a digital gameworld. In short, the player and avatar are introduced through the game interface, the player acts upon the avatar by conveying information, and the avatar acts upon the player by conveying information in return. Through such feedback loops, acts of play emerge (Gee, 2005) as a meaningful relationship is made.

The types of information exchanged by players and avatars depend on how the unique agencies of each coalesce in responses to scenarios encountered in the gameworld. These scenarios are generally multimodal, including verbally communicated world narratives, videos that advance discrete plots, gesturing characters that populate the world, navigable environments, and ambient sounds and music. Games also present tasks or decision scenarios that, as logic structures, may be considered a mode in themselves – a semiotic resource (Kress, 2010), with a grammar distinct from image, text, and sound. For example, in order to progress in Portal players must work through spatial puzzles, and in World of Warcraft players must often collect items, kill monsters, or deliver messages as instructed by game characters. Often, the abilities of a player alone are not enough to accomplish a task. Rather, the abilities of both player and avatar are required, such as a player's problem-solving skills and the avatar's ability to make manifest a portal or shoot a monster in the gameworld. These abilities must coalesce to accomplish the task, requiring each agent to communicate with the other (Banks, 2013). In this way, game tasks drive interactivity. It is these calls to action that shift the audience-as-consumer and medium-as-producer scenario to one of collaborative production between the player and the avatar. We propose that Steuer's definition of interactivity should be extended: interactivity is not merely the way that the player may influence gameworld content, but how the player influences the avatar, how the avatar influences the player, and how the player and avatar together influence the gameworld content. In other words, we must consider with more rigor the meaning of the prefix "inter-" as a reciprocal exchange of information rather than a unidirectional one.

These information exchanges and joint influence on gameworld content can be best understood as constituting a cyborgic system in which an organic agent (the player) and an inorganic agent (the avatar) are intimately linked. Cyborg theories (e.g., Haraway, 1991a, 1991b; Wiener, 1948) posit that in such systems, humans and technologies communicate according to unique agencies (e.g., a game's visualization of a world and a player's exploration of it), and mechanisms internal to the system (e.g., feedback loops between a game's rule system and a player's willingness to follow it or break it) allow information to be received, stored, and processed by both elements (Wiener, 1948). Within these systems, experiences co-produced by players and avatars vary according to unique interactions among player effectivities (e.g., motivations, subjectivities, skills, preferences), avatar effectivities (e.g., abilities, permissions, access to resources) and technological affordances (Gibson, 1977; Greeno, 1994; see Sundar, 2008, about games specifically). Through this interactive co-production, players may experiment with new identities (Grodal, 2000), appreciate a compelling narrative (Bowman, Rogers & Sherrick, 2013; Oliver et al, 2013), compete for achievements and status (Sherry, Lucas, Greenberg & Lachlan, 2006; Yee, 2006), escape from stress and repair moods (Bowman, 2012; 2013), spend time with friends (Ducheneaut & Moore, 2004), and a host of other experiences. In these ways, players' experiences with avatars are not so different than experiences players may have with other humans - two people may roleplay, listen to a story, compete, relax, and socialize. Reeves and Nass (1996) argue that we treat our technologies as we treat humans. It may be that when technologies respond to us in human-like ways, we can only understand these information exchanges according to accessible metaphors for human interaction (Bogost, 2012). Among various types of video game content, the feature most prone to such humanization is the avatar - a digital body that represents a player in a gameworld.

12.4 The Experience of the Player-Avatar Relationship

A player-avatar relationship (PAR) may be understood simply as the material and semiotic connection between a human gamer and the digital body representing that gamer in the gameworld. This connection varies according to the unique interactions between the two agents and the meaning those interactions have in their respective physical and digital worlds. Traditionally, a human-human relationship is a valenced connection between two people where each influences the other (Berscheid & Pelau, 1983; Harvey & Pauwels, 2009). If we consider the player and avatar as engaged in information exchanges through which joint action is made possible, the connection between the two agents satisfies this definition of a relationship, even from the first moment a player creates and avatar or a game assigns an avatar to a player (Reid, 1996).

PARs are generally understood to exist in the mind of the player as so-called headcanons – player-created narratives that help make sense of the gameworld outside of (but copacetic with) the formal world narrative. Others argue that PARs are liminal – existing in the space between the digital and physical bodies. Often, this threshold is thought to be the game interface itself (Boudreau, 2012; Gee, 2005), but it can also be understood as the line between "the world we think of as external and real and the thoughts in our mind that we take for fantasies. When we are in a threshold state [we are] filled with the real sensations and emotions for imaginary objects" (Murray, 1997, p. 292). Of particular importance across each of these perspectives is the notion that PARs are held as legitimate and important parts of gameplay experiences: PARS contribute to cognitive, affective, and behavioral outcomes of play as the avatar is created, as player influences the avatar, as the avatar influences the player, and as experience and meaning are co-produced.

Traditionally, conceptual approaches toward to studying relationships between audiences and mediated characters have been examined from a 'me versus not-me' perspective (see Klimmt, Hefner, & Vorderer, 2009 for review). That is to say that "media users perceive a social distinction between themselves (the observers) and the media characters" (Klimmt et al., 2001, p. 352). Klimmt et al. (2009) proposed that this dyadic paradigm might not be accurate in the context of video game play, citing that interactivity plays a role in closing the perceived distance between the individual and the avatar, or "self" and "other" – suggesting a monadic relationship akin to the psychological merging of the player and character known as character attachment (CA; Lewis, Weber, & Bowman, 2008). However, Klimmt and colleagues' line of argumentation does not consider the reconceptualization of interactivity offered in this chapter – in particular, it assumes that (a) the player is actively merging towards the avatar in the gameworld and (b) the avatar is a passive object to be merged with rather than a possible partner in gameplay. For example, Downs (2010) proposed a model of player-avatar relationships rooted in the logic of the Hegelian Dialectic, arguing that we can understand PARS as a function of three notions: thesis, antithesis, and synthesis (James, 2007). According to Hegel's logic thesis is a single intellectual proposition. The antithesis, then, is a conflicting idea or a negation of the original proposition. The dissonance between thesis and antithesis is resolved through synthesis – the incorporation and reinterpretation of the two into an entirely new proposition (Beiser, 1993). Applied to PARs, this model holds that players and avatars can be thought of as separate forces that are compelled into interaction through gameplay. When a player picks up a game controller, each entity acts on the other, and this interaction forms and evolves into myriad relational outcomes. The synthesis is at once part player and part avatar, but different than both. Such a perspective dictates that in order to understand the relationship, we have to take it for more than the sum of its parts: we must understand both social actors as well as their inter-relation.

12.4.1 Explaining the Player-Avatar Relationship

Digital games have avatars that, in some way, represent the player in the gameworld and translate the player's intention into that world. In this intrinsically dialectic relationship, players and avatars relate to one another in various ways. These relationships between these digital and physical agents begin at the moment they are introduced through the game interface and evolve through play over time.

These introductions can unfold in various ways depending on the characteristics of the game and the motivations of the player. Sometimes the avatar is assigned by the game, as with Mega Man's sole playable character of the same name. Sometimes, a limited number of choices are presented, as when players can choose from headline characters Mario or Luigi as playable characters in Super Mario Brothers. The greatest freedom in avatar choice is presented in games that permit varying degrees of both character selection and customization, such as selecting among predesigned facial and body features (such as piercings and skin patterns in World of Warcraft) or crafting highly customized bodies through control over many features (such as forehead height and eye color in The Elder Scrolls). In some games, however, avatars are not bodies in the traditional sense. For example, in Tetris, players' intentions are made manifest in the game by momentary control over configurations of blocks. Similarly, player's intentions in real-time strategy games (such as the sci-fi war simulator StarCraft) manifest in the manipulation of various combat resources, but the narrative is experienced through the assumption of multiple nameless characters over the course of the game narrative. In Trine and Botanicula, players may switch among a number of different characters, each with unique abilities, and Trine permits multiple players to share those avatars. In these ways, the meeting of player and avatar challenge traditional notions of 'one player, one avatar' embodiment in games (Yee, Ellis, & Ducheneaut, 2009).

For video games in which players can customize the way their avatars look and how they participate in the gameworld, customization most often happens before player "meets" the avatar as a formal entity in the world. Depending on a games' character customization system, players may choose an avatar's race, gender (usually from the male or female binary), combat class or role, backstory and personality features, social or functional alliances, and aesthetic features. Sometimes these customizations will influence how gameplay progresses, such as Guild Wars 2, in which character design includes making decisions about avatar race and personality that influence how the game narrative unfolds. Avatar design decisions are known to be related to various motivations, such as identity performance (Martey & Consalvo, 2011), creative expressions and roleplay (Neustaedter & Fedorovskaya, 2009), individual and group combat strategies (Fron, Fullerton, Morie, & Pearce, 2008), social norms (Merola & Peña, 2010), and aesthetic preferences (Kafai, Fields, & Cook, 2007).

Avatar customization and other relationship decisions are often related to players' motivations for entering the game in the first place (Banks, 2013). As digital games evolved - from the earliest text-based online roleplaying games to contemporary immersive graphical environments - so have perspectives on motivations for play. At a more general level, Sherry et al. (2006) adopted a uses and gratifications theory perspective (Blumler & Katz, 1974) in specifying more general reasons for video game play, including the prominent roles of challenge, competition, escape and fantasy.

Bartle (1996) suggested that there are four types of players who engage in text-based games: “socializers” who enjoy interacting with other players, “achievers” who work toward game-related goals, “explorers” who aim to discover the gameworld and challenge its boundaries, and “killers” who try to distress other players or interfere with play. These motivations can be understood as a function of whether the player focuses on acting (as with killers and achievers) versus interacting (socializers and explorers) and on the gameworld (achievers and explorers) versus other players (killers and socializers). These play motivations were explored in relation to massively multiplayer online games (MMOs). Yee (2006) found that 10 discrete play motivations fell into three main motivational categories: achievement (advancement, mechanical mastery, competition), social (socializing/chatting, relationships, teamwork), and immersion (discovery, roleplaying, customization, escapism).

These play motivations have been shown to drive PARs, and as motivations shift the relationships may shift (Banks, 2013). Players who focus on achievement and competition tend to relate to their avatars as objects or mere tools to master game tasks. Those motivated to socialize and work in teams tend to relate to their avatars as identity expressions and extensions of players’ senses of self. When players are motivated by immersion and escapism, they tend to relate to their avatars as autonomous social entities that exist independently from the player. Additionally, other motivations were discovered: some players are drawn to the game as a safe place for playing out personal problems and negotiating or practicing possible identities; players with these motivations tend to engage avatars in symbiotic relations, where the player and avatar are experienced as cooperatively contributing to play experiences. For example, a player beginning the MMO World of Warcraft may be driven by social factors. The player’s friends belong to a particular faction (a group of allied players) so she creates and engages an avatar in that faction, seeing the avatar as a simple representation that allows her to play socially. However, motivations may shift as players gain experience in the game, and the relationship between player and avatar may become more or less intense (Banks, 2013), and perceptions of liminal or joint identities may fade over time (Martinez, 2011). The player may find that completing quests with her friends is boring, but roleplaying is much more fulfilling because it allows her to ‘escape’ everyday pressures; through this escapism the player-avatar relationship becomes richer. Conversely, the player may find that hardcore raiding is highly fulfilling because it satisfies a penchant for achievement, and as she focuses on honing skill and downing bosses, the player may begin to see the avatar as more of a tool for combat rather than an expressive character. In these ways, the player-avatar relationship may shift over time, based on how the player acts upon the avatar and how the avatar acts upon the player.

12.4.2 The Player and the Avatar: Who Impacts Whom?

The different PARs can have qualitatively different impacts on gamers as well as on their virtual experiences. Moreover, the relationships themselves are likely impacted by how gamers see the virtual world (or characters in the virtual world) as well as the player's motives for visiting the virtual space to begin with. We can understand these effects by understanding both how players influence their avatars and how avatars influence the player themselves.

12.4.2.1 Player Agencies

Popular and scholarly literature attends to the ways that video games are uniquely suited to identity experimentation, broadly, and in terms of gender, race, and personality (e.g., Grodal, 2000; Nakamura, 2000). From this perspective, players approach virtual worlds as a space to 'try out' different identities, from constructing an aggressive and daunting warrior-class monster to experience feelings of dominance and power to forming smaller, docile, healer-class elves to construct identities associated with compassion and care. Although played out in digital environments, these simulated experiences trigger physical-world reactions from users as our minds do not readily distinguish between physical and digital stimuli (Grodal, 2000; Reeves & Nass, 2006). In this way, players can be seen "putting on" different personae and taking the lessons learned from the interactions between these personae and other characters (including other player personae) back into their non-gaming lives (Banks, 2013).

A few studies have shown that individual differences – such as personality traits – can have a significant impact on how avatars are engaged. Dunn and Guadagno (2012) found that trait introverts – particularly those who self-reported high levels of neuroticism – were more likely to craft attractive avatars. The same study also found that individuals more open to new experiences were found to choose avatars with skin tones different than their own. Huh and Bowman (2008) found that excessive MMO play was highly correlated with extraversion, suggesting that extraverted gamers turn to virtual worlds in an effort to engage, via their avatar, innumerable social connections possible in these expansive spaces unrestricted by space-time constraints. Similar work on social networks suggests that a major factor in their appeal is the communication possibilities afforded by the platforms, such as enhanced access, social stature, and community resources (Wellmann, Quan-Haase, Witte & Hampton, 2001). Belisle and Bodur (2010) suggested that the relationship between player and avatar personalities is particularly useful for extracting information about social networking users, such as in a marketing context.

12.4.2.2 Avatar Agencies

At the simplest level, avatars exert agency – the capacity to act – over the player by the nature of their coding (Lessig, 2000). If "code is law" as Lessig titles his work, then an avatar's programming technologically affords and constrains the ways it may impact the player – the code governs the types of information it may convey. A large, muscular avatar with a bladed weapon communicates an aggressive warrior-type and likely dictates a more aggressive and violent style of play, while a diminutive, slender avatar with an arsenal of bows and arrows communicates a more passive ranger-type and likely dictates a style of play that is more stealth and secretive. Put simply, avatars present themselves to players as they are programmed, and for players to take up avatars according to these "laws" is a condition of play.

We might also expect avatars to hold agency over players as relational partners of a co-dependent social relationship. For example, from a character attachment perspective (Lewis et al., 2008) data has shown that intense levels of attachment are associated with increased time spent playing video games as well as with self-reported video game addiction. Although not given as an initial interpretation of these findings, one might suggest that the highly intimate nature of CA brings about a situation in which gameplay becomes a relational maintenance strategy – simply put, one must spend increasingly amounts of time with their avatar in order to sustain high levels of CA (Lewis et al., 2008). Such an interpretation suggests that the avatar by its nature demands to be interacted and played with in order for the relationship to be a satisfactory one, just as one relational partner craves and demands attention from another in forming social ties (Granovetter, 1973) and romantic relationships (Darity, 2008). Extending CA research further, Bowman, Schultheiss, and Schumann (2012) found that gamers with lower levels of suspension of disbelief and perceived responsibility for their avatar's actions and well-being were more likely to engage in anti-social gameplay (such grief gaming, pursuing more battles with other players, and generally playing alone rather than in groups or guilds). The same study found that players with a heightened sense of control over their avatars were more likely to engage in pro-social gameplay (such as serving as healers and coordinating gameplay within guilds). In both cases, we see evidence that the nature of the relationship between the player and the avatar (albeit as reported by the player) holds influence over the virtual experience itself.

Finally, there is emerging evidence that suggests that avatars can have direct impact on players beyond their programming or the relational mechanics themselves; that is, avatars can have agency independently of a given player. Avatars can have a profound impact on players by transferring their socially constructed personae to the player themselves, an influence called the Proteus Effect (Yee & Bailenson, 2007). From this perspective, players are thought to take on perceived attributes of their avatars outside of the gameworld, such as showing increased aggressive and confident behaviors after having played a tall avatar rather than a short one (Yee & Bailenson, 2007) or showing greater need for social affiliation after engaging more socially-desirable avatars, such as identifying with medical professionals after playing as a healer character (Peña et al, 2009). Note that the notion of governing code (Lessig, 2000) is distinct from the Proteus effect in that the former is a collection of functional affordances and constraints (a sort of avatar-DNA) that regulates the human users' behavior by defining what the user can and cannot do with the avatar during play, and the latter is a priming effect in which exposure and response to the avatar's aesthetic influences the user's subsequent behavior inside or outside the game. Taken together, these studies suggest that as players establish relationships with their avatars, the digital body may in a sense act on the player through its mechanics and aesthetics and so impact players' experiences.

12.5 The Subjective Experience of the PAR

In virtual worlds, the relationship between the human (physical) and avatar (digital) agent is significant both for the agents and for the broader situation of play. Indeed, as players and avatars exchange information in cyborgic feedback loops, meaning emerges as a relational effect (Akrich & Latour, 1992; Latour, 2005).

Perhaps the most self-evident of these relationships are the ways that the player-avatar relationship is meaningful for the player. Sometimes, the relationship is a source of personal power, as when abused or disenfranchised women create and engage strong, beautiful female avatars and feel greater autonomy and agency when playing with them. PARs can also be meaningful when the relationship serves as a vehicle for learning about themselves and resolving dissonance, as when players are able to practice performances of non-normative identities or when drawing on game narratives as metaphors for everyday challenges. PARs appear to be particularly meaningful for players who engage avatars as social companions, appreciating narratives, achievements, and interactions as a "we" rather than as an "I."

It is possible that PARs are also meaningful for the avatar. At its simplest, the active PAR permits the avatar to continue to manifest in the gameworld every time the player logs into the game. The relationship influences how the avatar evolves statistically, aesthetically, narratively, and socially. It is also possible that the PAR may mean something to the avatar as a subjective, independent agent. Although it may seem counterintuitive that a nonhuman agent could find significance in a relationship, object-oriented perspectives contend that meaning exists outside of humans' perceptions of them (see Harman, 2002). However, because humans cannot grasp what it means to experience the world independent of the human experience, we explain nonhuman objects' existence according to human metaphors (Bogost, 2012) and apply those metaphors to the gameworld and its denizens (Martey & Stromer-Galley, 2007). Although we cannot comprehend how an avatar experiences a PAR, the notion that an avatar may encounter stimuli and respond to them and be materially influenced by the encounter is a useful theoretical frame. By attending to the ways that the avatar and its constitutive components evolve functionally, narratively, and socially through play. One way to do this is through the player's active construction of headcanons about their relationship with their avatars – stories that include speculations about how the player-avatar relationship matters to the avatar, including avatar's aesthetic, social, and ethical perspectives (Banks, 2013). These human metaphors and derivative stories– are embedded in and influenced by every day, physical-world expectations and norms. Likewise, most contemporary games are built around these norms, and in particular norms and expectations for embodiment. Specifically, if an avatar takes the general form of a human body, it should look human, act human, have the same experience in the gameworld as humans do in the physical world, and that embodiment is similarly congruous - one player can control just one avatar body (Yee, Ellis, & Ducheneaut, 2009). When technologies such as avatars adhere to these expectations, we tend to treat them as we would treat human beings (Reeves & Nass, 2005), and in the same way that we narratively frame our relationships with other people, we craft narratives to explain how the player and avatar exist in relation to one another and in relation to digital and physical worlds in which the agents are embedded (Banks, 2013). These metaphor-driven narratives are how the meaning of PARs are experienced and recalled, as has been demonstrated using linguistic analysis techniques to understand the social continuum of the PAR by analyzing the different attachment styles manifest in players' recollections of their favorite avatars in World of Warcraft (Banks & Bowman, 2013).

12.5.1 Meaning as a Relational Effect

The specific meaning that emerges from a PAR depends on the degrees to which it similar to human social relationships, particularly in terms of three relational dynamics: self-differentiation, emotional intimacy, and perceived agency (Banks, 2013). First, PARs vary in the degree of self-differentiation, or how the avatar is experienced as distinctly autonomous and separate from the player. Such distinction is required for an authentic relationship as it maximizes the sensation of empathy, or genuine concern, for the social other (Bowen, 1978). Second, PARs vary in the level of emotional intimacy, or the perception of closeness that results in feelings of care, affirmation, value, and belonging (Sinclair & Dowdy, 2005). Players' experiences of emotional intimacy with an avatar may be expressed through emotional language, senses of having shared experiences, and deep appreciation for the relationship rather than hedonic enjoyment of its strategic benefits. Finally, PARs vary in the perceived agency of the player and the avatar – who is thought to be "in charge" of gameplay activities – both morally and functionally. Moral agency is the ability to consider the consequences of one's actions and to take responsibility for those actions (Kohlberg, 1958) and functional agency is the self-directive ability to enact intention (Bandura,

1989) of the moral agent. Sometimes the player is experienced as morally and/or functionally in charge of play, and sometimes the avatar is thought to be in charge.

The importance of this tripartite understanding of PARs was found in an in-depth phenomenological study of World of Warcraft players and their relationships with favorite avatars, Banks (2013) found that patterns among the three relational features of self-differentiation, emotional intimacy, and perceived agency. PARs with low self-differentiation (where the avatar was experienced as an extension of or part of the player) also featured low emotional intimacy and high player agencies – these PARs resembled user-tool relationships rather than social relationships. Conversely, PARs with high self-differentiation (where the avatar was seen as a separate entity) featured high emotional intimacy and high avatar agencies – these PARs resembled authentic social relationships. As such, PARs can be understood according to a continuum of increasing socialness, where the relational feature of perceived avatar agency sometimes moves the relationship beyond parasocial to fully social.

These lower and higher levels of socialness are associated with different gameplay motivations (Banks, 2013), revealing four primary types of PARs, each with different meaning-making functions that can be identified according to avatars' roles (Banks, 2014): objects, extensions of Self, symbiotes, and separate social agents.

Table 12.1. A typology of Player-Avatar Relationships (PAR), from Banks and Bowman (2013)

	Avatar as Object	Avatar a Me	Avatar as Symbiote	Avatar as Other
Identification (I am that avatar)	**Low** My avatar is a digital form.	**High** My avatar is me in digital form.	**Mid** My avatar is a part of me.	**Low** My avatar is its own being.
Suspension of Disbelief (Accepts Digital World as a Real One)	**Low** The environment is a space of competition.	**Mid** I appropriate the world to fit my own view of it.	**Mid** I am able to visit my avatar's world.	**High** My avatar lives in a digital world with its own norms.
Sense of Control (Physical)	**High** My avatar is a tool for mastery of in-game challenges.	**Mid** My avatar is my social surrogate to accomplish my social play goals.	**Mid** My avatar and I use each other to accomplish negotiated goals.	**Low** I am a tool for my avatar; it tells me how to control it to accomplish its goals.
Sense of Care & Responsibility (Affective)	**Low** My avatar has no needs.	**Mid** My avatar is me – it needs what I need.	**Mid** My avatar and I know each other's needs.	**High** I help my avatar get the things it needs in his/her world.

In some relationships, the avatar serves merely as a strategic object – a tool. These "object relationships," are characterized by low self-differentiation, low emotional intimacy, and high player agency. They are associated with play motivations of intense competition and combat play. These relationships are generally detached and strategic, and these players effectively and enjoyably play the game without much consideration of the digital body as a body per se. This PAR type aligns with literature characterizing avatars as tools (Linderoth, 2005) and bundles of resources (Castronova, 2005). When the avatar is taken merely as a tool, meaning is made according to the tool's effectiveness and the resulting success or failure in its use.

In others, the avatar is a reification of a player's sense of identity in the gamespace, and often are created to embody the roles, appearance, and interactions that the player wishes to extend into the digital world. These "Me relationships" feature low self-differentiation, low to moderate emotional intimacy, and high player agency. Me relationships are associated with highly social play and gaming as a daily activity or ritual in which players work toward goals set forth by the game and goals they make for themselves. These relationships' characteristic of lower emotional intimacy can be attributed to players' strong identification with avatars – if players see an avatars as being an extension of themselves, then the avatar is not an "other" to care for or to share experience with. Me relationships did feature mild expressions of care, but these convey affection for how the item "is Me," as one might express care for a favorite t-shirt, a loved car, or a childhood toy. This relationship type is similar to characterizing avatars as surrogates in social interaction (Gee, 2006), vehicles for gameplay (Carr, 2002), and carefully crafted player identities (Turkle, 1997). When the avatar is taken as an extension of the self, meaning is made according to the immediacy of gameworld experiences as the player feels comfortable acting "in" and "through" the avatar as a second, representative skin.

Still other PARs feature the avatar as a partner in identity. Such "symbiote relationships" are characterized by shifting self-differentiation, moderate to high emotional intimacy, and mixed player and avatar agencies (both are "in charge" of play). Players in these PARs emphasized play motivations of working through challenges and solving problems. In particular, symbiote relationships often focused on negotiating identities by designing, testing, and practicing possible selves (see Markus & Nurius, 1987) in the gameworld through the avatar before the player translates those selves into everyday life. While this relationship type aligns, in part, with literature characterizing avatars as masks (Galanxhi & Nah, 2007) and costumes (Merola & Peña, 2010), it extends these metaphors by adding a type of identity exchange between player and avatar. That is, not only does the player wear the avatar as a mask or costume, but the avatar is seen as drawing on player characteristics as it existed in the game space, and both player and avatar were engaged in processes of negotiating and becoming more alike. As such, when the avatar acts in symbiosis with the player, meaning emerges according to the way embodiments, actions, and identities are relevant in the narratives of both the gameworld and the everyday physical world.

Finally, some PARs involve experiencing the avatar as a distinct moral agent with its own governing systems, life history, and trajectory, and as embodying independent existence within the gameworld. These "other relationships" are authentically social, featuring high self-differentiation, high emotional intimacy, and high avatar agency. Avatar agency is so high, in fact, that some players see themselves as a tool for achieving the avatar's goals, rather than the player's own objectives. Players in these PARs were motivated to play by the opportunities to escape everyday life and become immersed in the gameworld as a separate but very real space. Although this relationship type is reminiscent of literature characterizing avatars as narratives (Webb, 2001), it goes beyond narrative: avatar-as-other relationships rely on the experience of the avatar as a real amalgam of body, personality, behaviors, subjectivity, and supporting narrative about which new narratives emerge over time. When the avatar is engaged as an autonomous social agent, meaning is made as the player and avatar enter and participate in the game as partners, according to the benefits enjoyed by each agent in their respective worlds.

In each of these PAR types, play motivations contribute to how the player and avatar are connected, and then meaning-making unfolds as a function of the socialness of the relationship (Banks, 2013). Self-differentiation is seen as the key driver of differences among the PARs, as it underlies the meaning that an avatar holds for a player and aids in the relational narrative by which the player constructs, enacts, and is influenced by the lived gameplay experience.

12.6 Pixels or People? Implications for Understanding User-Avatar Relationships in Social Networks

As the corporeal world becomes increasingly enmeshed with the digital, it is important that we understand the many different relationships that exist between humans and their technologies. In terms of virtual worlds, one particularly salient relationship is that between the human user and the digital avatar. Prevailing thought seems to implicate the user as the singular dominant force in any given virtual world – the human as a player exerting his or her agency over the avatar in pursuit of myriad goals. Yet, emerging theory and research (such as that presented in this chapter) urges us to consider the user and the avatar as unique and distinct social entities, each with the potential to influence and be influenced by the other. In the study of virtual worlds, we suggest that the social interactions between a user and his or her avatar are just as integral to a given social environment as are the social interactions between one user and another. Users engage their avatars in tandem with (and often in advance of) engagement with the digital world, and these partnerships can substantially impact the experiences a player has with a given environment.

12.6.1 Extending PARs to social networking avatars

To this point, much of our discussion has centered on avatars in video games. Of course, as we alluded to in the introduction of the chapter, avatars exist in a variety of different digital contexts. Regarding social networks, we can consider one's Facebook profile or their Twitter logo and handle to be avatars, as each serves as a self-representation for a given user in a given social space (cf. Kang & Yang, 2006). In this way, we should expect the same PAR types found in video game play to exist to some degree in various social networking platforms. For example, user of the job-searching engine LinkedIn might approach their profiles with an "avatar as object" – viewing their online CV and basic professional information as part of a larger network of professionals with a singular employment goal in mind. Facebook, as a platform that places great emphasis on social relationships (Keitzmann, Hermkens, McCarthy & Silvestre, 2011), might be particularly useful for technology users desiring an "avatar as me" orientation – treating their persistent Facebook profiles as digital extensions of the self. Conversely, Facebook users, in particularly excessive users, often invest so much time into cultivating their online profiles that those very profiles tend to take on an agency of their own, leading to compulsive usage patterns as the user attempts to satisfy the perceived needs of their Facebook avatar, even if this results in negative consequences to the user (Andreassen, Torsheim, Brunborg, & Pallesen, 2012).

12.6.2 Anti-Social PAR Effects

As can be found in the history of media psychology research, media and technology scholars are quick to take up the study of the potential deleterious effects of usage on individual thoughts, feelings, and actions. Below, we focus on a set of common concerns in media psychology research: excessive usage, aggression, and moral disengagement.

12.6.2.1 Excessive usage

The rise in popularity of persistent virtual worlds such as World of Warcraft and Second Life have ushered in legitimate discussions about excessive and problematic gameplay – including discussions about the potential addictive pull of these environments. Anecdotal evidence reports several cases of gamers engaging in marathon gaming sessions, some lasting three or four days without a break for basic physiological needs (i.e. sleep, food, or restroom breaks) resulting in hospitalizations or even death from renal failure (BBC News, 2005). Less extreme effects such as those used to diagnose gaming addiction include failing grades in school, job performance, and lying about one's time spent playing. Indeed, most of the criteria used to diagnose gaming addiction are borrowed from the Internet Addiction Disorder scale (IAD, Young

& Abreu, 2011). However, these diagnoses tend to broadly implicate virtual worlds as the substance or process one can be addicted to, rather than examining the processes and experiences within the virtual worlds that one is addicted to. Depending on PAR type (that is, depending on the player's relationship with their avatar) the addiction might be to the virtual world itself, challenge and reward systems, social interactions within a social network, visual or audial aesthetics, or even to the social connection with one's avatar. While each of these would likely result in increased time spent engaging the virtual world, one can recognize prima facie that how one approaches their avatar might have a substantial impact on which of these dimensions that users find particularly intoxicating. For example, a World of Warcraft player engaging in an "avatar as object" relationship with her game avatar might be drawn to challenge and reward structures, just as a Facebook user might view his profile as a tool for fostering social desirability vis-à-vis receiving likes and comments from their friends (cf. Burke, Kraut, & Marlow, 2011). Banks (2013) found that gamers engaging the "avatar as other" experienced anxiety while maintaining separation between their off-line and on-line worlds, a concept similar to Marwick and Boyd's (2010) discussion of social context collapse, wherein social networking users strive to situate their status updates within (and restricted to) the proper audiences. In both cases, anxieties stemming from "avatar as other" users' need to persistently cultivate their on-line other self might lead to excessive usage of a given platform in an effort to ameliorate those anxieties.

12.6.2.2 Aggression

Another prominent area of research in media psychology is that of aggression – the potential for virtual aggressive experiences to result in actual aggressive thoughts, actions and feelings in the corporeal world. Research into the Proteus effect (Yee & Bailenson, 2007; Pena, Hancock, & Merola, 2009) suggest that avatars can influence players by providing them with a replicable social identity for both in-world and out-of-world actions. We suggest that the degree to which a player sees the avatar as undifferentiated from themselves (i.e., as a tool or as an extension) is positively correlated with the potential for players to be impacted by their avatars. For example, players engaging anti-social, aggressive, and combative avatars might be more likely to engage in similar behaviors themselves as they (a) ascribe agency to themselves, (b) enact aggressive and combative behaviors as they are condoned in-game, and (c) practice a similar aggressive and combative agency in their out-of-game confrontations. Conversely, a player seeing an avatar as a distinct social agent would be more likely to distinguish an anti-social, aggressive avatar as distinct from themselves and so (a) ascribe agency to the avatar, (b) enact aggressive behaviors consistent with that avatar's persona in the gameworld, but (c) not translate those behaviors into non-game activities when the avatar is absent. Research into the general aggression model (Anderson & Bushman, 2002) generally supports the notion that reinforcing spirals of violence paired with successful outcome in mediated scenarios can carry over to non-mediated ones, and we suggest that the potential for this effect varies greatly as a function of PAR. In addition, a new form of social aggression might also emerge in virtual worlds by which players attempt to protect their self-differentiated avatars from physical, social, or emotional harm from other players or avatars – similar to a mother bear protecting her cubs from perceived dangers. Again, the degree to which one self-differentiates from their avatar should be positively correlated with their motivation to engage in such protective behaviors. In terms of other social media applications, we might apply PAR typologies to better understand instances of flaming or cyber-bullying. For example, users adopting an "avatar as tool" approach might be more willing to engage in such aggressive behaviors if they (a) see those behaviors as the behavioral norm of a given online group and (b) see their avatar as a tool for currying favor within said group. Recent work by Roesner (2014) found that aggressive group norms were a far stronger predictor of aggressive commentary than individual avatar anonymity.

12.6.2.3 Moral disengagement

A third area of anti-social effects research that could be informed by a more complete understanding of PARs is the notion of morality and moral disengagement. Recent work has demonstrated the stability of real-world moral intuitions on observed in-game moral decisions (Joeckel, Bowman, & Dogurel, 2012; Boyan & Grizzard, 2014), suggesting that a player's moral code does not vary from physical to digital worlds. However, competing evidence suggests that gamers knowingly engage in anti-social acts in virtual worlds, ascribing their witnessed actions to being "mere fantasy" or as justified by the game's narrative – thoughts and feelings often associated with moral disengagement processes (Hartmann & Vorderer, 2010). However, moral disengagement processes are often the result of players working to "protect" their enjoyment of a narrative, such as movie audiences extending moral latitude to the questionable actions of a favorite protagonist in order to maintain their positive dispositions toward the character (Shafer, 2009). Here, the necessity of such a process is only present when one sees the virtual world and the avatars that inhabit it as legitimate social agents. For example, in "avatar as object" PARs, players derive enjoyment of video games simply as the achievement of game challenges, often absent of any narrative context. For these players, gameplay is neither moral nor immoral but rather amoral – as supported by Joeckel et al. (2012). Regarding social networks, Rafferty and Vander Ven (2014) reported entertainment value among the motivations given for cyber-bullying by college-aged victims, suggesting that the perpetrators of the activity seemed almost detached from the legitimate psychological harm that the practice might result in.

12.6.3 Pro-Social PAR Effects

Related to the discussion of excessive and problematic gameplay, it is important to recognize that time spent in virtual worlds and with avatars that inhabit those legitimate social spaces is not always deleterious to players' well-being. Indeed, PARs are quickly emerging as an integrated part of many people's everyday lived experiences – increasing the amount of time one spends with avatars to levels considered excessive by some. At worst, these relationships are becoming normative and, at best, they have demonstrated therapeutic benefits to the player; as such, we should not be so quick to discount them as toxic.

12.6.3.1 Identity exploration

Scholars (Grodal, 2000; Turkle, 1995) have discussed the notion of identity exploration in digital environments – the act of one exploring their possible selves (see Markus & Nurius, 1986) and practicing potential desired selves. While we arguably have always had some degree of control in exploring new identities through relationships, affinities, and roles, scholars such as Gergen (2000) have argued that digital technologies – including immersive worlds with divergent norms -- have presented us with a multitude of spaces with which we are encouraged to take on various identities. Although Gergen argues that this constant face work results in a tragically fragmented and relativized sense of self, we argue with others (e.g., Turkle, 2007; Zurcherer, 1977) that the potential for one to explore several identities is key to realizing authentic identities. In this way, PAR types play a key role in the construction of identity engaged in by users through and with their avatars (Banks, 2013).

12.6.3.2 Parasocial contact

Another potential benefit of PARs can be found in theories of parasocial contact. As far back as 1954, Allport argued that for many media users, exposure to divergent cultures and races was often confined to media portrayals such as news and entertainment programming. He reasoned that these mediated portrayals had a significant impact on our perceptions of other cultures and races, demonstrating that positive portrayals resulted in more positive dispositions (and vice versa). Extending this to virtual worlds, we suggest that the social encounters one has with their own avatar as well as other avatars and players can have a similar impact – particularly given that virtual worlds (as well as the users and avatars that inhabit those worlds) are becoming increasingly diverse with respect to culture and ethnicity as they are not restricted to space-time boundaries. Such opportunities for diverse parasocial contact – or perhaps, authentic social contact - are exponentially greater when we consider the weak-tie nature of many social networking platforms that often connect users based on shared interests and other psychographic variables rather than more visible and socially salient demographic ones (Hampton, Goulet, Rainie & Purcell, 2011).

12.6.3.3 Social issues

Another area of study that can be informed by considering PARs in virtual worlds is that of serious games, or games designed with an educational or social consciousness element to them. Much of the current perspective on serious games suggests that the most effective way to teach serious lessons is to place the player "in the shoes" of an avatar, experiencing that avatar's world – and the trials and tribulations programmed into that space – first-hand. However, we might suggest that this "avatar as Me" relationship perspective might actually limit the ability for genuine learning to take place as such forced perspective-taking might not allow for one to overcome their own perceptive biases in order to genuinely embrace and encounter the serious message of a game. Bowen (1978) argues that a key to fostering genuine empathy is not perspective-taking, per se, as one cannot by definition feel empathy for themselves. Rather, empathy is maximized when one recognizes another as a distinct social agent with whom they share an intimate social connection. This self-differentiation is less about being "in their shoes" (which results in an individual considering how they themselves would feel in a novel situation) but rather being "with someone in their own shoes" (which results in an individual considering how their friend or loved one feels in a novel situation). By extension, this self-differentiation – maximized in the "avatar as other" PAR and minimized in the "avatar as Me" PAR – is integral to fostering meaningful learning via its ability to maximize the empathy one feels for a distinct social actor; indeed, this meaningful empathy would not be restricted to serious games as has been observed by players of games such as Heavy Rain and Spec Ops: The Line that use avatar-directed empathy (rather than self-reflected emotions) as the driving force behind their narratives. The rise in Facebook activism around causes not normally salient to distant audiences – such as the Egyptian uprisings of 2011 reaching Western audiences via social networks (Iskander, 2011) – suggests an opportunity for future research. Indeed, designers of social messages who wish to engage communication technology users might benefit from understanding the unique role of self-differentiation inherent to the different PAR typologies.

12.7 Conclusion

As interactions with the features, aesthetics, and functions of technology becomes more like interactions with humans, it is important to examine how our relationships with technology – specifically, the avatars that we craft, perform, experiment with and reflect upon – moderate our online experiences. Sociologists Thomas and Thomas (1928) once stated that "If men define situations as real, they are real in their consequences" (p. 571), and we might argue that whether or not we come to an agreement as to the legitimacy of the user-avatar relationship as an objectively genuine one, many of us experience them as real, and this reality should inform the manner by which we study the phenomenon.

Mediography

All in the Family (1971-1979). Developed by Norman Lear; CBS.
American Dad "Dungeons and Wagons" (2006, November 12). Written by Michael Shipley and Jim Bernstein; Fox.
Botanicula (2012). Designed by Jaromir Plachty; Amanita Design.
Heavy Rain (2010). Written and directed by David Cage; Quantic Dream.
Guild Wars 2 (2012). Written by Ree Soesbee, Jeff Grubb, Bobby Stein; NCsoft.
Mega Man (1987). Created by Akira Kitamura, Tokuro Fujiwara, Keiji Inafune; Capcom.
Portal (2007). Written by Erik Wolpaw, Chet Faliszek; Valve Corporation.
Second Life (2003). Developed by Linden Research, Inc.; Linden Research, Inc.
Spec Ops: The Line (2012). Written by Walt Williams, Richard Pearsey, designed by Cory Davis; 2K Games.
Super Mario Bros. (1985). Created by Shigeru Miyamoto; Nintendo.
Tetris (1984). Created by Alexay Pajitnov; Dorodnicyn Computing Centre.
Trine (2009). Written by Joel Kinnunen; Directed by Lauri Hyvaerinen; Nobilis.
World of Warcraft (2004). Designed by Rob Pardo, Jeff Kaplan, Tom Chilton; Blizzard Entertainment.

References

Allport, G. W. (1954). The nature of prejudice. Reading, MA: Addison-Wesley.
Anderson, C. A., & Bushman, B. J. (2002). Human aggression. Annual Review of Psychology, 53, 27-51.
Ahn, H., Bowman, N. D., & Kwolek, E. (2013, November). Generally concerned, but not specifically: General vs. situational influences of vulnerable narcissism on social network privacy concerns. Top papers in Human Communication and Technology Division, National Communication Association, Washington D.C.
Akrich, M., & Latour, B. (1992). A summary of a convenient vocabulary for the semiotics of human and nonhuman assemblies. In W.E. Bijker & J. Law (Eds.), Shaping Technology/Building Society Studies in Sociotecnical Change (pp. 259-264). Cambridge, MA: MIT Press.
Andreassen, C. S., Torsheim, T., Brunborg, G. S., & Pallesen, S. (2012). Development of a Facebook addiction scale. Psychological Reports, 110(2), 501-517. doi: 10.2466/02.09.18. PR0.110.2.501-517
Bandura, A. (1989). Human agency in social cognitive theory. American Psychologist, 44(9), 1175–184.
Banks, J. (2011, May). Manufacturing Monsters: The co-construction of Lady Gaga and her audiences on Twitter. Paper presented at the Annual Convention of the International Communication Association, Boston, MA.
Banks. J. (2013). Human-technology relationality and Self-network organization: Players and avatars in World of Warcraft. (Unpublished doctoral dissertation.) Colorado State University, Fort Collins, CO.

Banks, J., & Bowman, N. D. (2013). Close intimate playthings? Understanding player-avatar relationships as a function of attachment, agency, and intimacy. Selected Paper of Internet Research, 3. Retrieved from https://spir.aoir.org/index.php/spir/article/view/689
Bartle, R. (1996). Hearts, clubs, diamonds, spades: Players who suit MUDs. Journal of Online Environments, 1(1).
BBC News. (2005, August 10). S. Korean dies after games session. BBC News. Retrieved from http://news.bbc.co.uk/2/hi/technology/4137782.stm
Belisle, J-F. & Bodur, H. O. (2010). Avatars as information: Perception of consumers based on their avatars in virtual worlds. Psychology & Marketing, 27(8), 741-765.
Berscheid, E., & Peplau, L. A. (1983). The emerging science of relationships. In Close relationships (pp. 1–19). New York: W.H. Freeman & Company. Retrieved from http://www.peplaulab.ucla.edu/Peplau_Lab/Publications_files/Berscheid_Peplau_83.pdf
Biocca, F. (1997). The cyborg's dilemma: Progressive embodiment in virtual environments. Journal of Computer Mediated Communication, 3(2), 12-26. doi: 10.1111/j.1083-6101.1997.tb00070.x
Blumler J.G. & Katz, E. (1974). The uses of mass communications: Current perspectives on gratifications research. Beverly Hills, CA: Sage.
Boecking, S. & Wirth, W. (2005, May). Conceptualizing suspension of disbelief for communication research. Paper presented at the 55th annual conference of the International Communication Association, New York.
Bogost, I. (2012). Alien phenomenology: Or what it's like to be a thing. Minneapolis, MN: University of Minnesota Press.
Bowen, M. (1978). Family therapy in clinical practice. New York: Aronson.
Bowman, N. D. (2013). Social media, spaghetti westerns, and modern spectator sports. In Coombs, D. & Batchelor, B. (Eds.), American History through American Sports (Vol. 3, pp. 31-48). Santa Barbara, CA: Praeger.
Bowman, N. D., Rogers, R., & Sherrick, B. I. (2013, April). "In control or in their shoes": How character attachment differentially influences video game enjoyment and appreciation. Top Paper in "Media and the Self" research category, Broadcast Education Association Research Symposium "Media and Social Life: The Self, Relationships, and Society."
Bowman, N. D., Schultheiss, D., Schumann, C. (2012)."I'm Attached, and I'm A Good Guy/Gal!": How Character Attachment Influences Pro- and Anti-Social Motivations to Play MMORPGs. CyberPsychology, Behavior, and Social Networking, 15(3), 169-174. doi: 10.1089/cyber.2011.0311
Bowman, N. D., & Tamborini, R. (2012). Task demand and mood repair: The intervention potential of computer games. New Media & Society, 14(8), 1339-1357. doi: 10.1177/1461444812450426.
Bowman, N. D., & Tamborini, R (2013). "In the mood to game": Selective exposure and mood management processes in computer game play. New Media & Society. doi: 10.1177/1461444813504274.
Boudreau, K. (2012). Between play and design: The emergence of hybrid-identity in single-player videogames. (Unpublished doctoral dissertation.) University of Montreal, Montreal, Quebec, Canada.
Britt, A. (2008). Avatar. N.Y. Times blog, published on 8/8/2008. Retrieved from: http://www.nytimes.com/2008/08/10/magazine/10wwln-guest-t.html?_r=2&scp=2&sq=avatar&st=cse&oref=login
Burke, M., Kraut, R., & Marlow, C. (2011, May). Social capital on Facebook: Differentiating uses and users. CHI 2011, Vancouver.
Cesar, P. & Geerts, S. (2011, January). Past, present and future of social TV: A categorization. Consumer Communications and Networking Conference, Las Vegas, NV.
Coleridge, S. T. (1960). Biographia literaria or biographical sketches of my literary life and opinions. London: J. M. Dent. (Original work published 1817).
Darity, W. A. (2008). Relationship satisfaction. Detroit: MacMillian Reference USA.

Downs, E. (2010). Eighteenth Century Video Games: Using the Hegelian Dialectic to Explain How Individuals Identify with Avatars During Game Play. Presented at the Game Studies Division of the 2010 ICA convention, Singapore, June 22-26.
Downs, E. & Oliver, M.B. (2009, May). How can Wii learn from video games? Examining relationships between technological affordances and socio-cognitive determinates on affective and behavioral outcomes. Paper presented at the meeting of the International Communication Association, Chicago, Il.
Ducheneaut, N. & Moore, R. J. (2004, November). The social side of gaming: a study of interaction patterns in a massively multiplayer online game. In Proceedings of the 2004 ACM conference on Computer supported cooperative work (pp. 360-369). ACM.
Ducheneaut, N., Moore, R. J., Oehlberg, L., Thornton, J. D., & Nickell, E. (2008). Social TV: Designing for distributed, sociable television viewing. International Journal of Human-Computer Interaction, 24(2), 136-154. doi: 10.1080/10447310701821426
Dunn, R. A. & Guadagno, R. E. (2012). My avatar and me – gender and personality predictors of avatar-self discrepancy. Computers in Human Behavior, 28(1), 97-106. doi: 10.1016/j.chb.2011.08.015
Fox, J., & Bailenson, J. N. (2009). Virtual self-modeling: The effects of vicarious reinforcement and identification on exercise behaviors. Media Psychology, 12, 1-25. doi: 10.1080/15213260802669474
Fron, J., Fullerton, T., Morie, J., & Pearce, C. (2008). Getting girls into the game: Towards a virtuous cycle. In Kafai, Y, Heeter, C., Denner, J., & Sun, J. (Eds.), Beyond Barbie and Mortal Kombat (pp. 137-149). Cambridge, MA: The MIT Press.
Gee, J. P. (2005). Pleasure, learning, video games, and life: The projective stance. E-Learning and Digital Media, 2(3), 211–223.
Gibson, J. J. (1977). The theory of affordances. In R. Shaw & J. Bransford (Eds.), Perceiving, acting, and knowing: Toward an ecological psychology (pp. 67-82). Hillsdale, NJ: Erlbaum.
Granovetter, M. (1973). The strength of weak ties. American Journal of Sociology, 78, 1360-1380.
Greeno, J. G. (1994). Gibson's affordances. Psychological Review, 101(2), 336–342. doi: 10.1037/0033-295X.101.2.336
Grodal, T. (2000). Video games and the pleasures of control. In D. Zillmann & P. Vorderer (Eds.), Media entertainment: The psychology of its appeal (pp. 197-213). Mahwah, NJ: LEA.
Hampton, K., Goulet, L. S., Rainie, L., & Purcell, K. (2011). Social networking site and our lives. Washington, DC: Pew Research Center.
Haraway, D. (1991a). A cyborg manifesto: Science, technology, and socialism-feminism in the late Twentieth Century. In Simians, Cyborgs, and Women: The Reinvention of Nature (pp. 149–182). New York: Routledge.
Haraway, D. (1991b). Situated knowledges: The science question in feminism and the privilege of partial perspective. In Simians, Cyborgs, and Women: The Reinvention of Nature (pp. 183–202). New York: Routledge.
Harman, G. (2002). Tool-being: Heidegger and the metaphysics of objects. Peru, IL: Open Court.
Hartmann, T., & Vorderer, P. (2010). It's okay to shoot a character: Moral disengagement in violent video games. Journal of Communication, 60(1), 94-119. doi: 10.1111/j.1460-2466.2009.01459.x
Harvey, J. H., & Pauwels, B. G. (2009). Relationship connection: A redux on the role of minding and the quality of feeling special in the enhancement of closeness. In S. J. Lopez & C. R. Snyder (Eds.), The Oxford handbook of positive psychology (pp. 385–392). New York: Oxford University Press.
Holzwarth, M., Janiszewski, C., & Neumann, M. (2006). The influence of avatars on online consumer shopping behavior. Journal of Marketing, 70, 19-36. doi:10.1509/jmkg.70.4.19
Horton, D., & Wohl, R. R. (1956). Mass communication and para-social interaction: Observations on intimacy at a distance. Psychiatry, 19(3), 215-229.

Huh, S. & Bowman, N. D. (2008). Perception and addiction of online games as a function of personality traits. Journal of Media Psychology, 13(2).
Iskander, E. (2011). Connecting the national and the virtual: Can Facebook activism remain relevant after Egypt's January 25 uprising? International Journal of Communication, 5, 13-15.
James, D. (2007). Hegel: A guide for the perplexed. NewYork, NY: Continuum Publishing Group.
Jin, S. A., & Park, N. (2009), Parasocial interaction with my avatar: Effects of interdependent self-construal and the mediating role of self-presence in an avatar-based console game, Wii. CyberPsychology & Behavior, 12, 723-727. doi:10.1089/cpb.2008.0289
Jordan, T. (1999). Cyberpower: The culture and politics of cyberspace and the Internet. New York: Routledge.
Kafai, Y. B., Fields, D. A., & Cook, M. S. (2007). Your second selves: Resources, agency and constraints in avatar design in a tween online world. In A. Baba (ed.), Situated play: Proceedings of the Digital Games Research Association (pp. 31-39). Tokyo: The University of Tokyo.
Kang, H. & Yang, H. (2006). The visual characteristics of avatars in computer-mediated communication: Comparison of Internet relay chat and instant messenger as of 2003. International Journal of Human-Computer Studies, 64, 1173-1183. doi: 10.1016/j.ijhcs.2006.07.003
Keitzmann, J. H., Hermkens, K., McCarthy, I. P., & Silvestre, B. S. (2011). Social media? Get serious! Understanding the functional building blocks of social media. Business Horizons, 54(3), 241-251. doi: 10.1016/j.bushor.2011.01.005
Klimmt, C., Hefner, D., & Vorderer, P. (2009). The video game experience as "true" identification: A theory of enjoyable alterations of players' self-perception. Communication Theory, 19, 351-373. doi: 10.1111/j.1468-2885.2009.01347.x
Kohlberg, L. (1958). The development of modes of moral thinking and choice in the years 10 to 16 (Unpublished dissertation). University of Chicago, Chicago, IL.
Kress, G. (2010). Mode. In Multimodality: A social semiotic approach to contemporary communication (79-102). New York: Routledge.
Latour, B. (2005). Reassembling the social: An introduction to Actor-Network Theory. New York: Oxford University Press.
Lewis, M. L., Weber, R., & Bowman, N. D. (2008)."They may be pixels, but they're MY Pixels": Developing a metric of character attachment in role-playing video games. CyberPsychology and Behavior, 11(4). doi: 10.1089/cpb.2007.0137
Lessig, L. (2000). Code and other laws of cyberspace. New York: Basic Books.
Lowery, S. A. & DeFleur, M. L. (1995). Milestones in mass communication research: Media effects. (3rd edition). White Plains, NY: Longman.
Matchett, F. (2001). Krishna, Lord or Avatara? The relationship between Krishna and Vishnu. New York: Taylor & Francis.
Markus, H., & Nurius, P. (1987). Possible selves: The interface between motivation and the self-concept. In K. Yardley & T. Honess (Eds.), Self and identity: Psychosocial perspectives (pp. 157–172). Oxford: John Wiley & Sons.
Martey, R. M., & Consalvo, M. (2011). Performing the looking-glass self: Avatar appearance and group identity in Second Life. Popular Communication, 9(3), 165-180. doi: 10.1080/15405702.2011.583830
Martey, R. M., & Stromer-Galley, J. (2007). The digital dollhouse. Games and Culture, 2(4), 314–334. doi:10.1177/1555412007309583
Martinez, N. M. (2011). Liminal phases of avatar identity formation in virtual world communities. In A. Peachey & M. Childs (Eds.), Reinventing ourselves: Contemporary concepts of identity in virtual worlds (pp. 59–80). London: Springer Verlag.

Merola, N., & Pena, J. (2010). The effects of avatar appearance in virtual worlds. Journal of Virtual Worlds Research, 2(5). doi: 10.4101/jvwr.v2i5.843.
Murray, J.H. (1997). Hamlet on the holodeck: The future of narrative in cyberspace. New York: The Free Press.
Nakamura, L. (2000). Race In/For Cyberspace: Identity Tourism and Racial Passing on the Internet. Retrieved from http://www.humanities.uci.edu/mposter/syllabi/readings/nakamura.html
Neustaedter, C. & Fedorovskaya, E. (2009). Presenting identity in the virtual world avatar appearances. Proceedings of Graphics Interface (2009), ACM Press.
Oliver, M. B., Bowman, N. D., Woolley, J. K., Rogers, R., Sherrick, B. I., & Chung, M-Y. (2013, June). Video games as meaningful entertainment experiences. Poster presented at the Annual Meeting of the International Communication Association, London.
Peña, J., Hancock, J. T., & Merola, N. A. (2009). The priming effects of avatars in virtual settings. Communication Research, 36(6), 838-856. doi: 10.1177/0093650209346802.
Raney, A. A. (2004). Expanding disposition theory: Reconsidering character liking, moral evaluations, and enjoyment. Communication Theory, 14(4), 348-369. doi: 10.1111/j.1468-2885.2004.tb00319.x
Raney, A. A. (2011). The role of morality in emotional reactions to and enjoyment of media entertainment. Journal of Media Psychology, 23(1), 18-23. doi: 10.1027/1864-1105/a000027
Rafferty, R., & Vander Ven, T. (2014). "I hate everything about you": A qualitative examination of cyberbulling and online aggression in a college sample. Deviant Behavior, 35(5), 365-377. doi: 10.1080/01639625.2013.849171
Reeves, B., & Nass, C. (1996). The media equation: How people treat computers, television, and new media like real people and places. Stanford, CA: Cambridge University Press.
Reid, E. M. (1996). Text-based virtual realities: Identity and the cyborg body. In P. Ludlow (Ed.), High noon on the electronic frontier: Conceptual issues in cyberspace (pp. 327-346). Cambridge, MA: MIT Press.
Roesner, L. (2014, May). Aggressive language in online comments: Social influence, group norms, and effects of anonymity. International Communication Association, Seattle.
Shafer, D. (2009). The role of moral disengagement in the judgment of characters and the enjoyment of violent film. UMI Dissertation Publishing, Florida State University.
Sherry, J. L., Lucas, K., Greenberg, B., & Lachlan, K. (2006). Video game uses and gratifications as predictors of use and game preference. In P. Vorderer & J. Bryant (Eds.), Playing computer games: Motives, responses, and consequences (pp. 213-224). Mahwah, NJ: Lawrence Erlbaum.
Sinclair, V. G., & Dowdy, S. W. (2005). Development and validation of the emotional intimacy scale. Journal of Nursing Measurement, 13(3), 193–206.
Sheth, N. (2002). Hindu avatara and Christian incarnation: A comparison. Philosophy East and West, 52, 98-125. doi: 10.1353/pew.2002.0005
Steuer, J. (1992). Defining virtual reality: Dimensions determining telepresence. Journal of Communication. 42(4), 73-93. doi: 10.1111/j.1460-2466.1992.tb00812.x
Sundar, S.S. (2008). Self as source: Agency and customization in interactive media. In E.A. Konijn, S. Utz, M. Tanis, & S.B. Barnes (Eds.), Mediated interpersonal communication (pp. 58-74). New York, NY: Routledge
Stevenson, J. (1995). The fourth wall and the third space. New Paltz, NY: Centre for Playback Theatre.
Thomas, W. I. & Thomas, D. S. (1928). The child in America: Behavior problems and programs. New York: Knopf.
Turkle, S. (2007). Simulation versus authenticity. In J. Brockman (Ed.), What is your dangerous idea? Today's leading thinkers on the unthinkable (pp. 244–247). New York: Harper Perennial.
Vidmar, N. & Rokeach, M. (1974). Archie Bunker's bigotry: A study in selective perception and exposure. Journal of Communication, 24(1), 36-47. doi: 10.1111/j.1460-2466.1974.tb00353.x

Walther, J. (1996). Computer-mediated communication: Impersonal, interpersonal and hyperpersonal interaction. Communication Research, 23(1), 3-43. doi: 10.1177/009365096023001001.

Wellmann, B., Quan-Haase, A., Witte, J, & Hampton, K. (2001). Does the Internet Increase, Decrease, or Supplement Social Capital? American Behavioral Scientist, 45(3), 436-455.

Wertram, F. (1955). Seduction of the innocent. London: Museum Press, Ltd.

Wiener, N. (1948). Cybernetics or control and communication in the animal and the machine. Cambridge, MA: MIT Press.

Yee, N. (2006). Motivations for play in online games. CyberPsychology & Behavior, 9(6), 772–775. doi:10.1089/cpb.2006.9.772

Yee, N. & Bailenson, J. (2007). The Proteus Effect: The Effect of Transformed Self-Representation on Behavior. Human Communication Research, 33, 271–90.

Yee, N., Ellis, J., & Ducheneaut, N. (2009). The tyranny of embodiment. Artifact, 2, 1–6. doi: 10.1080/17493460903020398.

Young, K. S., & Abreu, C. N. (2011). Internet addiction: A handbook and guide to evaluation and treatment. Hoboken, New Jersey: Wiley.

Zillmann, D. & Cantor, J. (1977). Affective responses to the emotions of a protagonist. Journal of Experimental Social Psychology, 13(2), 155-165. doi: 10.1016/S0022-1031(77)80008-5.

Zurcher, L. A. (1977). The mutable self. Beverly Hills, CA: Sage Publications.

Olatz Lopez-Fernandez

13 Problem Mobile Phone Use in Spanish and British Adolescents: First steps towards a cross-cultural research in Europe

Abstract: The problematic use of mobile phones in some adolescents is a cause for concern throughout the world, although this problem has rarely been studied in more than one culture. The Mobile Phone Problem Use Scale (MPPUS) has been considered a gold standard, and recently has been adapted to adolescents (MPPUSA) to estimate problem users' prevalence and their characteristics. A mixed methods approach was used through a questionnaire administered to a European sample of 2356 (48% Spanish and 52% British adolescents) aged between 11 and 18 years (M=14.05, SD=1.729; 60.9% male). The problem users' prevalence, with a cut-off point extracted from the 95th percentile score estimated 14.9% in Spain and 5.1% in United Kingdom. These potential problem users presented higher scores in the symptomatology measured by the scale in comparison with those considered non-problematic, and the classification proposed showed an excellent accuracy. However, cultural differences has been detected between both user's countries in relation with the addictive symptoms presented, standing out were withdrawal symptoms against the negative consequences, also commonalities appeared in this psychosocial problem. In conclusion, the findings shed light on the main addictive symptoms which appear in the use of mobile phones, similar to other technological behavioural addictions; therefore, the first steps are proposed to study the mobile phone problem based on cyber-addictions in a cross-cultural perspective.

13.1 Inroduction

Research on problematic mobile phone use (PMPU) began to appear around a decade ago, and although it is still at a relatively early stage (Carbonell, Guardiola, Beranuy, & Bellés, 2009) considerable international progress has been made. Essentially this uncontrolled or excessive use of the mobile phone, which affects the daily user's life, has been classed as a potential technological behavioural addiction (also called in French-speaking countries a cyber-addiction) by several researchers (e.g., Billieux, 2012; Pedrero Pérez, Rodríguez Monje, & Ruiz Sánchez De León, 2012). The scientific community has begun to consider the addictive potential of mobile phones, although research has not yet addressed specific aspects of PMPU or analysed certain psychological facets of the disorder. According to Billieux (2012); we should adopt an integrative pathways model based on the adverse consequences of excessive or uncontrolled mobile phone use generating a vicious circle through the perpetuation of negative affection, which should consider four factors associated with this problem: impulsivity, relationship maintenance, extraversion, and the cyber-addiction, with this final factor being the focus of this chapter. This pathways model could explain the debate of PMPU defending mobile phone abuse (Ahmed, Qazi, & Perji, 2011) versus mobile phone addiction (Chóliz, 2010).

13.1.1 Cross-cultural research on cyber-addictions

As there is no more than two decades of research on cyber-addictions, few studies have attempted a cross-cultural perspective on the cyber-addiction spectrum; usually these studies are between two European countries treating the sample as one (e.g., Lemmens & Bushman, 2006) or from different continents with a real cross-cultural comparative (e.g., Li, Kirkup, & Hodgson, 2001); or directly between several countries (Durkee, 2012; Sariyska, 2014). However, almost all of them are centred on Internet and gaming addiction. As such there is a gap in cyber-addictions cross-cultural studies regarding PMPU.

13.1.2 Problematic mobile phone use versus problematic Internet use

Comparing the potential PMPU with the well-recognized and scientifically developed Problematic Internet Use (PIU), also known as Internet Addiction (IA), the area of mobile phone cyber-addiction has the benefit of having more reliable scales which measure its problematic with more psychometric support than PIU scales. On the other hand, PMPU shares with PIU a need for greater conceptualization and suffers from the same disparity in the sources of the diagnostic criteria and instruments with standard cut-off points to classify problematic users; so that the comparability of estimating the prevalence of users who o present addictive symptomatology remains difficult.

13.1.3 Evaluating problematic mobile phone use

As with PIU, PMPU has been measured with scales describing generalised use (i.e., the mobile phone device and its functions) and, to a lesser extent, with scales describing specific use (e.g., text messaging). Sources of study include observation of user behaviour (Mobile Phone Dependence Questionnaire, MPDQ; Toda, Monden, Kubo, & Morimoto, 2006), diagnostic symptoms (MPPUS; Bianchi & Phillips, 2005), disorder criteria (like pathological gambling, the Cell-phone Over-Use Scale, COS; Jenaro, Flores, Gómez-Vela, González-Gil, & Caballo, 2007) or substance use (the Test of Mobile Phone Dependence; Chóliz, & Villanueva, 2011), other cyber-addictions scales (such as the Internet Addiction Diagnostic Questionnaire used for the Mobile

Phone Addiction Scale or MPAS; Leung, 2007), and other underlying psychological dimensions (as the impulsivity for the Problematic Mobile Phone Use Questionnaire, PMPUQ; Billieux, Van der Linden, & Rochat, 2008). Overall, the PMPU scales have obtained high indexes of reliability and satisfactory factorial and construct validity, and the Mobile Phone Problem Use Scale (MPPUS; Bianchi & Phillips, 2005) has been considered "a gold standard" (Pedrero Pérez et al., 2012).

However, the estimated prevalence of PMPU varies between 0% and 38% (Pedrero Pérez et al., 2012) in the adolescent and young population of different Asian (the Cell Phone Addiction Scale [CPAS]; Koo, 2009), European (the "Cuestionario de Experiencias Relacionadas con el Móvil" [CERM]; Beranuy Fargues, Chamarro Lusar, Graner Jordania, & Carbonell Sánchez, 2009) and Oceanic (the Mobile Phone Involvement Questionnaire [MPIQ]; Walsh, White, & Young, 2010) countries. Proposals for diagnostic criteria for PMPU have been scarce but the most notable comes from Taiwan (Yen et al., 2009), whose PIU proposals are considered one of the most reliable for achieving clinical validation (Ko, Yen, Chen, Chen, & Yen, 2005; Ko, Yen, Chen, Yang, Lin, & Yen, 2009). Currently, PMPU diagnostic criteria do not seem to differ across cultures (Bianchi & Phillips, 2005; Yen et al., 2009), even though cross-cultural studies will be needed to guarantee scale validity (Baron, 2010) and address cultural differences in mobile phone use in countries (Baron & Segerstad, 2010). Current research also suggests that it may be that young female mobile phone users (Geser, 2006) and secondary school students (Kawasaki, Tanei, Ogata, Burapadaja, Loetkham, Nakamura, & Tanada, 2006) who are at the greatest risk of PMPU.

13.1.4 Problematic mobile phone use in adolescents

Chóliz (2010) argued for the inclusion of PMPU in the DSM-5, because the disorder affected adolescents whose problems were apparent in their social, affective, and behavioural sphere. Beranuy Farguesand colleagues (2006) observed that this group age is more vulnerable by not being in complete control of their impulses, moreover they affirm that adolescents are influenced by advertising campaigns, and they consider this device as a status symbol that facilitates their identity. Indeed, the mobile phone is already the media by which adolescents and their parents establish relationships (Weisskirch, 2011). Therefore, it seems that this technology is for several reasons one of the most relevant in adolescents' life, which could in turn facilitate addictive and problematic behaviour through its daily use.

13.1.5 Research problem and objectives

The question is, in the case of European adolescents, does PMPU exist? More specifically, in the case of high-school students from Barcelona and London, what kind of symptoms are the most prevalent? And finally, how do they perceive this potential cyber-addiction? In order to examine these questionsit was necessary to use a validated scale which measures PMPU in adolescents, for this purpose the Mobile Phone Problem Use Scale for Adolescents (MPPUSA; Lopez-Fernandez, Honrubia-Serrano, & Freixa-Blanxart, 2012) was selected. Furthermore an adaptation of the MPPUSA (Bianchi & Phillips, 2005) has also been validated for both Spanish (Lopez-Fernandez et al., 2012) and British adolescents (Lopez-Fernandez, Honrubia-Serrano, Freixa-Blanxart, & Gibson, 2013). The main objective of this chapter, is to open the door to cross-cultural research in this area through the comparison of PMPU in these two cultural adolescent groups; to do this three specific objectives have been outlined: (i) to describe the characteristics and patterns of mobile phone usage in adolescents, (ii) to estimate the prevalence of potentially problematic mobile phone users demonstrating its accuracy in classification based on addictive symptomatology, and (iii) to examine adolescent perception of PMPU.

13.2 Method

13.2.1 Participants

A cross-sectional survey study was carried out in nine schools in Barcelona (Spain) and London (United Kingdom [UK]) between 2009 and 2010. The schools themselves were a number of different types (private, public and state schools) and located within a number of different areas in the cities. The sample from Spain was formed by high school students from "Educacion Secundaria Obligatoria" (ESO; Compulsory Secondary Education) and "Bachillerato" (Baccalaureate is to prepare them for University) which cover adolescent education between 12 and 18 years old. Whereas in the UK Year 7 to Year 13 were used (from Year 7th to 11th is the compulsory, and Years 12 and 13 are Sixth Form/A Level to access University) which ages from 11 to 18 years old. In both cases the school years are between Primary and Higher Education. A sample 2356 students were surveyed, 1132 from Spain and 1224 from UK; however only 833 students from Barcelona (73.6% of Spanish sample) and 725 Londoners (59.2% of British sample) answered all the MPPUSA items correctly.

A mixed methods research design was used, specifically with an embedded design (Creswell & Plano Clark, 2007) through a survey. This research design implies that the quantitative part was the most important aspect of the standardized questionnaire, while a small qualitative component was also included in the data collection through open questions. The data analysis then combines the qualitative and quantitative findings, being the latter being the primary emphasis of the discussion.

13.2.2 Instruments

The pencil-and-paper questionnaire had three sections: (a) socio-demographic variables; (b) mobile phone usage data; and (c) the Spanish/British MPPUSA (for a more detailed description see Lopez-Fernandez et al., 2012; Lopez-Fernandez et al., 2013).

The socio-demographic variables were gender, age, school level, residence location (central city the surrounding area), the family size living in the adolescents' home (including themselves), parents' educational level and their employment status, nicotine and alcohol consumption, as well if they use other non-technological entertainments (see Table 1).

In mobile phone usage, they answered if they were owners of at least one device, what their main type of mobile phone use was (to communicate or for entertainment), how old they were when they had their first mobile phone, who is responsible for its cost, if they perceive addiction to mobile phones in their peers, the negative aspects of mobile phone use, and an open question about what definition they could propose to recognize a potential mobile phone problem user of their age.

The MPPUSA is comprised of 26 items, each with a 10-point Likert scale (being 1 "totally false" to 10 "completely true") (see Appendix A: Spanish version: Lopez-Fernandez et al., 2012; English version: Lopez-Fernandez et al., 2013). These questions themselves cover six dimensions (tolerance, escape, withdrawal, craving, negative life consequences, and social motivational aspects). The psychometric results were quite similar in both countries, achieving the factorial validity through exploratory factor analysis with the principal components technique, that showed its unidimensionality with 61% of variance explained in the Spanish version, and 57% in the British version (this second analysis with construct validity achieved through associations with the perception of mobile phone use with peer and self-perception uses); moreover, the reliability was equal in both version, with an excellent value (Cronbach alpha of 0.97 in both Spain and UK).

For the quantitative analysis, the confidence interval used was 95%, and it was performed using PASW 21.0 for Windows; in terms of the qualitative data a thematic analysis was performed.

13.2.3 Procedure

Permission was obtained from head teachers and the students in both countries, and anonymity and confidentiality was guaranteed. Furthermore, in the UK permission was granted from the ethics committee of Tower Hamlets Research and Performance Development Team under special conditions (Lopez-Fernandez et al., 2013). All students were voluntarily invited to participate without any reward.

13.3 Results

13.3.1 Socio-demographic variables, usage patterns, and symptomatology data for each country

The quantitative data was analysed with the initial sample from each country. Initial findings indicated that that both countries have quite similar adolescent characteristics (see Table 1), even though they are from different European cultures.

Table 13.1. Socio-demographic characteristics of the initial sample (N=2356) per country (percentage and frequency, or mean and standard deviation)

	Spain	UK
	(N=1132)	(N=1224)
Variable	**(n)**	**(n)**
	% (n) M(SD)	% (n) M(SD)
Gender	**(n=1129)**	**(n=1216)**
Males	53.5(604)	67.8(824)
Age – Years old	**(n=1131)**	**(n=1202)**
	14.55(1.816)	13.58(1.498)
11	0(0)	2.9(35)
12	15.3(173)	23.3(280)
13	21.3(241)	29(349)
14	13.5(153)	19.2(231)
15	14.9(169)	16.5(198)
16	17.9(202)	1.1(13)
17	11.7(132)	7.9(95)
18	5.4(61)	0.1(1)
School levels	**(n=1132)**	**(n=1218)**
ESO/Years 7-11	74.5(843)	89.1(1085)
Bachilerato/Years 12-13	25.5(289)	10.9 (133)
Types of schools surveyed	**(n=1132)**	**(n=1220)**
State	94.5 (1070)	66.3(809)
Public/Private	5.5 (62)	33.7(411)
Family members (type)	**(n=1123)**	**(n=1178)**
	4.02(1.050)	5.19(1.855)
≤ 2 (mono-parental)	5.3(59)	3.9(46)
3-4 (traditional)	70.1(788)	53.7(422)
≥ 5 (extensive)	24.6 (276)	60.3(710)

	Spain	UK
Parents' educational level		
Father	**(n=1081)**	**(n=1224)**
Primary		16(173)
Secondary	48(519)	54.5(543)
University	36(389)	41.2(412)
Mother		**(n=1098)**
Primary		16.8(185)
Secondary	43.7(479)	55.6(551)
University	39.5(434)	39.4(390)
Parents' working		
Father	(n=1102)	(n=1140)
	93.7(1033)	74.2 (8456)
Mother	(n=1120)	(n=1163)
	82.7(936)	46.9(574)
Nicotine/alcohol habitual consumptio		
Yes	(n=1118)	(n=1201)
	23.3(261)	12.4(149)
Entertainment without technology (n=1009)		
No	(n=1120)	(n=1170)
	21(235)	30.6(358)

Note: The percentage (%) presented is the valid percentage.

Similarly, the patterns of usage were quite similar between Spain and the UK. Almost all adolescents used mobile phones (Spain: 92.2%; UK: 85.1%), with the greater part being for entertainment (Spain: 63.7%; UK: 75.7%). The initial age of obtaining a mobile device was also quite similar (Spain: M=11.18, SD=1.915; UK: 10.01, SD=2.157). The cost for the device was above all covered by (Spain: 68% parents, 23.4% adolescent, 6.7% parents and adolescent, 1.9% other family members; UK: 52.7% parents, 25.9% adolescent, 16.7% parents and adolescent, 4.7% other family members). More than an half of adolescents perceived mobile phone addiction (Spain: 60.7%; UK: 54.6%); however, compared against other negative considerations they are more worried about other matters than mobile phone addiction(Spain: 51.6% economic, 21.8% addiction, 3.6% isolation, 2.6% pain and aches, among 20.3% of other negative aspects; UK: 21.2% pain and aches, 16.6% economic, 15% addiction, 10.2% isolation, 37% of other negative aspects).

In relation with the MPPUSA symptoms measured (using the grouping items proposed by Lopez-Fernandez et al., 2013); in Spain the most prevalent were (in order of frequency): withdrawal (34%), escape (33.1%), craving (26.7%), tolerance (24.3%), and negative consequences (26%). On the other hand, the most prevalent symptoms in the UK were: escape (19.3%), withdrawal (17.8%), tolerance (17.7%), craving (12.1%), and negative consequences (7.5%).

13.3.2 Proposal for classification of problem mobile phone users

13.3.2.1 Estimation of prevalence in each country

PMPU was classified according to the statistical criteria previously used on Internet addiction (Chow, Leung, Ng, & Yu, 2009).This method involves classifying non-problem and potential problem users through the cut-off point of the 95th percentile (Spain: 182, UK: 181). Based on this method the number of adolescent problem users is estimated to be 14.9% in Spain and 5.1% in UK. Analysis of this cut-off point revealed a statistically significant difference between potential problem (Spain: Mdn=201; UK: Mdn=182) and non-problem (Spain: Mdn=61; UK: Mdn=62) mobile phone users (Spain: U: Z=17.809, p<.001; UK: U: Z=10.267, p<.001).

Using this method to extract an extreme cut-off point, the adolescents classified as potential problematic users in both countries showed that there were almost no differences among the variables measured, except for a few slight cross-cultural differences in the intensity of the relationships detected: in Spain, for example, significant differences were found between those who habitually consume alcohol/tobacco ($\chi^2_{(1)}$=7.609, p < .01, V=.96) and those who perceive mobile addiction tended to be problematic users ($\chi^2_{(1)}$=28.607, p < .001, V=.201); similarly, in the UK those consuming alcohol/tobacco ($\chi^2_{(1)}$=28.674, p < .001, V=.2) and those who only enjoy with technologies tended to be the more problematic users ($\chi^2_{(1)}$=4.104, p < .05, V=.076).

To check this proposed classification of problem and potential non-problem users, a statistical verification of the suggested cut-off scores for each country was made to calculate the sensitivity, specificity, and classification accuracy of the addictive symptomatology (see Lopez-Fernandez et al., 2013; Phillips, Saling, & Blaszczynski, 2008, for the procedure followed); therefore, the social dimension was removed. The sensitivity of the scale was almost perfect in both countries, which is the particularly important, the specificity was noteworthy, and classification accuracy was very good in all symptomatology (see Table 2); therefore, this cut-off point support this precise classification.

13.3.2.2 Potential problem users' perception of PMPU in each country

The qualitative part of this study, addressed through the open question regarding the definition of PMPU, collected 124 quotations from the Spanish sample and 37 from the British, which means that 100% of potential problem users classified.

The problematic Spaniards pointed out clearly that dependency on mobile phones is when adolescents are attending to this device all day, including bringing it to his or

Table 13.2. Proposal of the classification function of the MPPUSA (N=1558; symptoms, answers of non-problem and potential problem users, sensitivity, specificity, and overall accuracy for each country)

Symptoms	Spain (N=833)									UK (N=725)								
	Answers of non-problem users n = 709			Answers of problem users n = 124			Sensitivity	Specificity	Overall accuracy	Answers of non-problem users n = 688			Answers of problem users n = 37			Sensitivity	Specificity	Overall accuracy
	Mdn	n Yes	n No	Mdn	n Yes	n No				Mdn	n Yes	n No	Mdn	n Yes	n No			
Tolerance	2	86	623	7*	123	1	99.2	87.9	89.6	3	91	597	8*	36	1	97.3	86.8	87.3
Escape	3	161	548	7*	124	0	100	77.3	80.7	3	97	591	8*	36	1	97.3	85.9	86.5
Withdrawal	2	166	543	7*	124	0	100	76.6	80.1	2.3	90	598	9*	37	0	100	86.9	87.6
Craving	1	107	602	7*	123	1	99.2	84.9	87	1.7	54	634	8*	34	3	91.9	92.2	92.1
Negative conseq.	1	81	628	7*	122	2	98.4	88.6	90	1.9	22	666	7*	31	6	91.2	96.8	96.1

Note: *$p < .001$

her hand in any situation. To some of them, this dependency is social, like an escape symptom, illustrated by quotations such as "it is the need to talk through the mobile with the rest of people and to be always in contact with them" (boy, 15 years old); for others it seems that the most prevalent symptoms are withdrawal and craving, like "when you are nervous because you have forget the mobile phone" (girl, 16) or "it is recognized because you cannot leave it, and if you forget it you are anxious for having it again with you. Moreover addicts are always calling and sending messages" (girl, 17). However, in their quotations they highlighted negative consequences, such as the economic issues: "it is recognized above all for its excessive use, and as a consequence you must pay a great quantity of money" (boy, 17) or the time spend on it: "the need to use it, to communicate, to play... it could be recognized observing the time that (this behaviour) is consuming" (girl, 16).

The British students also highlighted several aspects that could be matched with the addictive symptomatology measured by the MPPUSA. For example, the negative consequence symptom for its common, constant, and daily use, checking it continuously "every minute of the day" (girl, 17), presenting some kind mobile phone withdrawal symptom "feeling lost without it" (girl, 17) or "people who can't live without their mobile phone" (girl, 15), and sometimes in order to "talk to people" (boy, 12) as a form of escape. In summary, from their own perception, the mobile phone seems to be addictive because it is a necessary device to be in contact with others (calling, texting, etc.) and enjoy oneself (listening music, playing games, etc.).

13.4 Discussion

The findings demonstrate that, although no differences among users' characteristics and usage of the mobile phones between Spanish and British adolescents were found, a number of cultural differences were observed in terms of the symptomatology of PMPU between the two samples, which is contradictory with Internet usage characteristics detected in a previous cross-cultural inter-continental study (Li et al., 2001). These researchers found that experience of computers and the Internet was more negative for British individuals compared to Chinese. This finding is markedly different from the present results, which found that Spanish adolescents have a higher potential for PMPU compared with their British peers. . This is potentially due to their cultural communicative background (among other cultural factors, etc.). To the author's knowledge, this is the first study that aimed to compare PMPU between two countries, and as such provides a novel cross-cultural examination of this potential technological addiction.

In relation to the MPPUSA test, similar to Yen et al. (2009), the prevalence of PMPU symptoms was examined using a cut-off point established according to classification criteria. In their study, Yen et al. established the four most relevant symptoms to PMPU: conflict with other activities, excessive use despite consequences, and tolerance. These findings are in contrast to the present study, which found that the most prevalent symptoms were withdrawal, escape, and negative consequences. Furthermore, both countries studied here show different rates of these addictive symptoms, with the Spaniards reporting higher scores to all symptoms measured, similar to the Taiwanese. However, it should be noted that Yen et al. (2009) used a different scale (Problematic Cellular Phone Use Questionnaire; PCPU-Q). As well as this their study examined an oriental culture, which are notably different from the western cultures studied here. As such it is possible that the differences between the two studies are cultural in nature. A further findings worth discussing is the new methodological approach to examining cyber addiction outlined in this chapter, in which the most quantitatively prevalent symptoms corresponded with the symptoms qualitatively perceived to be the most prevalent, that is, withdrawal, escape and negative consequences. In terms of the socio-demographic and educational factors associated with PMPU, previous research has examined variables such as social class, type of educational centre, family environment, substance abuse, etc. However, the present study found no associations between these factors and PMPU, with the exception of alcohol/nicotine consumption, which seem to be related with those classified as potential problem users in both countries (Sánchez-Martínez & Otero, 2009). In the literature (Koo, 2010; Walsh, White, Cox, & Young, 2011) a number of factors having been suggested as a possible predictors: frequently checking the phone for new calls or messages, the number of text messages sent or contacts, the time devoted to calls or other applications (such as games or social networking), the danger behaviour produced for the phone, etc. Furthermore, in contrast to Geser (2006, who found that PMPU was more prevalent in girls, the present study also found no gender differences in. However, this disparity may once again be due to the difference in measures employed, as the present study, Geser used a more generalised scale measuring PMPU, which entails the possibility that boys and girls excessively use mobile phones in different ways (e.g., social networking in girls and gaming in boys). Another explanation may lie in the technological improvements to mobile phones inherent in smartphones, as no longer are mobile devices used simply for communication, but also for more complex behaviour which includes online applications.

Following Billieux (2012), the most important concern associated with this technology is that it may be having an uncontrolled impact on daily life, for what his integrative model, which considers the heterogeneity of dysfunctional mobile use and the specificity of the factors involved, offers to the scientific and clinic community a framework to situate, in any case, if a potential mobile phone/smartphone problem user belong to one (or more) specific pathway. For example, Imamura et al. (2009) observed the considerable effect that mobile phone email has on Japanese adolescents' emotional state, and for what may be some of these users could be considered in the relationship maintenance pathway and/or the cyber addiction pathway. Considering this later pathway, the range of online activities promoted through smartphones, such as video games (such as MMORPGs) and social networks (like Facebook), and the excessive use of such online activities through these devices could produce PMPU. Conversely, however, these problems could be considered as real online internet addictions (Griffiths, 1999, 2000) independently of the device used (smartphone or computer).

Overall, the field of cyber-addictions is becoming to open up to more complex addictive phenomenon, with PMPU sharing some commonalities with PIU and being present in a number of different cultures. Future research should further address the issue of PMPU following the assertion of Billieux (2012), in that research must elucidate the factors and pathways that lead to a problematic engagement in an online activity in order to understand this addictive behavioural phenomenon.

References

Ahmed, I., Qazi, T. F. & Perji, K. A. (2011). Mobile phone to youngsters: Necessity or addiction. African Journal of Business management, 5, 12512-12519.

Baron, N. S. (2010). Introduction to special section: mobile phones in cross-cultural context: Sweden, Estonia, the USA and Japan. New Media & Society, 12, 3–11.

Baron, N. S. & Segerstad, Y. H. (2010). Cross-cultural patterns in mobile-phone use: public space and reachability in Sweden, the USA and Japan. New Media & Society, 12, 13-34.

Beranuy Fargues, M., Chamarro Lusar, A., Graner Jordania, C. & Carbonell Sánchez, X. (2009). Validación de dos escalas breves para evaluar la adicción a Internet y el abuso de móvil. Psicothema, 21, 480-485.

Beranuy Fargues, M., Sánchez Carbonell, X., Graner Jordania, C., Castellana Rossell, M. & Chamarro Lusar, A. (2006). Uso y abuso del teléfono móvil en adolescentes. XXI Congreso Internacional de Comunicación: Los jóvenes y el nuevo escenario de comunicación, Pamplona, 9-10 de noviembre de 2006 (Spain).

Bianchi, A., & Phillips, J. (2005). Psychological Predictors of Problem Mobile Phone Use. Cyberpsychology & Behavior, 8, 39-51.

Billieux, J. (2012) Problematic use of the mobile phone: a literature review and a pathways model. Current Psychiatry Reviews, 8, 299-307.

Billieux, J., Van der Linden, M. & Rochat, L. (2008). The role of impulsivity in actual and problematic use of the mobile phone. Applied Cognitive Psychology, 22, 1195-1210.

Carbonell, X., Guardiola, E., Beranuy, M. & Bellés, A. (2009). A bilbliometric analysis of the scientific literature on Internet, videogames, and cell phone addiction. J Med Libr Assoc, 97, 102-107.

Chóliz, M. (2010). Mobile phone addiction: a point of issue. Addiction, 105, 373-374.

Chóliz Montañés, M. & Villanueva Silvestre, V. (2011). Evaluación de la adicción al móvil en la Adolescencia. Revista Española de Drogodependencias, 36, 165-184.

Chow, S. L., Leung, G. M., Ng, C., & Yu, E. (2009). A Screen for Identifying Maladaptive Internet Use. International Journal Of Mental Health And Addiction, 7, 324-332.

Creswell, J. W., & Plano Clark, V. L. (2007). Designing and conducting mixed methods research. Thousand Oaks, CA: Sage.

Geser, H. (2006). Are girls (even) more addicted? Some gender patterns of cell phone usage. In Sociology in Switzerland: Sociology of the Mobile phone. Online Publications: Zuerich.

Griffiths, M. D. (1999). Internet addiction: Internet fuels other addictions. Student British Medical Journal, 7, 428-429.

Griffiths, M. D. (2000). Internet addiction – Time to be taken seriously? Addiction Research, 8, 413-418.

Durkee, T., Kaess, M., Carli, V., Parzer, P., Wasserman, C., Floderus, B., . . . Wasserman, D. (2012). Prevalence of pathological internet use among adolescents in Europe: Demographic and social factors. Addiction, 107(12), 2210-2222.

Imamura, A., Nishida, A., Nakazawa, N., Shimodera, S., Tanaka, H., Kinoshita, H.,... Okazahi, Y. (2009). Effects of cellular phone email use on the mental health of junior high school students in Japan. Psychiatry and Clinical Neurosciences, 63, 701–703.

Jenaro, C., Flores, N., Gómez-Vela, M., González-Gil, F. & Caballo, C. (2007). Problematic internet and cell-phone use: Psychological behavioral, and health correlates. Addiction Research & Theory, 15, 309-320.

Kawasaki, N., Tanei, S., Ogata, F., Burapadaja, S., Loetkham, C., Nakamura, T. & Tanada, S. (2006). Survey on Cellular Phone Usage on Students in Thailand. Journal of Psysiological Anthropology, 25, 377-382.

Ko, C., Yen, J., Chen, C., Chen, S., & Yen, C. (2005a). Proposed diagnostic criteria of Internet addiction for adolescents. Journal of Nervous and Mental Disease, 193, 728-733.

Ko, C., Yen, J., Chen, S., Yang, M., Lin, H., & Yen, C. (2009). Proposed diagnostic criteria and the screening and diagnosing tool of internet addiction in college students. Comprehensive Psychiatry, 50, 378-384.

Koo, H. Y. (2010). Cell phone addiction in high school students and its predictors. Journal of Korean Academy of Child Health Nursing, 16, 203-210.

Li, N., Kirkup, G., & Hodgson, B. (2001). Cross-cultural comparison of women students' attitudes toward the Internet and usage: China and the United Kingdom. CyberPsychology & Behavior, 4(3), 415-426.

Lemmens, J. S., & Bushman, B. J. (2006). The Appeal of Violent Video Games to Lower Educated Aggressive Adolescent Boys from Two Countries. CyberPsychology & Behavior, 9(5), 638-641.

Leung, L. (2007). Leisure boredom, sensation seeking, self-esteem, addiction symptoms and patterns of cell phone use. In E. A. Konijn, M. A. Tanis, S. Utz & A. Linden (Eds.), Mediated interpersonal communication (pp. 359-381). Mahwah, NJ: Lawrence Erlbaum Associates.

Lopez-Fernandez, O., Honrubia-Serrano, M. L. & Freixa-Blanxart, M. (2012). Adaptación española del "Mobile Phone Problem Use Scale" para población adolescente. Adicciones, 24, 123–130.

Lopez-Fernandez, O., Honrubia-Serrano, M. L., Freixa-Blanxart, M. & Gibson, W. (2013). A Prevalence of Problematic Mobile Phone Use in British Adolescents. Cyberpsychology, Behavior and Social Networking, in press.

Pedrero Pérez, E., Rodríguez Monje, M. & Ruiz Sánchez De León, J. (2012). Adicción o abuso del teléfono móvil. Revisión de la literatura. Adicciones, 24, 139-152.

Phillips, J. G., Saling, L, & Blaszczynski, A. (2008). Psychology of mobile phone use and misuse. In A. C. Harper & R. V. Buress (Eds.), Mobile telephones: networks, applications, and performance (pp. 191–210). New York, NY: Nova.

Sánchez-Martínez, M. & Otero, A. (2009). Factors associated with cell phone use in adolescents in the Community of Madrid (Spain). CyberPsychology & Behavior, 12, 131-137.

Sariyska, R., Reuter, M., Bey, K., Sha, P., Li, M., Chen, Y.-F., . . . Montag, C. (2014). Self-esteem, personality and internet addiction: A cross-cultural comparison study. Personality and Individual Differences, 61-62, 28-33.

Toda, M., Monden, K., Kubo, K. & Morimoto, K. (2006). Mobile phone dependence and health-related lifestyle of university students. Social Behavior and Personality, 34, 1277-1284.

Walsh, S. P., White, K. M., Cox, S. & Young, R. M. (2011). Keeping in constant touch: The predictors of young Australians' mobile phone involvement. Computers in Human Behavior, 27, 333–342.

Walsh, S. P., White, K. M. & Young, R. M. (2010). Needing to connect: The impact of self and others on young people's involvement with their mobile phone. Australian Journal of Psychology, 62, 194-203.

Weisskirch, R. S. (2011). No Crossed Wires: Cell Phone Communication in Parent-Adolescent Relationships. Cyberpsychology, Behavior and Social Networking, 14, 447–451.

Yen, C-H., Tang, T-C., Yen, J-Y., Lin, H-C., Huang, C-F., Liu, S-C. & Ho, C-H. (2009). Symptoms of problematic cellular phone use, functional impairment and its association with depression among adolescents in Southern Taiwan. Journal of Adolescence, 32, 863-873.

APPENDIX A. MPPUSA (item number, item statement for Spanish and British adaptation, and Likert scale response)

Ítem n	MPPUSA Item statement: Spanish / British adaptations	Response
		1 (...) 10
1	Nunca tengo tiempo suficiente para el móvil / I can never spend enough time on my mobile phone	
2	Cuando me he sentido mal he utilizado el móvil para sentirme mejor / I have used my mobile phone to make myself feel better when I was feeling down	
3	Empleo mi tiempo con el móvil, cuando debería estar haciendo otras cosas y esto me causa problemas / I find myself occupied on my mobile phone when I should be doing other things, and it causes problems	
4	He intentado ocultar a los demás el tiempo que dedico a hablar con el móvil / I have tried to hide from others how much time I spend on my mobile phone	
5	El uso del móvil me ha quitado horas de sueño / I lose sleep due to the time I spend on my mobile phone	
6	He gastado más de lo que debía o podía pagar / I have spent with the mobile phone more than I should have	
7	Cuando no estoy localizable me preocupo con la idea de perderme alguna llamada / When out of range for some time, I become worried about the thought of missing a call	
8	A veces, cuando estoy al teléfono y estoy haciendo algo más, me dejo llevar por la conversación y no presto atención a lo que estoy haciendo / Sometimes, when I am on my mobile phone and I am doing other things, I get carried away with the conversation and I don't pay attention to what I am doing	
9	El tiempo que paso en el móvil se ha incrementado en los últimos 12 meses / The time I spend on my mobile phone has increased over the last 12 months	
10	He usado el móvil para hablar con otros cuando me sentía sol/a o aislado/a / I have used my mobile phone to talk to others when I was feeling isolated	
11	He intentado pasar menos tiempo con el móvil pero soy incapaz / I have attempted to spend less time on my mobile phone but am unable to	
12	Me cuesta apagar el móvil / I find it difficult to switch off/switch to silent my mobile phone	
13	Me noto nervioso/a si paso tiempo sin consultar mis mensajes o si no he conectado el móvil / I feel anxious if I have not checked for messages or switched on my mobile phone for some time	
14	Suelo soñar con el móvil / I have frequent dreams about my mobile phone	
15	Mis amigos y familia se quejan porque uso mucho el móvil / My friends and family complain about my use of the mobile phone	

Ítem n	MPPUSA Item statement: Spanish / British adaptations	Response
16	Si no tuviera móvil, a mis amigos les costaría ponerse en contacto conmigo / If I don't have a mobile phone, my friends would find it hard to get in touch with me	
17	Mi rendimiento ha disminuido a consecuencia del tiempo que paso con el móvil / My academic performance has decreased as a direct result of the time I spend on my mobile phone	
18	Tengo molestias que se asocian al uso del móvil / I have aches and pains that are associated with my mobile phone use	
19	Me veo enganchado/a al móvil más tiempo de lo que me gustaría / I find myself using on my mobile phone for longer periods of time than intended	
20	A veces preferiría usar el móvil que tratar otros temas más urgentes / There are times when I would rather use my mobile phone than deal with other more urgent matters	
21	Suelo llegar tarde cuando quedo porque estoy enganchado/a al móvil cuando no debería / I am often late for appointments because I'm talking on my mobile phone when I shouldn't be	
22	Me pongo de mal humor si tengo que apagar el móvil en clases, comidas o en el cine / I become irritable if I have to switch off/to silent my mobile phone for classes, meals, or at the cinema	
23	Me han dicho que paso demasiado tiempo con el móvil / I have been told that I spend too much time on my mobile phone	
24	Más de una vez me he visto en un apuro porque mi móvil ha empezado a sonar en una clase, cine o teatro / More than once I have been in trouble because my mobile phone has gone off during a class, at the cinema, or in a theatre	
25	A mis amigos/as no les gusta que tenga el móvil apagado / My friends don't like it when my mobile phone is switched off/to silent	
26	Me siento perdido/a sin el móvil / I feel lost without my mobile phone	

Nota: "Instrucciones: Por favor conteste cada una de las siguientes afirmaciones acerca del uso que ha hecho del teléfono móvil durante el último año. En cada una ha de considerar entre si ésta es totalmente falsa (1) o completamente verdadera (10). Por favor, sea honesto."

Note: "Instructions: Please answer each of the following questions about mobile phones use in the past year. In each one you must consider whether it is totally false (1) or completely true (10). Please be honest."

Silvia Casale, Caterina Primi, Giulia Fioravanti

14 Generalized Problematic Internet Use Scale 2: update on the psychometric properties among Italian young adults.

Abstract. Problematic Internet Use (PIU) involves cognitive distortions and dysfunctional behaviors (e.g., compulsive Internet use or using the Internet to alleviate negative emotions) that lead to negative outcomes in various areas of an individual's life. The Generalized Problematic Internet Use Scale 2 (GPIUS2) is one of the few theory-driven instruments to measure the type of PIU associated with the unique communicative context available online. The purpose of this study was to expand upon previous empirical evidence of the psychometric properties of the GPIUS) among Italian young adults. The present psychometric evaluation of the Italian version of the GPIUS2 was conducted on a sample of 748 undergraduate students (48.3% males) from 18 to 26 years old (M= 21.84 years, SD = 2.20). With regard to scale dimensionality, the four first-order factors model (i.e. preference for online social interaction, mood regulation, deficient self-regulation, and negative outcomes) was confirmed (fit indices: Satorra-Bentler scaled χ^2/df = 3.03; Comparative Fit Index = 0.93; Tucker–Lewis index = 0.92; Root Mean Square Error of Approximation = 0.05). Internal-consistency Cronbach's alpha ranged from 0.72 to 0.89. Convergent validity is demonstrated with significant correlations between GPIUS2 and Internet Addiction Test score. Validity was also assessed by exploring the relationship between GPIUS2 and several indices of psychosocial well-being that were expected to be related to PIU on the basis of previous studies. The overall results confirm previous evidence that the GPIUS2 is an adequate measure of generalized PIU cognitions, behaviors, and outcomes among young adults.

14.1 Defining Problematic Internet Use

The proliferation of Internet technology has led to an increase in problematic Internet use (PIU) in several cultural contexts (e.g., Canbaz, Sunter, Peksen, & Canbaz, 2009; Ghassemzadeh, Shahraray, & Moradi, 2008; Liu, Desai, Krishnan-Sarin, Cavallo, & Potenza, 2011). Even if cross-national variations in prevalence have been reported (Durkee et al., 2012), it seems possible to conclude that maladaptive internet use is widespread among adolescents. In Italy a recent study (Villella et al., 2011) assessing the prevalence of behavioral addictions in an adolescent population found that 1.2% of the participants were addicted to the Internet. More recently, a prevalence of 5.01% was reported (Poli & Agrimi, 2012).

Among the theoretical approaches to PIU, the cognitive-behavioral model (Davis, 2001) has received a great deal of attention. Compared to the Internet Addiction (IA) label, a misleading category in which to group all problems associated with excessive Internet use, the cognitive-behavioral model has the merit of accounting for what people are actually doing online. This perspective, rather than conceptualizing PIU as a behavioral addiction, conceptualizes PIU as a multidimensional syndrome that consists of cognitive, emotional, and behavioral symptoms that lead to difficulties in managing one's offline life. Davis (2001) proposes that PIU can be further classified as specific PIU (SPIU) – the overuse of content-specific functions of the Internet (e.g. gambling, viewing sexual material) – and generalized PIU (GPIU), which occurs when an individual develops problems due to the unique communicative context of the Internet. GPIU is conceptualized as "the real Internet syndrome," as it would likely not even exist in the absence of the Internet, which acts, in its social role, as a means of communication. In fact, the interpersonal functions that are unique to the Internet have been consistently identified by a number of scholars as being associated with problematic, pathological, or addictive Internet use (Caplan & High, 2010; McKenna & Bargh, 1999; Morahan-Martin & Schumacher, 2000, 2003). In a review of the literature, Morahan-Martin (2007) explains that "there is a growing consensus that the unique social interactions made possible by the Internet play a major role in the development of Internet abuse" (p.335), adding that "people with problematic Internet abuse are drawn to the experience of being online, and prefer virtual rather than face-to-face interpersonal communication" (p.342). By drawing a distinction between GPIU and SPIU, Davis proposes an empirically testable answer to what it actually is that people are addicted to, which was neglected by the Internet addiction perspective.

14.2 The update model of Generalized Problematic Internet Use

Since the publication of Davis' research, Caplan (2002; 2003; 2005; 2007; 2010) has integrated the research on interpersonal communication in face-to-face (FtF) settings with Davis's model of GPIU by highlighting the role that interpersonal computer mediated communication (CMC) processes play in the relationship between Internet use and psychosocial well-being. In 2010 Caplan proposed an integrated conceptual model of GPIU that combines elements of Davis' cognitive-behavioral theory, his own works that address a preference for online social interaction (Caplan, 2003; 2005), and the socio-cognitive model of unregulated Internet use (Kim, LaRose & Peng, 2009; LaRose, Lin, & Eastin, 2003). The updated cognitive-behavioral model of PIU includes four core components: preference for online social interaction (POSI), mood regulation, deficient self-regulation, and negative outcomes (Caplan, 2010). POSI is defined as the belief that one is safer, more efficacious, and more confident with online interpersonal interactions than with FtF interactions. According to Caplan, POSI is a cognitive symptom of GPIU that may help explain, at least in part, why certain individuals show other cognitive or behavioral indicators of problematic use, such as going online for mood regulation and having problems regulating their use of the web. Specifically, people with high levels of social anxiety and low levels of perceived social support have been found to be at risk of developing POSI (Caplan, 2007), since the online environment might be seen as more safer and comfortable than FtF interactions. The central role of POSI as a key factor for the development of other GPIU dimensions is one of the distinctive features of the GPIU perspective in comparison to the IA approach. Another cognitive symptom of GPIU is the motivation to use the Internet to alleviate distressing feelings (mood regulation), which has an important role in the development of the behavioral symptoms of both GPIU (Kim et al., 2009; LaRose et al., 2003) and POSI. Indeed, both the POSI and the mood regulation dimensions have been found to be good predictors of the failure to adequately monitor one's use of the web. The state in which conscious self-control of the web is diminished has been labeled as Deficient Regulation. This construct consists of a compulsive use dimension - the inability to control or regulate one's online behavior - and a cognitive preoccupation dimension, which describes an obsessive thought pattern about the online world. According to Caplan, "if cognitive symptoms of GPIU are salient enough, they lead to behavioral symptoms that ultimately result in negative outcomes" (p.1090). Several studies have provided preliminary empirical support for the basic assumptions of this model. Recent studies have produced empirical evidence supporting the claim that compulsive use is a central component of PIU (e.g., Caplan, 2005; Kim et al., 2009; van den Eijnden, Meerkerk, Vermulst, Spijkerman, & Engels, 2008). POSI has been found to be predictive of this compulsive use (Caplan, 2010; Fioravanti, Dèttore, & Casale, 2012) and mood regulation was a significant cognitive predictor of negative outcomes associated with Internet use (Caplan, 2002; Gámez-Guadix, Villa-George, & Calvete, 2012). Caplan and High (2007) found that the association between compulsive Internet use and negative outcomes is more pronounced when cognitive preoccupation is present. Moreover, results from the SEM analysis provided support for the overall conceptual model in several cultural contexts. Gámez-Guadix et al. (2012) found that preference for online social interaction and the use of the Internet for mood regulation increased the probability of reporting deficient self-regulation, which, in turn, was significantly associated with negative life outcomes.

14.3 The Generalized Problematic Internet Use Scale 2

Although some attempts to measure PIU have been made, these measures have not received extensive and systematic psychometric testing (Davis, Flett, & Besser, 2002). Recently, some theory-driven instruments have been created (e.g., Demetrovics, Szeredi, & Ròzsa, 2008; Pratarelli & Browne, 2002). Among them, the Generalized Problematic Internet Use Scale 2 (GPIUS2; Caplan, 2010), a revised and updated version of the 15-item Generalized Problematic Internet Use Scale (Caplan, 2002), has been developed in order to formally test the updated model of generalized problematic Internet use. The GPIUS2 addresses four core components: (1) POSI (a sample item is "Online social interaction is more comfortable for me than face-to-face interaction"); (2) Mood Regulation (a sample item is "I have used the Internet to make myself feel better when I was down"); (3) Deficient Self-Regulation, which consists of a compulsive use dimension and a cognitive preoccupation dimension (sample items are, respectively, "I find it difficult to control my Internet use" and "I think obsessively about going online when I am offline"); and (4) Negative Outcomes (e.g. "I have missed social engagements or activities because of my Internet use").

The GPIUS2 features two new factors that were not included in the original version of the GPIUS: POSI and deficient self-regulation. In the new version, POSI is regarded as a single construct rather than as two separate factors (social benefits and social control). Indeed, Caplan (2003) demonstrates the value of combining the social benefits (the perceived social benefits of Internet use) and the social control factors (an individual's perceived degree of control over self-presentation when interacting with others online) into a single subscale operationalizing POSI. Another change is that the GPIUS2 operationalizes deficient self-regulation as a higher-order factor that influences both cognitive preoccupation and compulsive Internet use subscale scores. This change is based on the work of LaRose and his colleague (2003), which suggests that compulsive Internet use and cognitive preoccupation are both symptoms of deficient self-regulation. In addition, the original scale's excessive Internet use subscale was omitted from the new scale, as empirical evidence has emerged that frequency of Internet use is not necessarily indicative of problematic use (Caplan, 2005). Finally, the names of two of the original dimensions were revised. Specifically, the mood alteration factor was renamed "mood regulation" in order to emphasize the motivation to use the Internet to alleviate and process emotions (LaRose et al., 2003; Yates, Gregor, & Haviland, 2012), and the withdrawal dimension was renamed "cognitive preoccupation" in order to more clearly reflect its emphasis on obsessive thinking about the online world.

The GPIUS2 is one of the few theory-based measures of GPIU with good psychometric properties. In comparison to the Internet Addiction Test (IAT; Young, 1998), the most used instrument for assessing PIU, the GPIUS2 is specifically focused on problematic use that arises due to the unique communicative context of the Internet. For these reasons, both the first and the second version of the GPIUS have been used recently in a variety of contexts for the assessment of GPIU (e.g., Ang, Chong, Chye, & Huan, 2012; Casale & Fioravanti, 2011; Casale, Tella, & Fioravanti, 2013; Chittaro & Vianello, 2013; Fioravanti et al., 2012; Fioravanti, Primi, & Casale, 2013; Gámez-Guadix et al., 2012) with the aim of reporting the properties of the scale across various cultures. Among Mexican adolescents, the GPIUS2 has demonstrated adequate psychometric qualities, including construct validity, convergent validity, and internal consistency (Gámez-Guadix et al., 2012). The psychometric properties of the Italian version of the GPIUS2were examined in a previous study (Fioravanti et al., 2013). Dimensionality was assessed applying a confirmative approach. Two models were compared: a higher-order factor model, as defined by Caplan's confirmatory factor analysis (2010), and a four-factor model in which deficient self-regulation was not divided into two factors (compulsive use and cognitive preoccupation), since the high correlations found by Caplan suggested the presence of a unique factor containing both dimensions. Results show a poor overall fit for the hierarchical model and an acceptable fit for the four-factor model. With regard to convergent validity, significant correlations between GPIUS2 (total score and subscales scores) and the IAT were found. The overall findings suggested that the Italian version of the GPIUS2 is an adequate measure of cognitions, behaviors, and outcomes associated with problematic use of Internet communicative services. However, those results have to be regarded as preliminary, since the relationships between GPIUS2 dimension and indices of psychosocial difficulties associated with PIU (e.g., social support) were not investigated. Moreover, the study was only partially representative of undergraduates, since students were recruited in just two faculties from one university. Furthermore, descriptive statistics of the GPIUS2 subscales were not reported.

For these reasons, the aim of the present study is to expand upon previous empirical research, providing a larger and more representative sample of undergraduate students. Moreover, we intend to provide descriptive statistics for the GPIUS2 subscales and examine concurrent validity data through the use of measures of constructs correlated with PIU.

14.4 Methods

14.4.1 Participants and data collection

Seven hundred and forty-eight undergraduate students (48.3% males) ranging in age from 18 to 26 years old (M= 21.84 years, SD = 2.20) participated in the study. Students of several randomly selected faculties of the University of Florence, Perugia, and Arezzo (Italy) were recruited in the study rooms or approached at the end of the lectures by four female research assistants. Participants were verbally asked about their willingness in participating in a survey about Internet uses. They were informed that the time to complete the questionnaire was around twenty minutes. Participation was voluntary and anonymous. No formative credits or monetary rewards were given. Data collection consisted of written questionnaires administered individually in classroom settings. Informed consent was obtained from all participants.

14.4.2 Measures and Procedure

A socio-demographic questionnaire was administered to collect information about participants' age, gender, ethnic group, continent of residence, marital status, educational attainment, employment status, and annual income.

The GPIUS2 (Caplan, 2010) contains fifteen Likert-type items rated on an 8-point scale (from "definitely disagree" to "definitely agree"). Preliminary data (Fioravanti et al., 2013) show that the Italian version of the GPIUS2 seems to be a valid measure of GPIU cognitions, behaviors, and outcomes. Its psychometric properties are comparable with those seen in the original instrument (Caplan, 2010). Whereas Caplan identified five first-order subscales, two of which (i.e., compulsive use and cognitive preoccupation) constitute a second-order factor (deficient self-regulation), the best-fit measurement model for the Italian version of the GPIUS2 includes four first-order factors without any higher-order determinants. With regard to reliability, internal-consistency Cronbach's alpha ranged from 0.78 to 0.89 (Fioravanti et al., 2013).

The IAT (Young, 1998) is the most used measure of Internet dependence. The Italian version (Ferraro, Caci, D'Amico, & Di Blasi, 2007) contains twenty Likert-type items using a 5-point scale (from "not at all" to "always"), yielding a maximum score of 100. A sample item is "How often do you find that you stay online longer than you intended?" In the current study, the IAT shows good internal consistency (Cronbach's $\alpha = .89$).

In order to assess concurrent validity of the GPIUS2 a measure of the Big Five personality traits and a self-report for the assessment of social support were administered to a subsample of participants (N=465). The Big Five Inventory - Version 44 (BFI-44; John, Donahue, & Kentle, 1991) provides a score for each of the Big Five personality traits (Conscientiousness, Agreeableness, Emotional Stability, Extroversion and Intellect or Openness). The test is made up of 44 statements, each of which is rated on a 5-point Likert scale as to the subjects' degree of agreement with how well it describes them (from 1 = "strongly disagree" to 5 = "strongly agree"). Evidence for the Italian BFI-44 reliability, validity, and cross-cultural applicability was reported in Ubbiali, Chiorri, Hampton, & Donati (2013).

The Multidimensional Scale of Perceived Social Support (MSPSS, Zimet, Dahlem, Zimet, & Farley, 1988) is intended to measure the extent to which an individual perceives social support from three sources: Significant Others (SO), Family (FA), and Friends (FR). The MSPSS is a brief, easy to administer self-report questionnaire that contains twelve items rated on a seven-point Likert-type scale, with scores ranging from "very strongly disagree" (1) to "very strongly agree" (7). The Italian version of the MSPSS has proven to be psychometrically sound (Di Fabio & Busoni, 2008).

The measures were administered in this order in one session.

14.4.3 Data analysis

The four first-order factors model (Fioravanti et al., 2013) was tested by applying a confirmative approach. The Satorra-Bentler Scaled Chi-Square for continuous non-normal outcomes (Satorra & Bentler, 2001), conducted with Mplus 3.0 (Muthen & Muthen, 2004) and applying Maximum Likelihood Mean Adjusted Estimation, was used to conduct the Confirmative Factor Analysis (CFA). The criteria for assessing overall model fit were mainly based on practical fit measures: the ratio of chi square to its degree of freedom (S-Bχ^2/df), the Comparative Fit Index (CFI, Bentler, 1995), the Tucker-Lewis Index (TLI, Tucker & Lewis, 1973), and the Root Mean Square Error of Approximation (RMSEA, Steiger, 1990). For the ratio of chi square to its degree of freedom (S-Bχ^2/df), values less than 3 were considered to reflect fair fit (Kline, 2005). We considered CFI and TLI values of .90 and above to reflect fair fit (Bentler, 1995). For the RMSEA, values equal to or less than .08 were considered to reflect adequate fit (Browne & Cudeck, 1993).

Internal consistency for both the subscales and the total scale has been assessed by calculating the alpha coefficients. Finally, in order to test the GPIUS2 convergent validity, correlation analyses were conducted.

14.5 Results

Table 1 shows descriptive statistics for the GPIUS2 items. Univariate distributions of the 15 items were examined for assessment of normality. Skewness and Kurtosis indices of eleven items ranged outside the values of -1 and 1, suggesting that the departures from normality were not acceptable (Marcoulides & Hershberger, 1997). Descriptive statistics for GPIUS2 subscales and total score are reported in Table 2. The correlation coefficients for the GPIUS2 items are shown in Table 3.

Since the departures from normality were not acceptable, the Satorra–Bentler scaled chi-square (S-Bχ^2) for continuous non-normal outcomes was used. Results of the CFA showed a good overall fit for the four first-order factors model (S-Bχ^2/df = 3.03; CFI = .93; TLI = .92; RMSEA = .05). The path diagram and the standardized path coefficients are shown in Figure 1. Standardized factor loading ranged from .60 to .79, all of which were significant at the .001 level as well as the estimated correlations among errors.

Table 14.1. GPIUS2 Items Descriptive Statistics

Item wording	*M*	*SD*	Asymmetry	*SE*	Kurtosis	*SE*	Corrected Item Total correlation
1. *Online social interaction is more comfortable for me than face-to-face interaction.*	2.16	1.44	1.53	.09	2.41	.18	.45
2. *When I haven't been online for some time, I become preoccupied with the thought of going online.*	2.17	1.53	1.65	.09	2.49	.18	.58
3. *I prefer communicating with people online rather than face-to-face.*	1.62	1.13	2.77	.09	9.78	.18	.52
4. *I have used the Internet to make myself feel better when I was down.*	2.71	1.87	1.09	.09	.32	.18	.53
5. *I have used the Internet to talk with others when I was feeling isolated.*	2.73	1.93	1.11	.09	.35	.18	.51
6. *I have difficulty controlling the amount of time I spend online.*	2.72	1.92	1.14	.08	.44	.18	.62
7. *I have missed social engagements or activities because of my Internet use.*	1.51	1.17	3.15	.08	10.90	.18	.50
8. *I have used the Internet to make myself feel better when I've felt upset.*	2.29	1.72	1.51	.08	1.65	.18	.58
9. *I would feel lost if I was unable to go online.*	2.16	1.65	1.71	.08	2.48	.18	.57
10. *I find it difficult to control my Internet use.*	2.14	1.67	1.70	.08	2.30	.18	.63
11. *I think obsessively about going online when I am offline.*	1.45	.97	2.76	.08	8.64	.18	.63
12. *When offline, I have a hard time trying to resist the urge to go online.*	1.70	1.27	2.24	.08	5.15	.18	.65
13. *I prefer online social interaction over face-to-face communication.*	1.62	1.31	3	.08	9.81	.18	.43
14. *My Internet use has created problems for me in my life.*	1.47	1.06	3.15	.08	11.62	.18	.55
15. *My internet use has made it difficult for me to manage my life.*	1.48	1.09	3.20	.08	11.88	.18	.56

Table 14.2. GPIUS2 scales and total score: Descriptive Statistics

GPIUS2 Scales	*M (SD)*
POSI	1.79 (1.03)
MOOD REGULATION	2.57(1.55)
DEFICIENT SELF REGULATION	2.06(1.15)
NEGATIVE OUTCOME	1.48(.93)
GPIUS2 TOTAL SCORE	1.99 (.91)

Table 14.3. Correlation coefficients for the GPIUS2 items

	ITEM 1	**ITEM 2**	**ITEM 3**	**ITEM 4**	**ITEM 5**	**ITEM 6**	**ITEM 7**	**ITEM 8**	**ITEM 9**	**ITEM 10**	**ITEM 11**	**ITEM 12**	**ITEM 13**	**ITEM 14**	**ITEM 15**
ITEM 1	-														
ITEM 2	.43**	-													
ITEM 3	.53**	.31**	-												
ITEM 4	.29**	.35**	.32**	-											
ITEM 5	.35**	.36**	.31**	.57**	-										
ITEM 6	.25**	.45**	.28**	.31**	.34**	-									
ITEM 7	.15**	.24**	.26**	.20**	.19**	.38**	-								
ITEM 8	.27**	.35**	.29**	.61**	.53**	.35**	.31**	-							
ITEM 9	.25**	.45**	.31**	.30**	.34**	.38**	.38**	.34**	-						
ITEM 10	.19**	.41**	.26**	.24**	.23**	.74**	.44**	.31**	.46**	-					
ITEM 11	.25**	.50**	.41**	.24**	.21**	.42**	.48**	.29**	.51**	.49**	-				
ITEM 12	.29**	.47**	.33**	.31**	.26**	.51**	.36**	.33**	.44**	.58**	.63**	-			
ITEM 13	.39**	.20**	.46**	.24**	.21**	.20**	.29**	.26**	.23**	.23**	.34**	.32**	-		
ITEM 14	.20**	.28**	.28**	.25**	.19**	.37**	.46**	.31**	.32**	.46**	.46**	.45**	.31**	-	
ITEM 15	.17**	.27**	.30**	.24**	.21**	.41**	.48**	.31**	.31**	.50**	.46**	.47**	.31**	.71**	-

** $p < .001$

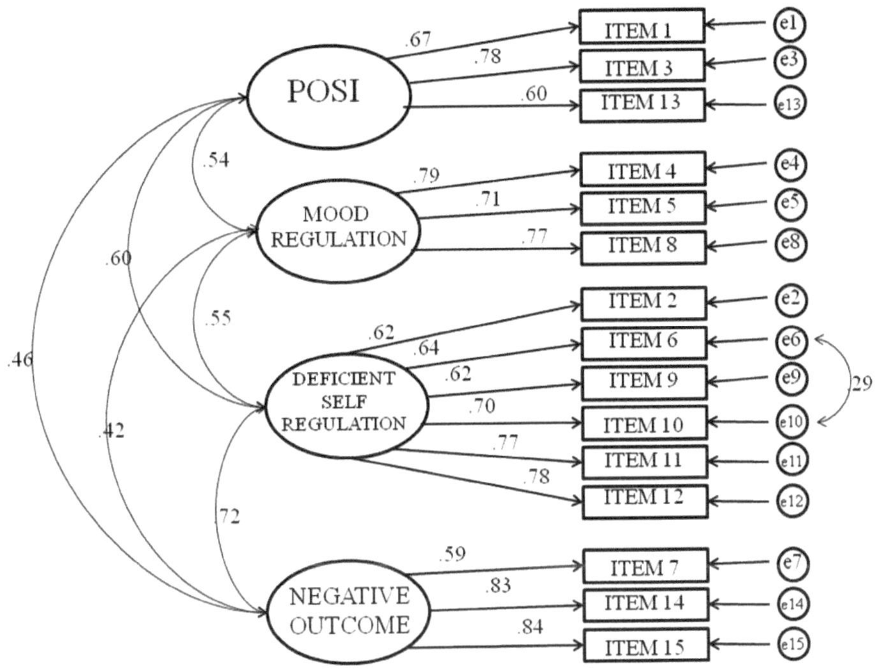

Figure 14.1. Confirmatory factor analysis of GPIUS 2

With regard to reliability, internal consistency Cronbach's Alpha was .71 (95% C.I.= .67 - .74) for POSI scale; α = .79 (95% C.I. = .77 - .82) for Mood Regulation scale; α = .84 (95% C.I. = .82 - .86) for Deficient Self-Regulation scale; and α = .78 (95% C.I. = .75 - .81) for Negative Outcome scale. When all items are used together to create an overall GPIUS2 composite score, the scale's reliability estimate was .88 (95% C.I.= .87 - .89). That value did not increase when an item was deleted, and all item-corrected total correlations were above .30.

Concerning validity, correlations between the GPIUS2 scores, gender, age, online-time in a typical week, and the IAT score were computed. GPIUS2 total score and gender were poorly correlated (r_{pb} = -.11; p<.01). GPIUS2 total score and age were not significantly correlated (r = .06; p = .07). A moderate correlation was found between GPIUS2 total score and the time spent online in a typical week (r = .25; p<.001). All the correlations between GPIUS2 (total score and all the subscale scores) and IAT scores (Table 4) were positive, indicating that a higher level of generalized pathological Internet use was associated with a higher level of Internet dependence. The correlations can be considered high according to the recently proposed cut-off values for convergent validity (Muñiz, 2011).

Pearson correlation coefficients between GPIUS2, BFI, and MSPSS scores are shown in Table 5.

Table 14.4. Pearson correlation coefficients between GPIUS2 scores and IAT scores

GPIUS2 Scales	**IAT total score**
POSI	.37*
MOOD REGULATION	.48*
DEFICIENT SELF REGULATION	.71*
NEGATIVE OUTCOME	.60*
GPIUS2 TOTAL SCORE	.73*

*p < .001

Table 14.5. Pearson correlation coefficients between GPIUS2, BFI and MSPSS scores (n = 465)

	POSI	**MR**	**DSR**	**NO**	**GPIUS2 TOTAL**
BFI_EX	-.27**	-.14*	-.02	-.06	-.13*
BFI_AG	-.10*	-.04	-.06	-.12*	-.12*
BFI_CO	-.08	-.13*	-.18**	-.24**	-.18**
BFI_NE	.13*	.16*	.05	.02	.12*
BFI_OP	-.13*	.00	-.07	-.04	-.07
MSPSS_SO	-.24**	-.10*	-.26**	-.22**	-.20**
MSPSS_FA	-.17**	-.17**	-.19**	-.25**	-.22**
MSPSS_FR	-.24**	-.12*	-.17**	-.17**	-.19**
MSPSS-TOT	-.27**	-.16*	-.25**	-.26**	-.25**

Note BFI_EX= Extraversion, BFI_AG= Agreeableness, BFI_CO= Conscientiousness, BFI_NE= Neuroticism, BFI_OP= Openness, MSPSS_SO= support form Significant Others, MSPSS_FA= support from Family, MSPSS_FR= support from Friends, MSPSS-TOT= social support total score, POSI= Preference for Online Social Interaction, MR= Mood Regulation, DSR=Deficient Self-Regulation, NO=Negative Outcomes.

*p<.05 **p<.001

14.6 Discussion

The present chapter provides an update on previous findings (Fioravanti et al., 2013) regarding the psychometric properties of the GPIUS2 among young people. Such a scale merits further investigation since it has the benefit of covering different cognitive and behavioral dimensions of the type of Internet abuse associated with the unique environment available online. Based on the results of the present study, the Italian adaptation of the GPIUS2 was confirmed to be a valid measure of GPIU cognitions, behaviors, and outcomes, and its psychometric properties are comparable with those seen in the original instrument (Caplan, 2010). In terms of scale dimensionality, Confirmatory Factor Analysis supported the four-scale structure, replicating our previous findings (Fioravanti et al., 2013). Indeed, a good overall fit for the four first-order factors model (POSI, mood regulation, deficient self-regulation, and negative outcomes) has been confirmed. From a theoretical point of view, this result confirms previous evidence regarding the strong interplay between obsessive thoughts about the Internet and compulsive Internet use, thus reflecting a unique manifestation of a diminished self-regulation capability. Concerning reliability, all four subscales and GPIUS2 total score demonstrated good to excellent internal consistency.

With regards to criterion validity, strong associations between GPIUS2 subscales and the IAT were found. In accordance with our previous findings, the higher correlation was found with the deficient self-regulation subscale, while the lower correlation was found with the subscale that measures preference for online social interaction levels. These results confirm that, in comparison with other measures of PIU, the GPIUS2 is more focused on problematic use due to the unique communicative context of the Internet. Since cognitive symptoms such as POSI have been systematically found to be a key factor in the development of negative outcomes (Caplan, 2003), a measure focused on these aspects might advance research about PIU. Indeed, the GPIUS2 provides a valuable approach to evaluating PIU from a multidimensional perspective, and a means of understanding the etiology and development of this problem.

The present findings are important because the relationship between GPIUS2 dimensions and indices of psychosocial difficulties associated with PIU (e.g., social support) was not investigated by previous researchers. The moderate negative associations between GPIUS2 (total score and all the subscales score) and a measure of social support demonstrated evidence for construct validity. Moreover, these significant negative associations might be seen as empirical support for the hypotheses put forth by the cognitive behavioral model of generalized PIU. According to Davis (2001), individuals with low levels of social support are more likely to appreciate an environment in which they feel safe and comfortable, which increases the likelihood that they will engage in inappropriate use of the Internet. Furthermore, the associations between Extraversion, Conscientiousness, and Neuroticism, on the one hand, and GPIUS2 dimensions, on the other hand, (respectively negative for Extraversion and Conscientiousness and positive for Neuroticism) support previous findings (e.g., Tsai, Cheng, Yeh, Shih, Chen, &Yang, 2009; van der Aa, Overbeek, Engels, Scholte, Meerkerk & Van den Eijnden, 2009) about the role of certain personality domains in the development of PIU. However, our results should not be seen as an empirical corroboration of previous findings, since they rely solely on cross-sectional data.

In conclusion, the present study builds on previous research on the psychometric properties of the GPIUS2, supporting its use among young, non-clinical populations. This scale permits researchers to evaluate different dimensions of PIU, is based on a well-developed theoretical model, and does not take much time to fill out. Moreover, the GPIUS2 addresses all the aspects that most researchers agree are related to PIU beyond the different conceptualizations they adopt for PIU (Chittaro & Vianello, 2013). The implications for research mainly deal with the use of GPIUS2 to analyze the prevalence of PIU and its relationships with other variables. The utilization of the GPIUS2 in clinical settings as a means of screening people at risk to develop the "real" Internet syndrome is also useful. In cognitive-behavioral therapy settings, the GPIUS2 could also help identify the specific maladaptive cognitions and ruminative thoughts that maintain PIU.

The present study relied solely upon undergraduate students. Undergraduates are generally considered a risk population, since they typically have flexible schedules and a natural affinity towards the Internet (Kuss, Griffiths, & Binder, 2013). Moreover, in comparison with adolescent students that might have some parental control of the Internet, college students typically have free and unlimited access. For these reasons, our primary purpose was to explore the psychometric properties of the measure in this risky population. However, further research should try to determine if our results can be extended to adolescent students and young workers.

References

Ang, R. P., Chong, W. H., Chye, S., & Huan, V. S. (2012). Loneliness and generalized problematic Internet use: Parents'perceived knowledge of adolescents'online activity as a moderator. Computers in Human Behavior, 28, 1342-1347.

Bentler, P. M. (1995) EQS structural equations program manual. Encino, CA: Multivariate Software.

Browne, M. W., & Cudeck, R. (1993) Alternative ways of assessing model fit. In Bollen K. A., Long J. S. (Eds), Testing structural equation models (pp. 136-162). Newbury Park, CA: Sage.

Canbaz, S., Sunter, A. T., Peksen, Y., & Canbaz, M. A. (2009). Prevalence of the pathological Internet use in a sample of Turkish school adolescents. Iran Journal of Public Health, 38, 64-71.

Caplan, S. E. (2002). Problematic Internet use and psychosocial well-being: Development of a theory-based cognitive-behavioral measure. Computers in Human Behavior, 18, 533–575.

Caplan, S. E. (2003). Preference for online social interaction: A theory of problematic Internet use and psychosocial well-being. Communication Research, 30, 625–648.

Caplan, S. E. (2005). A social skill account of problematic Internet use. Journal of Communication, 55, 721-736.

Caplan, S. E. (2007). Relations among loneliness, social anxiety, and problematic Internet use. Cyberpsychology & Behavior, 10, 234-242.

Caplan, S. E. (2010). Theory and measurement of generalized problematic Internet use: A two-step approach. Computers in Human Behavior, 25, 1089-1097.

Caplan, S. E., & High, A. C. (2007). Beyond excessive use: The interaction between cognitive and behavioral symptoms of problematic Internet use. Communication Research Reports, 23, 265-271.

Caplan, S. E., & High, A. (2010). Online social interaction, psychosocial well-being, and problematic internet use. In K. Young, & C.N. de Abreu, (Eds.), Internet addiction handbook (pp. 35-53). New York: John Wiley & Sons.

Casale, S., & Fioravanti, G. (2011). Psychosocial correlates of internet use among Italian students. International Journal of Psychology, 46, 288-298.

Casale, S., Tella, L., & Fioravanti, G. (2013). Preference for online social interactions among young people: Direct and indirect effects of emotional intelligence. Personality and Individual Differences, 54, 524-529.

Chittaro, L., & Vianello, A. (2013). Time perspective as a predictor of problematic Internet use: A study of Facebook users. Personality and Individual Differences, 55, 989-993.

Davis, R. A. (2001). A cognitive-behavioural model of pathological Internet use. Computers in Human Behaviour, 17, 187-195.

Davis, R. A., Flett, G. L., & Besser A. (2002). Validation of a New Scale for Measuring Problematic Internet Use: Implications for Pre-employment Screening. Cyberpsychology & Behavior, 5, 331-345.

Demetrovics, Z., Szeredi, B., & Rózsa, S. (2008). The three-factor model of Internet addiction: The development of the Problematic Internet Use Questionnaire. Behavior Research Methods, 40, 563-574.

Di Fabio, A., & Busoni, L. (2008). Measuring perceived social support: psychometric properties of the Multidimensional Scale of Perceived Social Support (MSPSS) in a sample of university students. Risorsa Uomo, 14, 339–350.

Durkee, T., Kaess, M., Carli, V., Parzer, P., Wasserman, C., Floderus, B., ... Wasserman, D. (2012). Prevalence of pathological internet use among adolescents in Europe: demographic and social factors. Addiction, 107, 2210-22.

Ferraro, G., Caci, B., D'Amico, A., & Di Blasi, M. (2007). Internet Addiction Disorder: An Italian study. Cyberpsychology & Behavior, 10,170-175.

Fioravanti, G., Dèttore, D., & Casale, S. (2012). Adolescent internet addiction. Testing the association between self-esteem, the perception of Internet attributes and preference for online social interaction. Cyberpsychology, Behavior, and Social Networking, 15, 318-323.

Fioravanti, G., Primi, C., & Casale, S. (2013). Psychometric evaluation of the Generalized Problematic Internet Use Scale 2 in an Italian sample. Cyberpsychology, Behavior, and Social Networking, 10, 761-766.

Gàmez-Guadix, M., Villa-George, F., & Calvete, E. (2012). Measurement and analysis of the cognitive-behavioral model of generalized problematic Internet use among Mexican adolescents. Journal of Adolescence, 35, 1581-1591.

Ghassemzadeh, L., Shahraray, M., & Moradi, A. (2008). Prevalence of internet addiction and comparison of internet addicts and non-addicts in Iranian high schools. Cyberpsychology & Behavior, 11, 731–733.

John, O. P., Donahue, E. M., & Kentle, R. L. (1991). The Big Five Inventory – Versions 4a and 54. Berkeley, CA: Institute of Personality and Social Research.

Kim, J., LaRose, R., & Peng, W. (2009). Loneliness as the cause and effect of problematic Internet use. The relationship between Internet use and psychological well-being. Cyberpsychology & Behavior, 12, 451–455.

Kline, R. B. (2005) Principles and Practice of Structural Equation Modeling (2nd Ed.). New York: Guilford Press.

Kuss, D. J., Griffiths, M. D., & Binder, J. F. (2013). Internet addiction in students: Prevalence and risk factors. Computers in Human Behavior, 29, 959–966

LaRose, R., Lin, C. A., & Eastin, M. S. (2003). Unregulated Internet usage: Addiction, habit, or deficient self-regulation? Media Psychology, 5, 225–253.

Liu, T. C., Desai R. A., Krishnan-Sarin, S., Cavallo, D. A, & Potenza, M. N. (2011). Problematic Internet use and health in adolescence: data from a high school survey in Cunnecticut. Journal of Clinical Psychiatry, 72, 836- 845.

Marcoulides, G. A., & Hershberger, S. L. (1997) Multivariate statistical methods. A first course. Mahawa, NJ: Lawrence Erlbaum Associates.

McKenna, K. Y., & Bargh, J. A. (1999). Causes and consequences of social interactions on the Internet: A conceptual framework. Media Psychology, 1, 249-269.
Morahan-Martin, J. (2007). Internet use and abuse and psychological problems. In A. Joinson, K. McKenna, T. Postmes, & U.D. Reips (Eds.), The Oxford Handbook of Internet Psychology (pp 331-345). New York: Oxford University Press.
Morahan-Martin, J., & Schumacher, P. (2000). Incidence and correlates of pathological Internet use among college students. Computers in Human Behavior, 16, 13–29.
Morahan-Martin, J., & Schumacher, P. (2003). Loneliness and social uses of the Internet. Computers in Human Behavior, 19(6), 659-671.
Muñiz, J. (2011, July). International strategies to improve tests and testing. Paper presented at the 12th European Congress of Psychology, Istanbul, Turkey.
Muthen, L. K., & Muthen, B. O. (2004) Mplus 3.0 [Computer Software]. Los Angeles, CA: Muthen & Muthen.
Poli, R., & Agrimi, E. (2012). Internet addiction disorder: Prevalence in an Italian student population. Nordic Journal of Psychiatry, 66, 55-9.
Pratarelli, M. E., & Browne, B. L. (2002). Confirmatory factor analysis of Internet use and addiction. CyberPsychology & Behavior, 5, 53-64.
Satorra, A., & Bentler, P. M. (2001). A scaled difference chi-square test statistic for moment structure analysis. Psychometrika, 66, 507-514.
Steiger, J. H. (1990). Structural model evaluation and modification: An interval estimation approach. Multivariate Behavioral Research, 25, 173-180.
Tsai, H. F., Cheng, S. H., Yeh, T. L., Shih, C. C., Chen, K. C., & Yang, Y. C. (2009).The risk factors of Internet addiction – A survey of university freshmen. Psychiatry Research, 167, 294–299.
Tucker, L. R., & Lewis C. (1973). A reliability coefficient for maximum likelihood factor analysis. Psychometrika, 38, 1-10.
Ubbiali, A., Chiorri, C., Hampton, P., & Donati, D. (2013). Psychometric properties of the Italian adaptation of the Big Five Inventory (BFI). Bollettino di Psicologia Applicata, 266, 37-48.
van der Aa, N., Overbeek, G., Engels, R.C.M.E., Scholte, R.H.J., Meerkerk, G.-J., & Van den Eijnden, R.J.J.M. (2009). Daily and compulsive Internet use and well-being in adolescence: A diathesis-stress model based on Big Five personality traits. Journal of Youth and Adolescence, 38, 765–776.
van den Eijnden, R. J. J. M., Meerkerk, G., Vermulst, A. A., Spijkerman, R., & Engels, R. C. M. E. (2008). Online communication, compulsive internet use, and psychosocial well-being among adolescents: A longitudinal study. Developmental Psychology, 44, 655–665.
Villella, C., Martinotti, G., Di Nicola, M., Cassano, M., La Torre, G., Gliubizzi, M. D., ... Conte, G. (2011). Behavioral addictions in adolescents and young adults: Results from a prevalence study. Journal of Gambling Studies, 27, 203-14.
Yates, T. M., Gregor, M. A., & Haviland, M. G. (2012). Child Maltreatment, alexithymia, and Problematic Internet Use in young adulthood. Cyberpsychology, Behavior, and Social Networking, 15, 219-225.
Young, K. S. (1998) Caught in the Net. New York, NY: John Wiley
Zimet, G. D., Dahlem, N. W., Zimet, S. G. & Farley, G. K. (1988). The Multidimensional Scale of Perceived Social Support. Journal of Personality Assessment, 52, 3

Pietro Cipresso, Brenda K. Wiederhold, Giuseppe Riva

15 Smartphone for social networking: methodological aspects

Abstract: In this chapter we parsed methodological aspects in studying behavior with mobile social networking sites like Facebook by using physiological measures. Current computational methods and the huge availability of sources and devices for psychophysiological recording allowed a deeper understanding of complex behaviors and an even more detailed knowledge of human emotions. These methods can be applied to understand the user navigation experience.

15.1 Introduction

Recent smart phones and mobile platforms integrate multiple advanced functions and allow individuals to share a lot of different information, such as photos and GPS data, within their social networks in real-time (Humphreys & Liao, 2011). Although a mobile device has by definition a smaller display (Ballagas, Borchers, Rohs, & Sheridan, 2006; Bulusu, Heidemann, & Estrin, 2000), which could create many problems during the experience (Chae & Kim, 2004; Codispoti & de Cesarei, 2007; De Cesarei & Codispoti, 2010; Lombard, Grabe, Reich, Campanella, & Ditton, 1996), they are easy-to-use and customizable: in particular, touch screen capabilities may improve the usability and navigation experience when browsing photos and information (Albinsson & Zhai, 2003; Chae & Kim, 2004; Vogel & Baudisch, 2007). Hence, it is easy to understand how mobile phones enable people to stay virtually connected at all times irrespective of their location. They assure "perpetual contact" (James, 2004; Katz & Aakhus, 2002) and affect every aspect of personal and professional life directly or indirectly. On the other hand, it is important to highlight that pathological experience may also arise from a pervasive use of mobile phones (Lepp, Barkley, & Karpinski, 2014; Salehan & Negahban, 2013).

Multifunctional mobile platforms allow individuals to be constantly in touch with their social network and to go beyond the main constraint of face-to-face communication, enacting the spatial-temporal contiguity (G. Riva, 2010). Moreover, mobile devices create an ubiquitous bridge between real and virtual life (Barkhuus & Polichar, 2011); they enhance the capability of social networking sites (SNSs) to create a new social space, the *Interreality*, marked by the fusion of real and virtual networks (Gaggioli et al., 2011; Repetto et al., in press). From a wider viewpoint, it is possible to assume that connections between millions of people via social networking sites constitute a new and powerful "social-self" where individuals can share experiences and have the "sense of being with another" (Biocca, Harms, & Burgoon, 2003), i.e., the *Social Presence*. The feeling of being with another person while using a social medium means, first of all, feeling part of the mediated communication (Biocca et al., 2003; Villani, Repetto, Cipresso, & Riva, in press), i.e., the *Presence*. According to Biocca and Colleagues (Biocca et al., 2003), *presence* is marked by two main aspects, *telepresence*, the sense of "being there" in a virtual space as the result of the possibility of executing automatic responses to spatial cues and creating the mental models of the mediated space, and *social presence*, the sense of "being with another" in a mediated space, including effective responses to social cues and mental models of other intentions. From this perspective, mobile platforms could be defined as *social presence technologies* (Biocca et al., 2003) specifically designed to increase social presence, since they assure ubiquitous (Ballagas et al., 2006; Repetto et al., in press; Villani et al., 2011) and perpetual (Katz & Aakhus, 2002) social contact via multimodal access (Brown, Green, & Harper, 2002).

As IJsselsteijn and Colleagues (IJsselsteijn, de Ridder, Freeman, & Avons, 2000; Ijsselsteijn, Freeman, & De Ridder, 2001) and Biocca and Colleagues (Biocca et al., 2003) underlined, there is not a unified model that assesses presence in mediated communication, although different approaches, such as, subjective self-report measures (Slater & Garau, 2007), continuous presence assessment (IJsselsteijn et al., 1997), analysis of postural and gestural responses (Freeman, Avons, Meddis, Pearson, & IJsselsteijn, 2000; Giakoumis et al., In press), psychophysical methods (Stanney et al., 1998), physiological indexes (Baumgartner, Valko, Esslen, & Jancke, 2006; Mikropoulos, 2001; Schilbach et al., 2006; Wiederhold et al., 2000), and many others (Schultze, 2010) have been used also with clinical patients (Albani et al., 2012; Raspelli et al., 2012; Repetto et al., in press). In this chapter, we were interested in examining subjects' experience during the use of SNSs; thus, our objective was to identify presence during such experience and the ways in which it leads to an optimum. A measure of presence in this study needs to consider the temporal continuity of the experience, additionally, for an objective and accurate assessment, we had to measure the key factors that previous research took into account for presence and optimal experience. Thus, we focused on three main aspects of time-space continuum of subjects' states: physiological arousal, emotional valence, and sustained attention.

According to the classic valence-arousal model (Lang, 1995a; Russell, 1979), to identify affective states of subjects during an experimental session, we can consider the two dimensions of "activation", namely, physiological arousal and emotional valence. Valence and arousal dynamics have been used extensively in psychophysiological research as an objective way to measure affective states during a mediated experience (Backs, da Silva, & Han, 2005a; Bradley & Lang, 2000; Cipresso, Serino, et al., 2012a; Codispoti, Surcinelli, & Baldaro, 2008; Gruhn & Scheibe, 2008a; Keil et al., 2002a; Morris, 1995; Rubin, Rubin, Graham, Perse, & Seibold, 2009; Salimpoor, Benovoy, Larcher, Dagher, & Zatorre, 2011; Salimpoor, Benovoy, Longo, Cooperstock, & Zatorre, 2009; Tajadura-Jimenez, Pantelidou, Rebacz, Vastfjall,

& Tsakiris, 2011). More recently, research has been conducted to discern different emotions by the means of cardiovascular measures (Cacioppo, Tassinary, & Berntson, 2007; Rainville, Bechara, Naqvi, & Damasio, 2006a), confirming results that can be obtained using specific patterns of the cardiovascular indexes (Magagnin et al., 2010; Mauri, Cipresso, Balgera, Villamira, & Riva, 2011; Mauri et al., 2010a).

The third dimension used to assess the SNSs experience was the attention. According to Draper and Colleagues (Draper, Kaber, & Usher, 1998), presence occurs when more attentional resources are allocated to the computer-mediated environment: "The more attentional resources that a user devotes to stimuli presented by the displays, the greater the identification with the computer-mediated environment and the stronger the sense of presence." If we are able to demonstrate that users are engaged during an experience and that during the same experience their level of attention (Schupp et al., 2007) to the source of the experience is high, then we can affirm that their sense of presence is high, which increases the optimal experience of subjects through higher involvement (Riley, Kaber, & Draper, 2004; Giuseppe Riva, Davide, & Ijsselsteijn, 2003).

15.2 Psychophysiology and Affective States

According to the classic valence-arousal model (Lang, 1995b; Russell, 1979) for experimentally identifying affective states in subjects, we can consider the two dimensions of "activation", namely, physiological arousal and emotional valence.

This approach has been extensively used in psychophysiological research as an objective way to measure affective states during a mediated experience (Backs, da Silva, & Han, 2005b; Bradley & Lang, 2000; Cacioppo et al., 2007; Cipresso, Serino, et al., 2012b; Gruhn & Scheibe, 2008b; Keil et al., 2002b; Kuhr et al., 2011; Morris, 1995; Rozenkrants & Polich, 2008; Rubin et al., 2009; Sharpley et al., 2000). More recently, extensive research has been done to discern different emotions by the means of cardiovascular measures (Rainville, Bechara, Naqvi, & Damasio, 2006b), with the results from these studies benefitting the analysis of affective states through cardiovascular indexes patterns (Magagnin et al., 2010; Mauri et al., 2011; Mauri et al., 2010b). For example, a recent study by Causse and colleagues (Causse, Baracat, Pastor, & Dehais, 2011) examined pilots' cardiovascular and oculometric measurements related to decision making.

Physiological arousal can be measured by using electroencephalogram (EEG), galvanic skin response (GSR), cardiovascular activity (ECG or BVP), and respiration signal (RSP); emotional valence can be measured by using EEG, self-reports, facial expression identification, eye-blink startle, and facial EMG corrugator and/or zygomatic. According to Blumenthal and colleagues (Blumenthal et al., 2005), facial EMG-CS (corrugator) can be considered the best measure of emotion valence.

Frontal EEG activation asymmetry has been generally used, giving evidence that greater left frontal activity seems to be more related with positive emotional valence, whereas greater right frontal activity seems to be more involved in negative emotional valence (Debener, Beauducel, Fiehler, Rabe, & Brocke, 2001). Alpha index has been suggested to be the most adept for studying frontal EEG activation asymmetry (Debener et al., 2001). Alpha Asymmetry index can be calculated in a number of different ways in order to take into account the prevalence of one hemisphere over the other one, and correct the index accordingly. In calculating this index it is crucial to consider that higher cortical activation is revealed by lower Alpha waves, and thus this need to be considered in the computation and formula derivation.

As recently demonstrated by Mojzisich and colleagues (Mojzisch et al., 2006), self-involvement during social interactions is specifically related to attention allocation. For this reason we are also interested in investigating sustained attention as another dimension of analysis. To this ends, slow Alpha EEG bands (following Slow Alpha) have been demonstrated to be a valid measure of sustained attention (Klimesch, 1999; Klimesch, Doppelmayr, Russegger, Pachinger, & Schwaiger, 1998).

15.3 Hypotheses and Research Questions

Eight hypotheses can be formulated, four regarding navigating SNSs using a PC and four considering navigation using a mobile device (Table 1). Each hypothesis is based on one dimension of Arousal-Valence-Attention factors. We added the fourth dimension of anxiety to act as a control dimension. For this purpose, we used two basic affective states, namely "Relax" and "Stress," that can be easily elicited in healthy subjects, representing the ground truth in the tridimensional space (Cipresso, Gaggioli, et al., 2012; Magagnin et al., 2010; Mauri et al., 2010a; Villani et al., 2011). This operation is conducted to compare along each axis the SNSs condition with a standard affective states generated in the subject.

Table 15.1. Test Hypotheses (~ is for similar, > is for greater than, < is for lower than)

Hypothesis	SNSs by	Dimension	Relax	Stress
Hp1	PC	Physiological Arousal	SNSs > Relax	SNSs ~ Stress
Hp2	PC	Emotional Valence	SNSs ~ Relax	SNSs > Stress
Hp3	PC	Attention	SNSs > Relax	SNSs ~ Stress
Hp4	PC	Anxiety	SNSs ~ Relax	SNSs < Stress
Hp5	Mobile	Physiological Arousal	SNSs > Relax	SNSs ~ Stress
Hp6	Mobile	Emotional Valence	SNSs ~ Relax	SNSs > Stress
Hp7	Mobile	Attention	SNSs > Relax	SNSs ~ Stress
Hp8	Mobile	Anxiety	SNSs ~ Relax	SNSs < Stress

The significant quadratic trend in the within-subjects contrasts can be used to further test each hypothesis. The Bayes factor can also be considered as alternative to the conventional t-test to express preference for either the null hypothesis or the alternative.

For Physiological Arousal, we hypothesized that subjects are more physiologically activated when navigating SNSs, which make them have an arousal quite similar to the one in the stress condition and different enough from the one during the relax condition (Hypotheses 1 and 5).

Positive emotions during the SNSs navigation were also proposed, in that the subjects were proposed to have a higher emotional valence during SNSs navigation, as high as in a Relax condition. On the other hand, low emotional valence due to the elicited negative emotions is expected during the Stress condition (Hypotheses 2 and 6).

For attention, it was easy to hypothesize that a higher level of attention characterizes both of the SNSs conditions (if an interest is provoked) and the stress condition, where the attentional resource is needed to focus on the complex task. On the other hand, the relax condition is expected to have a low level of attention, which is different from the SNSs condition (Hypotheses 3 and 7).

Anxiety level is an important dimension to be considered, since it allow us to correctly discern stressful experiences from optimal experiences. In this context, this dimension is crucial for avoiding erroneous conclusions about the effect of SNSs navigation. The hypothesis, therefore, is that the level of anxiety during SNSs navigation is quite different from the level of anxiety during the stress condition. In this sense, the level of anxiety during the SNSs navigation is supposed to be quite similar to the level during the relax condition (Hypotheses 4 and 8).

A synthesis of the hypotheses is reported in Table 1, where were coded the SNSs navigation for both sessions: during the PC navigation (shortly PC session), and during the navigation using a specific app in a mobile smart phone (shortly Mobile session).

The goal of studies which are interested in SNSs experience should be to investigate the effects of navigating SNSs on subjects' experience by measuring psychophysiological correlates. In particular the following research questions (RQ) arise:

> **RQ1:** Can SNSs navigation leads to an engagement state, aside from the specific platform used and the related levels of pervasiveness?

> **RQ2:** Can SNSs navigation through the mobile be more effective, leading to a higher pervasiveness able to induce an optimum state?

To answer these questions, we can use standard psychophysiological measures. We need to consider that the more the subjects will be engaged and attentive, the more likely they will be able to achieve an optimal state characterized by positive valence, high arousal, and high attention. Thus, we are interested in objectively identifying specific pattern of users' affective states in the Arousal-Valence-Attention space while experiencing SNSs navigation through a PC or a mobile platform.

15.4 Conclusion

We presented a multidimensional model to understand the experience of SNSs navigation by means of psychophysiological correlates. The dimensions considered were physiological arousal, emotional valence, and life satisfaction. Psychophysiological measures can be extremely useful for understanding users' behavior without interfering with their experience, and for this reason are considered to be very effective psychometric instruments. The idea of creating a map of the affective states during user navigation can be considered either in terms of simple observation or as an intervention device for any bad state arising during SNSs use. A real-time intervention to inform users of their affective states during SNSs navigation requires so-called affective computing. According to Rosalind Picard (1997), who coined the term, "affective computing is computing that relates to, arises from, or deliberately influences emotion or other affective phenomena." Of course affective computing is a fascinating field; however, it does have intrinsic limitations due to a lack of classification. It is in fact complex to recognize an affective state after months of signal processing and data analysis, let alone in real time. However, the big advantage of affective computing is that it has fostered the development of plenty of classification methods through vivid and productive international discussion at extremely high scientific levels. The continuous development of new artificial intelligence techniques further enriches this scenario; however, these methods have not often been applied to understanding SNSs navigation.

The spread of SNSs use among the population has been significant in the last ten years, and we can now affirm that most people in a way or another use social connections with direct consequences on their lives. To quantify these consequences is important not only at the social level but also at the individual level, since better information about our own states is crucial for personal decision-making. In particular, if I don't feel stressed during an SNSs navigation, but indeed I am, it would be better if an automatic system would be able to suggest I change my activity and try to relax for a while. Science fiction? Not at all. Automatic detection of physiological states and understanding of affective states is becoming a reality, and thousands of researchers are working to make this scenario possible.

References

Albani, G., Priano, L., Cipresso, P., Raspelli, S., Pignatti, R., Ferronato, P., . . . Mauro, A. (2012). Diurnal sleepiness and executive dysfunctions: A virtual and neuropsychological study in Parkinson's disease and sleep apnea syndrome. Movement Disorders, 27, S9-S9.

Albinsson, P. A., & Zhai, S. (2003). High Precision Touch Screen Interaction. Paper presented at the Proc. CHI '03.

Backs, R. W., da Silva, S. P., & Han, K. (2005a). A comparison of younger and older adults' Self-Assessment Manikin ratings of affective pictures. Experimental Aging Research, 31(4), 421-440. doi: Doi 10.1080/03610730500206808

Backs, R. W., da Silva, S. P., & Han, K. (2005b). A comparison of younger and older adults' self-assessment manikin ratings of affective pictures. Exp Aging Res, 31(4), 421-440. doi: 10.1080/03610730500206808

Ballagas, R., Borchers, J., Rohs, M., & Sheridan, J. G. (2006). The smart phone: A ubiquitous input device. Ieee Pervasive Computing, 5(1), 70-77.

Barkhuus, L., & Polichar, V. E. (2011). Empowerment through seamfulness: smart phones in everyday life. Personal and Ubiquitous Computing, 15(6), 629-639. doi: DOI 10.1007/s00779-010-0342-4

Baumgartner, T., Valko, L., Esslen, M., & Jancke, L. (2006). Neural correlate of spatial presence in an arousing and noninteractive virtual reality: An EEG and psychophysiology study. Cyberpsychology & Behavior, 9(1), 30-45.

Biocca, F., Harms, C., & Burgoon, J. K. (2003). Toward a more robust theory and measure of social presence: Review and suggested criteria. Presence-Teleoperators and Virtual Environments, 12(5), 456-480.

Blumenthal, T. D., Cuthbert, B. N., Filion, D. L., Hackley, S., Lipp, O. V., & van Boxtel, A. (2005). Committee report: Guidelines for human startle eyeblink electromyographic studies. Psychophysiology, 42(1), 1-15. doi: 10.1111/j.1469-8986.2005.00271.x

Bradley, M. M., & Lang, P. J. (2000). Affective reactions to acoustic stimuli. Psychophysiology, 37(2), 204-215.

Brown, B., Green, N., & Harper, R. (2002). Wireless world : social and interactional aspects of the mobile age. London ; New York: Springer.

Bulusu, N., Heidemann, J., & Estrin, D. (2000). GPS-less low-cost outdoor localization for very small devices. Ieee Personal Communications, 7(5), 28-34.

Cacioppo, J. T., Tassinary, L. G., & Berntson, G. G. (2007). Handbook of psychophysiology (3rd ed.). Cambridge England ; New York: Cambridge University Press.

Causse, M., Baracat, B., Pastor, J., & Dehais, F. (2011). Reward and uncertainty favor risky decision-making in pilots: evidence from cardiovascular and oculometric measurements. APPLIED PSYCHOPHYSIOLOGY AND BIOFEEDBACK, 36(4), 231-242. doi: 10.1007/s10484-011-9163-0

Chae, M., & Kim, J. (2004). Do size and structure matter to mobile users? An empirical study of the effects of screen size, information structure, and task complexity on user activities with standard web phones. Behaviour & Information Technology, 23(3), 165-181. doi: Doi 10.1080/01449290410001669923

Cipresso, P., Gaggioli, A., Serino, S., Pallavicini, F., Raspelli, S., Grassi, A., . . . Riva, G. (2012). EEG alpha asymmetry in virtual environments for the assessment of stress-related disorders. Stud Health Technol Inform, 173, 102-104.

Cipresso, P., Serino, S., Villani, D., Repetto, C., Sellitti, L., Albani, G., . . . Riva, G. (2012a). Is your phone so smart to affect your state? An exploratory study based on psychophysiological measures. Neurocomputing, 84, 23-30. doi: DOI 10.1016/j.neucom.2011.12.027

Cipresso, P., Serino, S., Villani, D., Repetto, C., Sellitti, L., Albani, G., . . . Riva, G. (2012b). Is your phone so smart to affect your states?: An exploratory study based on psychophysiological measures. Neurocomputing, 84, 23-30. doi: 10.1016/j.neucom.2011.12.027
Codispoti, M., & de Cesarei, A. (2007). Arousal and attention: Picture size and emotional reactions. Psychophysiology, 44(5), 680-686. doi: DOI 10.1111/j.1469-8986.2007.00545.x
Codispoti, M., Surcinelli, P., & Baldaro, B. (2008). Watching emotional movies: Affective reactions and gender differences. International Journal of Psychophysiology, 69(2), 90-95. doi: DOI 10.1016/j.ijpsycho.2008.03.004
De Cesarei, A., & Codispoti, M. (2010). Effects of Picture Size Reduction and Blurring on Emotional Engagement. PLoS ONE, 5(10). doi: ARTN e13399. DOI 10.1371/journal.pone.0013399
Debener, S., Beauducel, A., Fiehler, K., Rabe, S., & Brocke, B. (2001). Frontal EEG alpha asymmetry and affective style: Are individual differences related to fundamental dimensions of emotion? Psychophysiology, 38, S35-S35.
Draper, J. V., Kaber, D. B., & Usher, J. M. (1998). Telepresence. Human Factors, 40(3), 354-375.
Freeman, J., Avons, S. E., Meddis, R., Pearson, D. E., & IJsselsteijn, W. I. (2000). Using behavioral realism to estimate presence: A study of the utility of postural responses to motion stimuli. Presence-Teleoperators and Virtual Environments, 9(2), 149-164.
Gaggioli, A., Raspelli, S., Grassi, A., Pallavicini, F., Cipresso, P., Wiederhold, B. K., & Riva, G. (2011). Ubiquitous health in practice: the interreality paradigm. Stud Health Technol Inform, 163, 185-191.
Giakoumis, D., Drosou, A., Cipresso, P., Tzovaras, D., Hassapis, G., Gaggioli, A., & Riva, G. (In press). Using Activity-Related Behavioural Features towards more Effective Automatic Stress Detection. PLoS ONE.
Gruhn, D., & Scheibe, S. (2008a). Age-related differences in valence and arousal ratings of pictures from the International Affective Picture System (IAPS): Do ratings become more extreme with age? Behavior Research Methods, 40(2), 512-521. doi: Doi 10.3758/Brm.40.2.512
Gruhn, D., & Scheibe, S. (2008b). Age-related differences in valence and arousal ratings of pictures from the International Affective Picture System (IAPS): do ratings become more extreme with age? Behav Res Methods, 40(2), 512-521. doi: 10.3758/Brm.40.2.512
Humphreys, L., & Liao, T. (2011). Mobile Geotagging: Reexamining Our Interactions with Urban Space. Journal of Computer-Mediated Communication, 16(3). doi: ARTN 407. DOI 10.1111/j.1083-6101.2011.01548.x
IJsselsteijn, W. A., de Ridder, H., Freeman, J., & Avons, S. E. (2000). Presence: Concept, determinants and measurement. Human Vision and Electronic Imaging V, 3959, 520-529.
IJsselsteijn, W. A., Freeman, J., Avons, S. E., Davidoff, J., de Ridder, H., & Hamberg, R. (1997). Continuous assessment of presence in stereoscopic displays. Perception, 26, 42-43.
Ijsselsteijn, W. A., Freeman, J., & De Ridder, H. (2001). Presence: Where are we? Cyberpsychology & Behavior, 4(2), 179-182.
James, D. (2004). Perpetual contact: Mobile communication, private talk, public performance. Sociology-the Journal of the British Sociological Association, 38(1), 203-206.
Katz, J. E., & Aakhus, M. A. (2002). Perpetual contact : mobile communication, private talk, public performance. Cambridge, UK ; New York: Cambridge University Press.
Keil, A., Bradley, M. M., Hauk, O., Rockstroh, B., Elbert, T., & Lang, P. J. (2002a). Large-scale neural correlates of affective picture processing. Psychophysiology, 39(5), 641-649. doi: Doi 10.1017/S0048577202394162
Keil, A., Bradley, M. M., Hauk, O., Rockstroh, B., Elbert, T., & Lang, P. J. (2002b). Large-scale neural correlates of affective picture processing. Psychophysiology, 39(5), 641-649. doi: 10.1017.S0048577202394162
Klimesch, W. (1999). EEG alpha and theta oscillations reflect cognitive and memory performance: a review and analysis. Brain Research Reviews, 29(2-3), 169-195.

Klimesch, W., Doppelmayr, M., Russegger, H., Pachinger, T., & Schwaiger, J. (1998). Induced alpha band power changes in the human EEG and attention. Neuroscience Letters, 244(2), 73-76.

Kuhr, B., Jacobi, J., Krause, C., Kaiser, J., Gasse, S., Gruber, T., & Quirin, M. (2011). Arousal, Valence, Dominance ... And Desire? Evidence from an Erp Study Concerning the Necessity of a New Motivational Dimension to Describe Affective States. Psychophysiology, 48, S88-S88.

Lang, P. J. (1995a). The Emotion Probe - Studies of Motivation and Attention. American Psychologist, 50(5), 372-385.

Lang, P. J. (1995b). The emotion probe. Studies of motivation and attention. Am Psychol, 50(5), 372-385.

Lepp, A., Barkley, J. E., & Karpinski, A. C. (2014). The relationship between cell phone use, academic performance, anxiety, and Satisfaction with Life in college students. Computers in Human Behavior, 31(0), 343-350. doi: http://dx.doi.org/10.1016/j.chb.2013.10.049

Lombard, M., Grabe, M. E., Reich, R. D., Campanella, C. M., & Ditton, T. B. (1996). Screen size and viewer responses to television: A review of research. Paper presented at the Theory and Methodology division at the Annual conference of the Association for Education in Journalism and Mass Communication, Anahiem , CA.

Magagnin, V., Mauri, M., Cipresso, P., Mainardi, L., Brown, E., Cerutti, S., . . . Barbieri, R. (2010). Heart Rate Variability and Respiratory Sinus Arrhythmia Assessment of Affective States by Bivariate Autoregressive Spectral Analysis. Comput Cardiol (2010), 37(5737930), 145-148.

Mauri, M., Cipresso, P., Balgera, A., Villamira, M., & Riva, G. (2011). Why Is Facebook So Successful? Psychophysiological Measures Describe a Core Flow State While Using Facebook. Cyberpsychology Behavior and Social Networking, 14(12), 723-731. doi: DOI 10.1089/cyber.2010.0377

Mauri, M., Magagnin, V., Cipresso, P., Mainardi, L., Brown, E. N., Cerutti, S., . . . Barbieri, R. (2010a). Psychophysiological signals associated with affective states. 2010 Annual International Conference of the Ieee Engineering in Medicine and Biology Society (Embc), 3563-3566.

Mauri, M., Magagnin, V., Cipresso, P., Mainardi, L., Brown, E. N., Cerutti, S., . . . Barbieri, R. (2010b). Psychophysiological signals associated with affective states. Conf Proc IEEE Eng Med Biol Soc, 2010, 3563-3566. doi: 10.1109/IEMBS.2010.5627465

Mikropoulos, T. A. (2001). Brain activity on navigation in virtual environments. Journal of Educational Computing Research, 24(1), 1-12.

Mojzisch, A., Schilbach, L., Helmert, J. R., Pannasch, S., Velichkovsky, B. M., & Vogeley, K. (2006). The effects of self-involvement on attention, arousal, and facial expression during social interaction with virtual others: A psychophysiological study. Social Neuroscience, 1(3-4), 184-195. doi: 10.1080/17470910600985621

Morris, J. D. (1995). Observations: SAM: The self-assessment manikin - An efficient cross-cultural measurement of emotional response. Journal of Advertising Research, 35(6), 63-68.

Picard, R. W. (1997). Affective computing. Cambridge, Mass.: MIT Press.

Rainville, P., Bechara, A., Naqvi, N., & Damasio, A. R. (2006a). Basic emotions are associated with distinct patterns of cardiorespiratory activity. International Journal of Psychophysiology, 61(1), 5-18. doi: DOI 10.1016/j.ijpsycho.2005.10.024

Rainville, P., Bechara, A., Naqvi, N., & Damasio, A. R. (2006b). Basic emotions are associated with distinct patterns of cardiorespiratory activity. Int J Psychophysiol, 61(1), 5-18. doi: 10.1016/j.ijpsycho.2005.10.024

Raspelli, S., Pallavicini, F., Carelli, L., Morganti, F., Pedroli, E., Cipresso, P., . . . Riva, G. (2012). Validating the Neuro VR-Based Virtual Version of the Multiple Errands Test: Preliminary Results. Presence-Teleoperators and Virtual Environments, 21(1), 31-42.

Repetto, C., Gaggioli, A., Pallavicini, F., Cipresso, P., Raspelli, S., & Riva, G. (in press). Virtual reality and mobile phones in the treatment of generalized anxiety disorders: a phase-2 clinical trial Personal and Ubiquitous Computing. doi: 10.1007/s00779-011-0467-0

Riley, J. M., Kaber, D. B., & Draper, J. V. (2004). Situation awareness and attention allocation measures for quantifying telepresence experiences in teleoperation. Human Factors and Ergonomics in Manufacturing, 14(1), 51-67. doi: Doi 10.1002/Hfm.10050

Riva, G. (2010). I Social Network. Bologna: Il Mulino.

Riva, G., Davide, F., & Ijsselsteijn, W. A. (2003). Being there : concepts, effects and measurements of user presence in synthetic environments. Amsterdam; Washington, D.C.; Tokyo: IOS Press; Ohmsha.

Rozenkrants, B., & Polich, J. (2008). Affective ERP processing in a visual oddball task: arousal, valence, and gender. Clin Neurophysiol, 119(10), 2260-2265. doi: 10.1016/j.clinph.2008.07.213

Rubin, R. B., Rubin, A. M., Graham, E. E., Perse, E. M., & Seibold, D. R. (2009). Self-Assessment Manikin. Communication Research Measures Ii: A Sourcebook, 336-341.

Russell, J. A. (1979). Affective Space Is Bipolar. Journal of Personality and Social Psychology, 37(3), 345-356.

Salehan, M., & Negahban, A. (2013). Social networking on smartphones: When mobile phones become addictive. Computers in Human Behavior, 29(6), 2632-2639. doi: http://dx.doi.org/10.1016/j.chb.2013.07.003

Salimpoor, V. N., Benovoy, M., Larcher, K., Dagher, A., & Zatorre, R. J. (2011). Anatomically distinct dopamine release during anticipation and experience of peak emotion to music. Nature Neuroscience, 14(2), 257-U355. doi: Doi 10.1038/Nn.2726

Salimpoor, V. N., Benovoy, M., Longo, G., Cooperstock, J. R., & Zatorre, R. J. (2009). The Rewarding Aspects of Music Listening Are Related to Degree of Emotional Arousal. PLoS ONE, 4(10). doi: Artn E7487. Doi 10.1371/Journal.Pone.0007487

Schilbach, L., Wohlschlaeger, A. M., Kraemer, N. C., Newen, A., Shah, N. J., Fink, G. R., & Vogeley, K. (2006). Being with virtual others: Neural correlates of social interaction. Neuropsychologia, 44(5), 718-730. doi: DOI 10.1016/j.neuropsychologia.2005.07.017

Schultze, U. (2010). Embodiment and presence in virtual worlds: a review. Journal of Information Technology, 25(4), 434-449. doi: Doi 10.1057/Jit.2010.25

Schupp, H. T., Stockburger, J., Codispoti, M., Junghofer, M., Weike, A. I., & Hamm, A. O. (2007). Selective visual attention to emotion. Journal of Neuroscience, 27(5), 1082-1089. doi: Doi 10.1523/Jneurosci.3223-06.2007

Sharpley, C. F., Kamen, P., Galatsis, M., Heppel, R., Veivers, C., & Claus, K. (2000). An Examination of the Relationship Between Resting Heart Rate Variability and Heart Rate Reactivity to a Mental Arithmetic Stressor. APPLIED PSYCHOPHYSIOLOGY AND BIOFEEDBACK, 25(3), 143-153. doi: 10.1023/a:1009598607998

Slater, M., & Garau, M. (2007). The use of questionnaire data in presence studies: Do not seriously likert. Presence-Teleoperators and Virtual Environments, 16(4), 447-456.

Stanney, K., Salvendy, G., Deisinger, J., DiZio, P., Ellis, S., Ellison, J., . . . Witmer, B. (1998). Aftereffects and sense of presence in virtual environments: Formulation of a research and development agenda. International Journal of Human-Computer Interaction, 10(2), 135-187.

Tajadura-Jimenez, A., Pantelidou, G., Rebacz, P., Vastfjall, D., & Tsakiris, M. (2011). I-Space: The Effects of Emotional Valence and Source of Music on Interpersonal Distance. PLoS ONE, 6(10). doi: DOI 10.1371/journal.pone.0026083

Villani, D., Grassi, A., Cognetta, C., Toniolo, D., Cipresso, P., & Riva, G. (2011). Self-help stress management training through mobile phones: An experience with oncology nurses. Psychological Services.

Villani, D., Repetto, C., Cipresso, P., & Riva, G. (in press). May I experience more presence in doing the same thing in virtual reality than in reality? An answer from a simulated job interview. Interacting with Computers. doi: 10.1016/j.intcom.2012.04.008

Vogel, D., & Baudisch, P. (2007). Shift: A Technique for Operating Pen-Based Interfaces Using Touch. Conference on Human Factors in Computing Systems, Vols 1 and 2, 657-666.

Wiederhold, B. K., Kaneda, M., Lurie, Y. M., Cabral, I., May, T., & Wiederhold, M. D. (2000). The use of physiological monitoring to determine the concepts of presence and immersion in virtual worlds. Applied Psychophysiology and Biofeedback, 25(4), 263-264.

List of Figures

List of Tables